THE COR/COTR ANSWER BOOK

Third Edition

THE COR/COTR ANSWER BOOK

Third Edition

Bob Boyd, CFCM

MANAGEMENTCONCEPTSPRESS

MANAGEMENTCONCEPTSPRESS

8230 Leesburg Pike, Suite 800
Tysons Corner, VA 22182
(703) 790-9595
Fax: (703) 790-1371
www.managementconceptspress.com

Printed in the United States of America

Library of Congress Cataloging-in-Publication Data
2012939563
978-1-56726-373-2

10   9   8   7   6   5   4   3   2   1

About the Author

Bob Boyd worked for over 20 years as an electronics technician, COTR, contract administrator, and contract specialist for the U.S. Navy. He then worked for 15 years as an instructor in basic, advanced, and executive level acquisition courses at the Army Logistics Management College (ALMC) in Fort Lee, Virginia, and the Navy Acquisition Management Training Office (NAMTO) in Norfolk, Virginia. He also held the positions of course director and department chairman at ALMC and NAMTO, as well as the position of Associate Dean for the School of Acquisition Management at ALMC.

After retiring from federal government service, Bob founded Training Concepts, Inc. (TCI), which provided tailored COR/COTR training and consulting services for government and commercial clients. He also worked as an independent contractor, developing and teaching numerous acquisition courses, especially COR/COTR courses. He taught thousands of COR/COTRs and consistently received high praise from his students.

Bob's career uniquely qualifies him as a creditable and skilled COR/COTR trainer and consultant. He spent about 20 years in the technical arena and another 20 years in the contracting arena. This dual experience track gives him significant and valuable insight into the roles and responsibilities of the COR/COTR because the COR/COTR, a technical expert, must also perform as a contract monitor. Having "been there, done that," Bob is very familiar with the needs, challenges, and day-to-day functions of the COR/COTR.

Bob has been a member of the National Contract Management Association (NCMA) for more than 30 years and is a Certified Federal Contracts Manager (CFCM). He received his BS from Saint Paul's College and his MBA from Averett University.

To all the COs, CORs/COTRs, and private sector acquisition professionals. I hope you will be able to use this book to make your critical role in the acquisition process more effective and more rewarding. This book was a labor of love on my part for your benefit.

Contents

Figures

Exhibits

Preface

The contracting officer (CO), at his or her discretion, may delegate contract monitoring duties to individuals possessing technical expertise or other specific qualifications, to ensure that all contract performance and delivery requirements are met in an acceptable and timely manner. These individuals may be called contracting officer's representatives, or CORs. This book focuses on the responsibilities of the COR during initial technical requirements definition, preaward technical assistance to the CO, and postaward technical contract administration. This individual may also be referred to as the contracting officer's *technical* representative (COTR). Throughout this book, COR is used to refer to either designation.

The Office of Federal Procurement Policy (OFPP), in its *Guide to Best Practices for Contract Administration*, states the following regarding CORs:

> The government is becoming increasingly aware of the importance of proper contract administration in ensuring the maximum return on our contract dollars. *The COTR plays a critical role* in affecting the outcome of the contract administration process. [Emphasis added.]

> The technical administration of government contracts is an essential activity. It is absolutely essential that those entrusted with the duty to ensure that the government gets all that it has bargained for must be competent in the practices of contract administration and aware of and faithful to the contents and limits of their delegation of authority from the contracting officer.

The U.S. Merit Systems Protection Board, in its December 2005 report to the President and the Congress of the United States, titled "Contracting Officer Representatives: Managing the Government's Technical Experts to Achieve Positive Contract Outcomes," stated:

> Without question contracting is an appropriate and effective way to accomplish an important share of the Government's work. The volume of contract spending—$328 billion in fiscal year 2004, up 87% from FY 1997—demonstrates the importance of developing and managing Federal contracts in ways that will ensure the best contract outcomes and the best return on the taxpayers' dollar. In recent years, the Government has modernized its contracting rules and procedures and improved the management of contracting officers who carry out the business aspects of contracting. However, almost no work has been done to assess agencies' management of contracting officer representatives (CORs). These individuals provide the technical expertise necessary to convey the technical requirements of the Government, oversee the technical work of the contractor, and ensure that deliverables meet the technical requirements of the Government. Even the best managed contract is not successful if its deliverables fail to meet the technical requirements of the Government.

All federal government contracts have, or should have, three basic objectives:

1. To get what the government needs
2. When it needs it
3. At a fair and reasonable price.

How can the government ensure the successful achievement of these objectives?

The answer lies in three basic areas of responsibility:

1. Clear, precise, and complete definition of the requirements (what the government needs)
2. Selection of the best possible source (contractor) to fulfill the needs
3. Performance of the contract in a manner that accomplishes the three objectives.

The acquisition team, including contracting, technical (or program/project), legal, quality assurance, audit, and finance personnel, has overall responsibility for accomplishment of the government's objectives, and it is essential to take advantage of the team approach. Further, technical continuity and oversight are extremely important during the contracting process. While the CO is the person of authority, the COR has intimate knowledge of, and technical expertise related to, the contract requirements, and he or she should be involved with the contract from "cradle to grave." It is essential that the COR be identified right at the beginning of the acquisition process—during the initial definition of the contract technical requirements. He or she should then be responsible for technically coordinating and monitoring the contract action all the way through contract closeout.

Unfortunately, many contracts lack the necessary degree of technical oversight, and as a result, performance problems and cost overruns can arise. My career experiences as both a technical and a contracting person have convinced me that one of the most effective ways to help alleviate performance and cost problems is by implementing a better COR/COTR program for technical coordination and contract monitoring.

The U.S. Merit Systems Protection Board report also stated:

> We surveyed CORs from 10 agencies that accounted for 90 percent of the Government's contracting dollars. Based on the findings from this survey, we make recommendations for agencies to improve the regulatory and day-to-day management of CORs. *In particular, agencies need to fulfill the regulatory aspects of managing CORs to include formal delegation of authority, improved COR training, and strategic management of the COR workforce.* [Emphasis added.]

Good COR/COTR oversight and implementation programs with structure, uniformity, formalized training, and certification criteria have been desperately needed for the COR/COTR designation process. Significant changes were announced in the September 6, 2011, OFPP memorandum, *Revisions to the Federal Acquisition Certification for Contracting Officer's Representatives (FAC-COR)*. The memorandum establishes a risk-based, three-tiered certification program with varying requirements for training, experience, and continuous learning. The new requirements were effective January 1, 2012, and apply to all executive agencies except the Department of Defense. Such programs will allow us to realize the significant benefits to be derived from better contract technical oversight by assigning those well-trained COR/COTRs to our contracts on a dedicated "cradle to grave" basis.

I was motivated to write this book in the hope that it would bring this type of attention to the need for better COR/COTR designation programs and improved technical administration of government contracts. I also hope that by using this book as guidance, the acquisition team, especially the COR/COTR, will be able to accomplish its contract objectives in a manner that ensures that the government gets what it needs, when it needs it, at a fair and reasonable price.

PURPOSE OF THIS BOOK

This book is intended to serve as a practical guide for both government and private sector personnel involved in the acquisition process:

- CORs/COTRs, task monitors, quality assurance representatives, inspectors, legal counsel, project officers, program managers, and finance personnel can use it as a handbook to get answers and practical advice pertaining to their day-to-day contract technical administration duties and responsibilities.

- COs, administrative contracting officers (ACOs), contract specialists, and contract administrators can use it to better understand typical COR/COTR functions and the process of delegating authority and contract technical oversight responsibilities to CORs/COTRs.

- Contractors can use this book to gain insight into government procedures, policies, and functions pertaining to overall contract monitoring, particularly those related to COR/COTR roles, authority, duties, and responsibilities.

This book is designed to be used as a handbook to check for answers to specific questions, rather than read from cover to cover—hence the question and answer format. The information provided in the book has been thoroughly researched and edited to be as current and accurate as possible, but it should not be used as a legal reference. Given that government contracting is a dynamic environment that is in a constant state of change, it is imperative that the most current edition of the Federal Acquisition Regulation (FAR), agency supplements to the FAR as applicable, and individuals with contracting and legal authority be consulted on all matters related to particular contract or contracting situations.

CONTENT AND STRUCTURE OF THE BOOK

The content and structure of this book were defined by a detailed analysis of, and correlation to, the Federal Acquisition Institute (FAI) skills and competencies set forth in both the *FAI Contract Specialist Training Blueprints*, "Training Blueprints For Performing 71 Essential Contracting and Purchasing Duties," and the *FAI COR Workbook*, which contains 18 "units of instruction" specifically related to the career development and training of CORs. These publications prescribe the curriculum design "training blueprints" to be used, and tasks to be completed, by contracting professionals and other members of the contracting team, such as CORs, and were developed in consultation with the Office of Personnel Management (OPM).

The 18 units of instruction from the *FAI COR Workbook* that were used in the development of this book are directly related to the 20 duties in Appendix A, COR Duties and Tasks, printed in bold. The remaining 12 duties in Appendix A were derived from the *FAI Contract Specialist Training Blueprints* and other references.

This book is designed to provide the COR with a source of specific information that will help him or her develop the necessary skills to perform the duties and tasks inherent in the COR's critical role in the contracting process. Appendix A contains a detailed listing of these duties and tasks and can be used as an index to locate specific information related to the COR's assigned responsibilities. For example, suppose a COR were assigned the responsibility of preparing a technical work package, including a purchase request, to yield the best market response in terms of competition, quality, timeliness, price, and mission needs. If the COR needed more information about developing a work package, he or she could scan the list of duties and tasks in Appendix A and would find among the listed duties for Chapter 3: "Duty: Develop the Work Package for Transmittal to the Contracting Office." Turning to Chapter 3 of this book, the COR would find a section titled Developing the Work Package, which includes information related to the seven items included in the work package. This section identifies the seven tasks the COR will need to perform to develop the work package and provides specific guidance and information related to the COR's assigned duties.

Because CORs are usually not contracting or legal people, I have tried to minimize direct reference to and quotation from the FAR. Two reasons for doing this are specifically worth noting:

1. The language of the FAR can be difficult to interpret. The FAR allows a considerable degree of discretion (by necessity) and should be interpreted with the assistance of case law from the courts, boards, and Government Accountability Office.

2. The fact that the FAR changes frequently (again by necessity) compelled me to use a more generic approach, i.e., practical guidance based on experience and common sense. This approach is intended to ensure that this book will be useful for a longer period of time.

"May the FAR be with you!"

Bob Boyd, CFCM
May 2012

Acknowledgments

This book represents an accumulation of life-long learning experiences that I sometimes reflect upon, and I remind myself that so far, it has been a great journey. There have been so many teachers, mentors, colleagues, and friends along the way who have taught me many lessons. I think that the greatest lesson I have learned is that with time, patience, and perseverance all things are truly possible. The completion of this book is like reaching the top of the mountain and looking back to all the people who helped along the way. I thank all of you so very much.

I would particularly like to thank some folks that played very significant roles in the "mountain climb."

First is Joyce Hamlin, my word processing consultant, who worked many long hours to complete the original version of the material that is now this book. I honestly believe that without her efforts, this book would not have been possible.

There are many people at Management Concepts who had a part in this book and I thank all of them, especially Myra Strauss, the editorial director, for her review and final processing of the manuscript as well as her continuing support.

CHAPTER 1

The Contracting Officer's Representative and Contract Fundamentals

The contracting officer (CO) administers the contract during contract performance, but he or she rarely has the expertise to administer all areas of the contract necessary for successful performance. Therefore, the CO's decisions must be based upon the input of many people. The contracting officer's representative's (COR) responsibility is to provide technical support to the CO and to the contract specialist.

This chapter answers questions about the COR's specific duties, the COR's role in contract administration, and the COR's communication and documentation duties. This book provides answers to important questions about the typical duties and responsibilities of CORs. The actual duties and responsibilities of the COR are set forth in the letter of designation and may differ from those presented in this book. General principles, however, should still apply.

The COR will need to determine the requirements for designation as a COR in his or her particular agency. These COR designation requirements should, at a minimum, identify:

1. The COR training and certification requirements
2. The COR nomination and designation procedures of the contracting officer (i.e., the CO) making the designation
3. The title that will be used for the designated COR position.

THE CONTRACTING OFFICER'S REPRESENTATIVE

1. What is the COR?

The COR is a non-contracting person who is given the chief role in the technical monitoring and administrative aspects of a statement of work or specification of a contract. FAR 2.101 states: "Contracting Officer's Representative (COR) means an individual, including a contracting officer's technical representative (COTR), designated and authorized in writing by the contracting officer (CO) to perform specific technical or administrative functions."

2. What other terms do some agencies use in place of "COR"?

Agencies may describe the same official using terms such as:

- Contracting officer's technical representative (COTR)
- Government technical representative (GTR)
- Government technical evaluator (GTE).

Some agencies may reserve the COTR designation for technical representatives, while using the COR label for individuals who have other contract administration duties. Other agencies use the term COR to identify any government person who has been given authority under a contract by the CO. An agency usually handles the issue of deciding which title to use for the individual through a supplement to the Federal Acquisition Regulation (FAR) or other policy documents that generally reflect organizational practice. For the purposes of this book, the representative of a CO will always be called a COR.

3. What terms or roles can be confused with those of the COR?

The terms "ordering officer," "BPA caller," "contracting officer," "POC" (point of contact), "PCO" (principal or procuring contracting officer), "ACO" (administrative contracting officer), and "TCO" (termination contracting officer) have specific and decidedly different meanings and should not be used if the title COR is intended.

An individual may be designated as a COR under one contract and have another role (e.g., ordering officer) under another contract. Care should be taken not to confuse the titles, as the authorities of each position are quite different.

The COR's Authority

It is critical that the COR understand his or her authority when representing the CO. The COR must avoid making unauthorized changes to the contract; making such changes could create serious problems for both the government and the COR. The COR needs to determine the source and extent of the authority assigned to him or her.

4. What is the source of the COR's authority?

The authority vested in a COR comes directly from the CO. This authority is bestowed upon the COR through specific provisions set forth in the contract or in a letter of designation. The CO can revoke the authority for cause if the COR fails to perform as required.

5. What authority may be delegated to the COR?

To understand what authority may be delegated to a COR, we need first to examine the CO's authority. The CO's authority is discussed in FAR Subparts 1.6 and 2.1.

FAR 1.602-2 states: "CO's are responsible for ensuring performance of all necessary actions for effective contracting, ensuring compliance with the terms of the contract, and safeguarding the interests of the United States in its contractual relationships."

FAR 2.101 states: "'Contracting officer' means a person with the authority to enter into, administer, and/or terminate contracts and make related determinations and findings. The term includes *certain authorized representatives of the Contracting Officer* [emphasis added] acting within the limits of their authority as delegated by the Contracting Officer."

The CO may designate other government personnel to act as his or her authorized representatives for such functions as technical monitoring, inspection, approval of testing, and other functions of a technical nature not involving a change in the scope of the contract. Such designation must be in writing and must contain specific instructions regarding the extent to which the representative may take action for the contracting officer.

For every contract, the CO must determine whether to:

- Retain the contract and perform all applicable contract administration functions
- Retain the contract and perform the administrative functions with the assistance of other government personnel, such as CORs

- Assign the contract to a contract administration office (CAO)
- Assign the contract to a CAO with specific limitations or specific additions.

6. What is the COR's authority on a contract?

The extent of the COR's involvement, the specific functions he or she is called on to perform, and the processes used to perform those functions will vary from activity to activity and contract to contract. For example, in one instance the COR may be involved with a certain contract from "cradle to grave," while in another, the COR may be tapped for duty only after the contract has already been awarded.

The CO is responsible for tasking the COR through the official designation letter and through the dynamics of day-to-day teamwork. CORs are generally not authorized to change the price, quantity, quality, delivery, or any terms of the contract.

SELECTION OF THE COR

The following section explains the selection and designation process for a COR and identifies the elements of a COR letter of designation. The COR should follow his or her specific agency policies and procedures relating to CORs, but sometimes agency guidance is lacking or inconsistent. The following questions and answers provide general information and guidance that can be used to establish a better COR selection and designation process for a particular contracting situation.

7. When should a COR be selected and designated for a contract?

A COR should be selected:
- When technical guidance is needed for a contract
- To perform inspection functions
- When testing approval is required
- When continuous surveillance of the contractor's work is required.

8. How are CORs selected and designated?

FAR 1.602-2(d) states:

> COs shall designate and authorize, in writing, a contracting officer's representative (COR) on all contracts and orders other than those that are firm-fixed price, and for firm-fixed price contracts and orders

as appropriate. However, the CO is not precluded from retaining and executing the COR duties as appropriate. See FAR 7.104(e).

A COR

1. Must be a government employee, unless otherwise authorized in agency regulations

2. Shall be certified and maintain certification in accordance with the Office of Management and Budget (OMB) memorandum entitled "The Federal Acquisition Certification for Contracting Officer Technical Representatives" (FAC-COTR), dated November 26, 2007, or for DoD, DoD Regulations, as applicable.

3. Must be qualified by training and experience commensurate with the responsibilities to be delegated in accordance with department/agency guidelines

4. May not be delegated responsibility to perform functions that have been delegated under FAR 42.202 to a contract administration office, but may be assigned some duties at 42.302 by the CO.

5. Has no authority to make any commitments or changes that affect price, quality, quantity, delivery, or other terms and conditions of the contract, and

6. Must be delegated in writing, with copies furnished to the contractor and the contract administration office:

   • Specifying the extent of the COR's authority to act on behalf of the CO

   • Identifying the limitations of the COR's authority

   • Specifying the period covered by the designation

   • Stating the authority is not redelegable, and

   • Stating that the COR may be personally liable for unauthorized acts.

OMB memorandum "Revisions to the Federal Acquisition Certification for Contracting Officer's Representatives (FAC-COR)," dated September 6, 2011, revises and replaces the November 2007 memorandum. This new memorandum establishes a risk-based, three-tiered certification program for civilian agencies that better reflects the important role of the COR. The new requirements, which were effective January 1, 2012, apply to all executive agencies except for the Department of Defense.

Where the previous FAC-COTR had just one level of certification for all CORs, the new FAC-COR has three levels of certification with varying requirements for training, experience, and continuous learning, depending on the types of contracts being managed. The COR level required for a particular acquisition is determined by the CO during acquisition planning and in consultation with the program manager. Details pertaining to FAC-COR are available at *www.fai.gov/drupal/certification/fac-cor*.

For more information on how your agency will implement the new certification requirements, contact your Acquisition Career Manager (ACM). A listing of ACMs is available at *www.fai.gov/drupal/community/ acquisition-career-managers-acms*.

9. **What selection criteria does an agency use to select the COR?**

In addition to the regulatory requirements outlined in Question #8, the COR is usually selected on the basis of a recommendation by the program office, i.e., the requiring activity that initiates the contract requirement.[1] It is preferable that the COR be the technical expert on the requirements of the contract on which he or she will be working. Some agencies use a nomination process, including a nomination letter, to nominate an individual for the CO's consideration.

10. **When is a letter of designation used?**

A letter of designation is prepared when a CO must administer a contract and needs to rely on other government personnel to ensure the successful completion of the contract. For example, the CO officially designates a COR by issuing a letter of designation based on the CO's acceptance of the technical qualifications of the individual nominated by the program office in the nomination letter.

11. **What are the elements of a letter of designation?**

Letters of designation must be tailored for the individual COR for each applicable contract to which a COR is assigned. Therefore, each letter will contain certain elements as necessary. The sample letter provided in Figure 1-1

---

[1] The term "requiring activity" generally refers to the technical activity or program (project) office that originally initiated the contract requirements to satisfy a need. Most of the time, the requiring activity is the end user of the contract deliverables. In other instances a technical activity will generate a contractual requirements package on behalf of other end users (e.g., a DoD program office acquiring weapons in support of troops).

Date: Reply to: Attention of:

Subject: Designation of Contracting Officer's Representative (COR)

Contract Number:

Contractor:

To: [COR Designee]

1. Pursuant to, and in accordance with the subject contract, you are hereby designated to act as the Contracting Officer's Representative (COR) in relation to the supplies and/or services to be provided under the subject contract. This designation is personal to you and may not be delegated to others.

2. You are hereby authorized by this designation to take any and all action which could lawfully be taken by me as Contracting Officer (CO) with regard to the following, except any action specifically prohibited herein or by the terms of subject contract:

   A. Technical requirements
      – Verify that the contractor performs the technical requirements of the contract in accordance with the terms, conditions and specifications of the contract.
      – Assist the contractor in interpreting technical requirements of the subject contract's scope of work. All technical questions arising out of the contract that cannot be resolved without increasing costs, causing alterations or changes to the contract scope, or creating irresolvable differences should be reported in writing to the CO. Such a report should contain the facts and recommendations pertinent to the technical questions at issue. Only the CO is authorized to accept non-conforming work, waive any requirement of the contract, or modify any term or condition of the contract.
      – Inform the CO in writing of any performance failure by the contractor.
      – Inform the CO if you foresee that the contract will not be completed according to schedule or within funding limitations. Your written notice should include your recommendations for remedial action.
      – Ensure that the government meets its contract obligations to the contractor. This includes, but is not limited to, the provision of government-furnished equipment and services called for in the contract, and timely government comment on, or approval of, draft contract deliverables, as may be required by the contract.

   B. Inspection/acceptance
      – Conduct government inspection and acceptance of contract deliverables, or assure that government inspection and acceptance are accomplished for:

         _____ All items

         _____ Line item numbers _____

         _____ The final report

         _____ Other (specify as required).

FIGURE 1-1. Sample COR Letter of Designation

C. Property management
    You are/are not (*delete one*) requested to:
    – Review and comment on the contractor's request for government-furnished facilities, supplies, materials, and equipment, and forward the request to the CO for disposition.
    – Review and comment on the contractor's request for consent to the purchase of supplies, materials, and equipment, and forward the request to the CO for disposition.

D. Payments
    – Review invoices for payment of costs and profit.
    – Review and approve vouchers for reasonableness and applicability of cost and for the appropriateness of the fee claimed (i.e., whether fees can rightfully be claimed based on progress, delivery, or the percentage of work completed).
    – Review copies of paid invoices for verification of the percentage of contract work completed and any fee claimed that is based upon said percentage of work completed.
    – If you do not agree with the contractor's costs, progress, delivery, and/or any other issues claimed, contact will be made with the CO prior to invoice approval for appropriate resolution of the disagreement.

E. Records
    You are required to maintain adequate records to sufficiently describe the performance of your duties as a COR during the life of this contract and to distribute such records as applicable. At a minimum, the COR file shall contain the following:
    (1) A copy of the designation letter from the CO
    (2) A copy of the contract or the appropriate part of the contract and all contract modifications
    (3) All correspondence initiated concerning performance of the contract
    (4) A record of inspections performed and the results of the inspections
    (5) Memoranda for the record or minutes of any pre-performance conferences, meetings, or discussions with the contractor or other individuals pertaining to the contract or to contract performance.

F. Contract closeout
    Upon completion of the work:
    – Return, upon request from the CO, a memorandum advising him or her of the actions yet to be taken on the expiring contract.
    – Forward to the CO a closeout statement attesting to the contractor's completion of technical performance under the contract and delivery and acceptance of all goods and services for which inspection and acceptance are herein delegated.
    – Forward to the CO all records and documents pertinent to the administration of the contract which were retained by you in your capacity as COR during the period of contract performance.
    – If the contract contains classified requirements, forward the necessary documents to (*insert name of the security activity*).

FIGURE 1-1. Sample COR Letter of Designation *(continued)*

G. Additional instructions
    Additional instructions are/are not (*delete one*) attached to this letter.

3. As one engaged in contracting and related activities, you shall conduct business deal-ings with industry in a manner above reproach in every aspect and shall protect the United States government's interests and maintain its reputation for fair and equal dealing with all contractors.

    Should you have direct or indirect financial interests that would place you in a posi-tion in which there is a conflict between your private interest and the public interest of the U.S. government, you shall advise your supervisor and the CO of the conflict so that appropriate action may be taken. A COR should avoid the appearance of such a conflict to maintain public confidence in the conduct of business between the U.S. government and the private sector.

4. The following limitations are placed on your designation:

    A. You may not make any commitments or changes that affect price, delivery/per-formance, quality, quantity, or other terms and conditions of the contract. This includes a prohibition on oral or written change orders.

    B. You may not perform any function that may be delegated under FAR 42.202(a) to contract administration offices.

    C. You may be held personally liable for any unauthorized acts in your duties as a COR or as a government employee.

5. This designation as a COR shall remain in effect through the life of the contract, unless sooner revoked or terminated by the CO. Such termination of the designation shall be in writing. If your designation is revoked for any reason before completion of this con-tract, turn your records over to the successor COR or obtain disposition instructions from the CO. If you are reassigned or separated from service, you shall request ter-mination and relief of your duties from the CO in advance of reassignment or separa-tion to permit sufficient time for the selection, training, and designation of a successor COR.

6. You are required to acknowledge receipt of this designation on the original copy and to return it to the CO for retention in the contract file. Your signature also serves as evidence that you are aware of the standards of conduct for a COR, and you agree to be bound thereby. The duplicate copy should be retained in your file.

{Signature of CO}

Copies furnished:
Contractor Finance Office
Receipt of this designation is hereby acknowledged: {Signature of COR}

FIGURE 1-1. Sample COR Letter of Designation (*continued*)

contains several elements that are most often found in a letter; however, it is unlikely that an individual letter would contain all the elements shown. For example, other individuals may be assigned inspection and acceptance or property administration duties. It is essential that the elements in the letter be tailored to the particular individual in a given COR designation because this is the document that establishes the COR's authority as delegated by the CO.

12. What other means of designation do agencies use to outline the duties of a COR?

Agencies may use other means of designation, such as:

- *Team assignments.* Some agencies have developed a *joint partnership agreement* that is signed during the preaward phase, defining how the program office and the contracting office will work together on the contract. The agreement contains details pertaining to the duties and areas of responsibility of each party in defining the contract requirements and planning for contract administration during the performance period. The teamwork concept is enhanced by designating the COR early in the process. By becoming familiar with the program requirements, the COR is able to assist the CO in developing the statement of work and contract administration plan.

- *Contract requirements.* The COR's authority and responsibilities can be presented in the contract through:
  - Part 1, Section G ("Contract Administration Data") of the Uniform Contract Format, or an addendum to a commercial item contract that specifies the name and duties of the COR
  - The technical direction clause in the contract, which establishes the scope of the COR's responsibilities in relation to the contractor. The clause further defines the role of the COR during contract performance.

The CO delegates the authority and responsibilities of the COR by signing the contract. A separate letter may not be necessary when the information contained in the contract is sufficient.

- *Internal policy.* Instructions and responsibilities addressed to individuals involved in the contract administration process may also be contained in:
  - Regulations and policy documents
  - Office procedures

    – Job descriptions of contract administration team players.

Regardless of internal policies, the CO must still officially designate the individual who will serve as COR by name under a specific contract. Agency policy, procedures, and job descriptions cannot substitute for a specific designation from the CO, unless the agency has an agreement with the contracting office—as in a situation in which the same commodity or services were being acquired on follow-on contracts, and the COR designation flows from one contract to the next per the conditions of the agreement.

    Also, remember that if the assigned duties of the COR are changed, or another person is assigned the responsibility by the program office to technically monitor the contract, the program office or the COR must inform the CO immediately so that the CO may assign the duties of the COR to another person.

    In summary, the designation process should follow these steps:

1. The COR is nominated in writing by the program organization.
2. The COR is notified by letter, written and signed by the CO.
3. The COR acknowledges acceptance of the position by signing and returning a copy of the letter to the CO.

THE COR'S DUTIES

The COR will need to perform general duties and responsibilities that may be assigned to him or her as a COR. The following questions and answers describe the COR's duties and responsibilities and identify the major areas of contract administration that are usually assigned to CORs.

    The competencies needed to best perform these duties are described at the Federal Acquisition Institute (FAI) web page at *www.fai.gov/drupal/node/184.*

General Duties

13. What are the general duties of a COR?

The COR must:

- *Know the contract.* The COR must be thoroughly familiar with all facets of the contract. He or she will not only act as a liaison between the contractor and the CO on matters pertaining to the contract requirements, but will also be responsible for contract compliance to the extent such responsibilities are designated to the COR.

- *Build rapport.* The COR may be introduced to the contractor at or before the postaward orientation conference, or he or she may already have an established professional relationship with the contractor. The COR should begin to build or strengthen rapport with the contractor immediately, displaying his or her knowledge of the contract and emphasizing his or her understanding of the team concept. Of course, the COR will always relate to the contractor within the framework of the COR's designated authority. (See the section in Chapter 2 entitled Ethics and Integrity for more on the importance of maintaining an "arm's-length" relationship with the contractor and the standards of conduct and ethics that govern the relationship between the COR and the contractor.)

- *Interpret technical requirements.* Among the COR's most important duties are talking with the contractor and gathering information from the contractor regarding differences in interpretation of the contract technical requirements. The COR may also be called upon to advise the contractor on environmental concerns, quality assurance, or issues related to safety, security, and government property. The COR will report this information, including differences of opinion, to the CO for resolution.

- *Recommend changes.* Remember, the COR may *not* make commitments to the contractor with regard to changes in price, quantity, quality, or delivery, but because he or she is intimately involved with the day-to-day workings of the contract, the COR may encounter situations that, in his or her opinion, warrant such changes. The COR's responsibility is then to recommend these changes to the CO in writing. The COR should support his or her suggestions with technical and cost justification and input from the contractor, if such input is appropriate. And, more importantly, the COR will be responsible for monitoring the contractor to be sure he or she does not act on such changes until the changes are formally issued by the CO.

- *Monitor and evaluate performance.* As the CO's "eyes and ears," the COR will spend time at the contractor's establishment to ensure that the contract is being performed as required. Site visits are essential to monitor whether:

  - The contract is on schedule

- The contractor is performing quality assurance requirements as specified by the contract
- Employees charged to the contract account are actually working on the contract
- Government property is being maintained properly.

The COR's presence at the contract performance site also helps him or her evaluate the contractor's performance. As an evaluator, the COR will record his or her observations of the contractor's technical performance and perhaps offer ideas for technical performance improvement. The contractor's required reporting, in addition to the COR's first-hand observations, will provide the data for the COR's evaluation reports to be furnished to the CO. The COR will also present a performance evaluation report as part of the contract closeout process.

- *Review invoices.* The COR is usually responsible for the review of each invoice submitted by the contractor and for recommending payment based on performance and allowability of cost (under certain types of contracts). The COR is required to report any discrepancies between the contractor's invoices and existing contract terms to the CO.

- *Recommend corrective action.* The COR may find deficiencies in contractor performance and must report these to the CO. In addition, the COR may recommend courses of corrective action to the CO. An important point to remember is that the COR (or any government official) may *not* tell the contractor *how* to correct a deficiency. The contractor may interpret such direction as a "constructive change" (see Chapter 6, Resolving Constructive Changes), proceed with the change, and charge the government for what amounts to an unauthorized commitment. The COR *may* ask the contractor for a plan of action to correct deficiencies, and relay such plans to the CO, who then determines the next action. Possible actions could include the CO issuing a change order or issuing a show cause or cure notice, which are delinquency notices used when the contractor is failing to make progress or perform other provisions of the contract. (See the discussion of contract termination in Chapter 8 for further discussion of these notices.)

- *Inspect and accept deliverables.* The COR may also be assigned the responsibility of inspecting deliverables (e.g., units of a product or the performance of services) and deciding whether or not they are acceptable according to contract requirements.

14. In what areas of contract administration are CORs usually assigned duties and responsibilities?

The COR's specific duties and responsibilities are set forth in his or her letter of designation. Figure 1-2 lists major areas of concern for the CO relating to contract administration. The CO will likely delegate significant duties and responsibilities to the COR from the major areas shown in bold type. Minor duties and responsibilities related to the other areas listed may be delegated to the COR from time to time by the CO.

The COR may be responsible for the following tasks and authorities, as covered in the letter of designation:

- **Administration**
  The COR may:
  - Act as the government's technical representative for contract administration
  - Supervise all technical and clerical personnel assigned to assist the COR
  - Assist the CO in conducting a postaward orientation conference
  - Represent the government in conferences with the contractor and prepare memoranda of pertinent facts for the record
  - Confer with representatives of the requesting office and other user groups on contract performance matters
  - Maintain a file system

• **The contract administration plan**	• Contract disputes
• Cross-servicing agreements with other agencies	• **Reviewing and analyzing technical and cost reports**
• **Conducting postaward orientation conferences**	• Security
• **Engineering support**	• Labor relations
• **Technical surveillance**	• Equal employment opportunity compliance reviews
• **Schedule surveillance**	• **Contract termination**
• Small business and disadvantaged firm's subcontracting programs	• **Inspection and acceptance**
• **Interpretation of statements of work**	• Progress payments
• Property administration	• **Review of the contractor's invoices**
• **Cost monitoring**	• Maintenance and retention of contract records
• Contract modifications and equitable adjustments	• **Contract closeout**
	• Audits

FIGURE 1-2. Major Areas of Concern in Contract Administration

- Prepare a project diary
- Keep a current set of drawings and specifications, noting all changes or deviations.

- **Inspection and acceptance**
  The COR may:
  - Inspect all work for full compliance with contract requirements
  - Promptly reject all work that does not comply with contract requirements and immediately notify the CO of the rejection
  - Advise the CO if the contractor fails to remove, correct, or replace rejected work promptly
  - Provide appropriate technical direction, advising the contractor of its formal appeal rights when there is disagreement
  - Prepare and maintain a list of items that are at variance with contract requirements, apprising both the contractor and the CO of possible corrective action or of the need for it
  - Maintain a list of product defects or omissions
  - Ensure that all defects and omissions are corrected.

- **Labor relations**
  The COR may:
  - Ensure that Equal Employment Opportunity posters are prominently displayed at the job site
  - Report violations of labor standards provisions to the CO
  - Monitor the contractor's time- and record-keeping.

- **Contract modifications**
  The COR may:
  - Administer contract modifications previously authorized and issued by the CO
  - Ensure that the contractor provides formal proposals for contemplated changes.

- **Payments**
  The COR may:
  - Review and verify the contractor's invoices, determining the government's agreement or non-agreement with the contractor's percentage of physical completion for progress reports and cost vouchers.

- **Schedule surveillance**
  The COR may:

  - Review and forward to the CO the contractor's schedule or project management chart with a recommendation for acceptance or rejection

  - Require the contractor to submit, if specified in the contract, a progress chart showing the actual progress on the project at the end of each accounting or payment period

  - Advise the CO of any delay factors (e.g., strikes, weather) and record the impact of these factors on contract completion.

- **Safety and environmental monitoring**
  The COR may:

  - Enforce safety and health requirements

  - Enforce environmental requirements.

Communication and Documentation Duties

One of the most important areas of responsibility for the COR is his or her communication and documentation duties. The COR must perform these duties effectively and thoroughly to ensure that the government's interests in the contract are accurately and adequately recorded and preserved. The following questions and answers provide the COR with information related to:

1. Occurrences that require communication with the CO

2. Formal versus informal communication with the contractor

3. The requirements of proper technical interpretation

4. The technical direction clause

5. The requirements of proper documentation.

15. What are the COR's communication and documentation responsibilities?

The COR must communicate constantly with the CO to apprise the CO of real or potential problems regarding contract performance, requirements for contract changes, and other important events and situations. The COR must also communicate with the contractor to answer questions and initiate technical guidance. The COR must practice a degree of sensitivity in such communication to ensure that "personal services" (i.e., creating an employer-employee relationship; see Chapter 3, Special Considerations

When Contracting for Services) are not rendered, that constructive changes do not result from technical guidance, that proper procedures are followed to implement changes, and that the government is protected by accurate documentation of all communication.

16. What typical occurrences require the COR to communicate with the CO?

The COR must advise the CO of the following occurrences:

- Failure by either the contractor or the government to meet contractual commitments
- Required contract changes
- Cost growth under cost reimbursement contracts or other cost-related problems
- Unsatisfactory progress
- Discrepancies in invoices or vouchers.

The CO may stipulate other routine periodic reports, and the COR must be sure to make complete, effective, and timely reports to the CO.

17. Why is it important to be aware of limits on communications with contractors?

CORs must be careful in their communications with contractors. First of all, the distinction must be made between prime contractors and subcontractors; the essential issue here is the observance of "privity of contract," which defines the relationship between the two parties to a contract (see Figure 1-3).

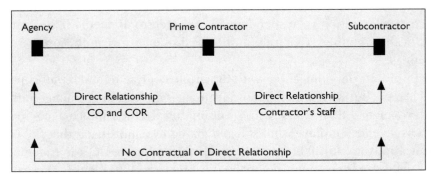

FIGURE 1-3.   Privity of Contract and Relationships among Government Agencies, the Prime Contractor, and Subcontractors

Because of limits on the COR's authority, he or she must understand the differences between formal and informal communication. The protocols of both formal and informal communication must be carefully followed to prevent serious contractual and legal problems.

Under current contract regulations, communication protocols are commonly cross-referenced by levels of contract authority. The highest contract authority is the head of the contracting activity (HCA). The principal delegation made by the HCA is the appointment of COs. All other employees working on a contract support the HCA through the COs. Certain responsibilities are delegated to CORs in the letter of designation, with written limitations on the area and amount of their authority. Other government employees may have assigned contract duties that require monitoring and evaluation input to the CORs and COs.

18. What are the differences between formal and informal communications with a contractor?

Formal communications occur between individuals (the HCA, COs, and CORs) who are *authorized* to represent the contracting parties, and as such, these communications are usually *binding*, i.e., constitute a legal duty or obligation. Formal communications usually are in writing (which can include electronic media such as e-mail), but oral communication is also acceptable. Oral communication occurs in meetings, in briefings, by phone, or through video teleconferencing. Formal direction given orally should then be confirmed in writing.

Informal communications can occur between any government employee *without* contractual authority and any contractor or subcontractor employee, and these communications are thus *non-binding*. Informal communication can occur in written correspondence or via electronic media (e.g., e-mail), retrievable databases, or telephone facsimile; in presentations; and in meetings.

Informal communications with the prime contractor and its subcontractors are encouraged and expected from agency staff and management in performance of their oversight responsibilities. In their informal communications, agency employees must avoid giving the impression that the communications are formal. (In particular, when a CO or COR is engaging in informal communications, he or she must be careful to identify those communications as non-binding.) Misconstrued communication could result in unauthorized direction to the contractor, which can provide the basis for claims made by the prime contractor against the government based on changes or additions to the work requirements.

19. How does the COR respond to contractor requests for information or action?

The COR should make every reasonable effort to respond in writing within 30 days to written requests from contractors regarding contract administration matters. Sometimes, however, depending on the nature of the request, the COR may have to coordinate with the CO. This coordination might delay the COR's response or mean that the CO will need to respond directly to the contractor. In the event of such a delay, the COR should provide the contractor, within 30 days, written notice of the specific date by which either the COR or the CO will respond to the request. (Note: This requirement does *not* apply to a request for a CO decision under the Contract Disputes Act, which has different response time requirements.)

20. What kinds of communication does the COR have with subcontractors?

Although an agency has the authority to approve subcontracts prior to contract award, there is no direct link between the agency and the subcontractor (see Figure 1-3). *Privity*, the legal term that defines the relationship between two parties of a contract, does not exist between the agency and subcontractors. Therefore, the prime contractor is responsible for ensuring, through its own internal processes, that quality work is performed and delivered on time by any subcontractors to meet the objectives of the prime contract.

Formal direction to subcontractors flows only through the prime contractor. There can be simultaneous communication (e.g., the exchange of informational copies of correspondence) between the prime contractor and subcontractors, but the agency and the subcontractor cannot bypass the prime contractor to communicate directly with each other.

21. What are the requirements for proper documentation of communications?

Effective communication is a wasted effort without good documentation. Without documentation of communications, there is no record of the events of contract performance, and the government is left vulnerable in the event of a claim, dispute, or a last-resort contract termination for default.

Proper documentation:

- Is the key to establishing and protecting the government's position in a dispute
- Includes written records of all oral communication with the contractor and the CO
- Includes copies of all written correspondence with the contractor and the CO.

Meetings and telephone conversations should be documented. Meetings need not be formal "sit-down" meetings with an agenda. A meeting can also be an informal or impromptu gathering to discuss technical issues. Whichever type of meeting the COR attends, formal or informal, he or she must be sure to take notes, include them in the COR file, and provide a copy to the CO, as appropriate.

It is also important for the COR to document telephone conversations. Significant decisions and issues are discussed on the telephone as a normal part of conducting business. Thus, it is important for the COR to keep a record of such decisions and issues as part of the COR file.

22. What should the COR document?

Documentation is not a complicated process, but it does require organization. The COR should not rely on his or her memory to document events that took place in the past. It is very important to document events as they occur to provide an accurate record for the file.

The COR should prepare memoranda for the record (MFR) of all meetings, trips, and telephone conversations relating to the contract.

Key rules for the COR to remember in maintaining the COR file include:

- Note the contract number on each record and on all correspondence relating to the contract
- Be sure that the CO receives a copy of all records and other correspondence
- Pay utmost attention to restrictions regarding proprietary data, as well as classified and business-sensitive information.

Interpreting Technical Requirements

23. What is the COR's role in interpreting technical requirements?

The COR must understand that interpretation of technical requirements permits explanation of intent after awarding the contract to contractors but does *not* permit changing the statement of work or methods the contractor has agreed to perform.

The COR assists the contractor in interpreting the technical scope of work required. This guidance may be in response to a contractor's direct request, or it may result from the COR's observation of a deficiency in performance caused by a differing interpretation of requirements made by the contractor. Whatever the situation, the COR may initiate technical guidance to the contractor as long as the advice does not result in an increase in costs, change the contract scope, or create irresolvable differences between the government and the contractor. If one of these changes is required, the COR must report the situation to the CO, with pertinent information and recommendations for action.

Guidance for Proper Technical Interpretation

- Do not attempt to interpret the contract for contractors or their subcontractors unless you are specifically appointed as the COR. Interpret contract specifications for a contractor only to explain the agency's intent.

- Where the contract is silent on methods of performance, allow the contractor to decide how to proceed.

- Do not establish an "employer/employee" relationship with contractors or any of their subcontractors. Remember, the establishment of such a relationship is illegal and is known as a "personal services" relationship. (See Chapter 3 for further discussion.)

---

24. What is the technical direction clause?

When the CO formally designates a COR to administer the technical aspects of a contract, the contract, in many cases, will contain a *technical direction clause.* Usually developed by the program office in coordination with the contracting office, a technical direction clause specifically identifies the technical areas involved in the administration of a contract and any limitations associated with the COR's authority to technically direct the contractor. The clause also provides for prompt reporting of government conduct that the contractor considers as constituting a change to the contract. This clause is normally found in Section H of the Uniform Contract Format for cost-reimbursement contracts. See Figure 1-4 for a sample technical direction clause.

1. The work to be performed by the contractor under this contract is subject to the surveillance and written technical direction of a technical representative (e.g., a COR) who shall be specifically appointed by the contracting officer in writing. The term *technical direction* is defined to include, without limitation, the following:
    a) Directions to the contractor that redirect the contract effort, shift work emphasis between work areas or tasks, require pursuit of certain lines of inquiry, fill in details, or otherwise provide technical guidance to the contractor in order to accomplish the statement of work
    b) Provision of information to the contractor that assists in the interpretation of drawings, specifications, or technical portions of the scope of work
    c) Review and, where required by the contract, approval of technical reports, drawings, specifications, or technical information to be delivered by the contractor to the agency under the contract
    d) The technical representative shall monitor the contractor's performance with respect to compliance with the requirements of this contract
    e) Technical direction and management surveillance shall not impose tasks or requirements upon the contractor additional to or different from the general tasks and requirements stated in the schedule of this contract.

2. Technical direction must be within the contract's scope of work and must be issued in writing. The technical representative does not have the authority to and may not issue any technical direction that:
    a) Constitutes an assignment of additional work outside the general scope of the statement of work
    b) Constitutes a change as defined in the contract clause entitled "changes"
    c) In any manner causes an increase or decrease in the total estimated contract cost or the time required for contract performance
    d) Changes any of the expressed terms, conditions, or specifications of the contract
    e) Interferes with the contractor's right to perform the terms and conditions of the contract.

3. If the contractor receives any guidance or direction as outlined in items 2(a) through 2(e), the contracting officer shall be notified within five working days of the occurrence. Within 30 days, the contracting officer (CO) shall either advise the contractor that the technical direction is within the contract's work scope and does not constitute a change under the "changes" clause, or within a reasonable amount of time, the CO must advise the contractor that a written change order will be issued. The contractor may dispute the contracting officer's findings.

FIGURE 1-4. Sample Technical Direction Clause

CONTRACT FUNDAMENTALS

This section provides information to assist the COR in identifying the six classifications of contracts and the five elements of a valid contract and in understanding the concepts of authority under agency law as related to the

COR. As a member of the contracting team, the COR can rely on other members of the team (e.g., the CO, legal personnel) for responsibilities relating to the finer points of contract law. However, the COR needs a basic understanding of the concepts of contract and agency law to assist the CO effectively in the planning, formation, and administration of a specific contract.

25. What is an agreement?

An *agreement* is defined as "mutual assent between two or more legally competent persons, ordinarily leading to a contract. In common usage, it is a broader term than *contract, bargain,* or *promise* because it includes executed sales, gifts and other transfers of property, as well as promises without legal obligation. While agreement is often used as a synonym for contract, some authorities narrow it to mean only mutual assent."[2]

26. What is a contract?

A *contract* is defined as "a promise for the breach of which the law provides a remedy, or the performance of which the law recognizes as a duty; a transaction involving two or more individuals, whereby each has reciprocal rights to demand performance of what is promised."[3] A *promise* is defined as "a declaration of one's intention to do or to refrain from doing something."[4] If an individual promises in a contract to do something, the courts will ensure that he or she upholds that promise; if he or she does not, the courts will provide a solution for the person to whom he or she made the promise.

27. What are the types of contracts?

Contracts can be classified as:

- Unilateral
- Bilateral
- Unenforceable
- Voidable
- Void
- Valid.

---

[2] Steven H. Gifis, *Barron's Dictionary of Legal Terms*, 3rd ed. (Hauppauge, NY: Barron's, 1998), p. 17.

[3] Ibid, p. 98.

[4] Ibid., p. 382.

A *unilateral contract* is one in which only one party makes a promise. It may be a promise for an act (e.g., "I will pay you $10 to mow my lawn") or an act for a promise (e.g., someone offers a reward for the return of a lost dog). In the case of the reward, one person makes a promise to pay, and a contract would be formed when the other person acts on that promise.

A purchase order under the government's simplified acquisition procedures that is signed only by a CO is a governmental example of a unilateral contract. The contractor accepts the offer by delivering in accordance with the terms of the offer, or rejects the offer by not responding to it. If the person to whom the offer was made performs to the terms of the offer, a valid contract will be created.

A *bilateral contract* is one in which both parties make promises. A promise to perform a service in exchange for a promise to pay the agreed upon amount for the service is a bilateral contract.

An *unenforceable contract* is one that cannot be enforced by the courts because of a particular statute or doctrine. Unenforceable contracts are not invalid, but if a breach of an unenforceable contract occurs, then the courts cannot determine if a remedy exists.

An example of an unenforceable contract would be one based on the statute of frauds. This statute requires that certain types of contracts be in writing to be enforceable (e.g., real estate contracts). If an individual enters into an oral contract for the sale of land, even if all the elements of a valid contract are present in the oral contract, civil courts are prohibited from enforcing the provisions of that contract.

A *voidable contract* is one in which only one of the parties is bound to the terms of the contract, while the other may withdraw from the contract at any time. Examples of voidable contracts are ones made with persons under the legal age and contracts induced by fraud, such as ones containing intentional misrepresentation of facts. Minors and persons induced by fraud to make a contract for which fraud is proven can choose not to be bound by the contract.

A *void agreement* is one that never became a contract because it lacked an essential element, or the agreement contains misrepresentations of fact. In either situation, the CO can void the contract. For example, a contract found to be in violation of an Environmental Protection Agency (EPA) regulation, or one in which an offeror represents his or her company as a small business under a small business set-aside when it is actually a large business may be voided.

A *valid contract* is one that contains all of the following essential elements.

28. What are the elements of a contract?

The five essential elements of a valid contract are:

- An offer
- Acceptance
- Mutual consideration
- Legal purpose
- Contractual capacity.

To initiate a contract, an *offer* must be made. An offer is a promise of what will be done and what is expected if the promise is fulfilled.

Advertisements are not considered to be offers but rather invitations to negotiate, unless they are very specific regarding offer and acceptance guidelines or terms and conditions. But advertisements of rewards are generally considered to be offers that can result in unilateral contracts. An advertisement for bids is considered a request for an offer rather than a specific offer itself.

An offer must:

- Show the offeror's intent to perform if the offer is accepted by the other party
- Be complete and clear in all of its terms
- Be communicated to the offeree.

Acceptance is an expression of consent to a proposal or offer. There are two ways to accept an offer:

If the contract is . . .	Acceptance occurs when the offeree . . .
Unilateral	delivers or performs.
Bilateral	expresses to the offeror acceptance of the same items and conditions stated in the offer.

Acceptance must be:

- *Expressed* to the offeror.

- *Consistent* with the same terms and conditions stated in the offer. Changing these terms and conditions creates a counter-offer, and it is up to the original offeror to accept or reject the terms.

- *Timely.* The offeror may stipulate a period of time after which the offer is no longer valid. When no such time frame is expressed in the contract, the acceptance period must be of a reasonable length. The offeror may fill in a time for acceptance on the government's official contract form; a 60-day acceptance period is established if the offeror does not specify a desired length of time for acceptance. If the CO determines that a specific period of time must be allowed by the offeror, he may insert a minimum acceptance period clause.

Mutual consideration means that each party receives something of value and gives up something of value when a contract is established between the parties. Without mutual consideration, one party would be giving a gift to the other, which does not have the same legal obligation as a contract.

Contracts also must be for a *legal purpose*. If a contract violates a statute, it is unlawful and void. An example of a void contract would be one that was awarded on a cost-plus-percentage-of-cost basis. The FAR forbids the use of such a contract because it rewards a contractor for increasing costs on a contract and discourages cost reduction.

Parties entering into a contract must have the capacity to do so. *Contractual capacity* is the ability to incur legal liability or to acquire legal rights. Examples of individuals who lack contractual capacity are minors and insane or intoxicated persons.

Agency and Authority

29. What is "agency"?

Agency is a fiduciary (based on trust and confidence) relationship between two persons in which one person (the *agent*) acts for or represents another (the *principal*) in dealings with third parties. A principal can confer authority on an agent only if the agent accepts it. A principal can also approve the unauthorized actions of an agent and thereby create an agency relationship. This process is called *ratification*. An agent has certain duties to his or her principal. These include a duty to act in the principal's best interest, a duty of good conduct, a duty to keep the principal informed, a duty to act only as authorized, and a duty of loyalty to the principal.

30. What is an independent contractor, and what is an agent?

An *independent contractor* contracts to do a piece of work according to his or her own methods and without being subject to the control of the other party to the contract; the independent contractor's only concern is to provide an acceptable product or service. An independent contractor does not represent the other party in business dealings.

The primary distinction between an agent and an independent contractor is the amount of control placed over each. An *agent* is generally subject to more control. For example, a chauffeur is an agent of his employer. A taxi cab driver is not an agent of his fare.

Chauffeur	Taxi Driver
Under control of his employer.	Paid only to take fare to a particular destination.
Fills limousine with gas and charges his employer.	Fills taxi with gas and is responsible for the cost.
Gets a ticket and the employer pays it.	Gets a ticket and must pay for it himself.
Has an accident and his employer is liable.	Has an accident and the fare is not liable.

There are two types of agents. A *general agent* can transact all the business of the principal or all of the principal's business of a particular kind or in a particular place. A *special agent* can act only in a special transaction or for a particular purpose or class of work. CORs are special agents because they can only be given authority to perform certain actions.

31. What is actual authority?

Agents can *only* be given *actual authority*. There are two types of actual authority:

- *Express authority* is conferred in direct terms, definitely and explicitly.

- *Implied authority* is conferred by inference. For example, if a COR is given express authority to authorize payment of invoices, he or she is given implied authority to return improper invoices for correction.

32. What is apparent authority?

Apparent authority is authority perceived by a third party (e.g., a contractor) to exist, when authority was never actually conferred upon the government agent in question. For example, the contractor may perceive that the COR has authority to conduct a particular inspection, when in fact the COR does not have that authority because the authority has been delegated to a particular government inspector. Apparent authority does *not* apply to government contracts unless a CO ratifies the action of an unauthorized agent.

33. What is ratification?

Ratification is defined as the affirmation by a person of a prior act that did not bind him or her but was done on his or her account; the act is then treated as if he or she originally authorized it. Government employees can ratify actions of any unauthorized agent if the individual ratifying the action has the actual authority to enter into a contract and the government benefits from the action.

34. How can agency be terminated?

Agency can be terminated:

- By mutual agreement of the principal and the agent
- Upon expiration of the contract
- By the principal's revocation of the authority
- By the agent's own renunciation, in some cases (e.g., an act of conscience)
- By operation of law (e.g., the death of either principal or agent).

CHAPTER 2

The Federal Acquisition Process

As discussed in Chapter 1, the COR must become a member of the contracting team, and therefore must have insight into the federal acquisition process. This chapter provides an overview of that process by focusing on its vision, standards of performance, and goals. Also, the phases, steps, and functions included in the process and the COR's performance objectives relating to those functions will be identified.

As a representative of the CO and a member of the contracting team, the COR must adhere to applicable ethical principles and procurement integrity requirements. These principles include impartiality, fairness, honesty, and the protection of certain contract-related information. The COR must also know and follow the rules regarding gratuities. He or she must also know how to resolve conflicts of interest.

Adherence to ethical principles and procurement integrity requirements is of critical importance to the COR. As a government employee, he or she has no doubt become familiar with the usual standards of conduct that apply to federal employment. But as a member of the contracting team, the COR may face new challenges regarding conduct.

Ethical dilemmas will likely arise, regardless of whether or not there is a rule or standard of conduct that applies to the situation. These new dilemmas arise because the COR has access to advance procurement information, is significantly involved in drafting the requirements document, performs the technical evaluation and selection of the contractor, and has direct and influential interface with the contractor during performance of the contract. For example, during the performance phase, the COR may have sole authority for the approval of test results, inspection, and final acceptance of the contractor's work. In all these activities, the COR must be very careful when performing his or her duties because of the special responsibilities he or she has in overseeing the contract.

THE FEDERAL ACQUISITION PROCESS

The following questions and answers provide an overview of the federal acquisition process and are intended to enable the COR to:

1. Understand the vision and standards of performance for the federal acquisition process
2. Identify the goals of the federal acquisition process
3. Identify the phases, steps, and functions of the federal acquisition process
4. Describe the performance objectives for the COR as a member of the contracting team.

35. What is the federal acquisition process?

The term *federal acquisition process* refers to the regulations, procedures, and specific steps involved in acquiring supplies and services for use by the United States government. This process is a part of and in conformance with the Federal Acquisition Regulations System, described in Subpart 1.1 of the Federal Acquisition Regulation (FAR), which was established for the codification and publication of uniform policies and procedures for acquisition by all executive agencies.

36. What is the vision of the federal acquisition process?

The vision of the federal acquisition process is to deliver, in a timely manner, the best-value supply or service to the customer, while maintaining the public's trust and fulfilling public policy objectives. "Best value" is viewed from a broad perspective, balancing the many competing interests in the process, such as tradeoffs among cost, performance, and delivery.

37. What are the goals of the federal acquisition process?

The federal acquisition process is designed to achieve two basic goals:

1. To obtain the optimum market response to requirements for supplies and services in terms of:
   - Quality
   - Timeliness
   - Price while
   - Accomplishing socioeconomic objectives
   - Minimizing business and technical risks
   - Maximizing competition
   - Maintaining procurement integrity.
2. To ensure that purchased supplies and services are:
   - Delivered or performed when and where they should be, as specified in the contract
   - Acceptable, in terms of conforming to the contract specifications or statement of work
   - Furnished in compliance with other terms and conditions of the contract.

38. What are the phases, steps, and functions of the federal acquisition process?

The federal acquisition process is divided into three phases:

1. Acquisition planning
2. Contract formation
3. Contract administration.

In each of the phases, contracting personnel and the COR will perform several steps involving related functions:

- *Steps in the acquisition planning phase:*
   A. Determination of need
   B. Analysis of requirements
   C. Extent of competition

    D. Source selection planning

    E. Solicitation terms and conditions.

- *Steps in the contract formation phase:*

    F. Solicitation of offers

    G. Bid evaluation

    H. Proposal evaluation

    I. Contract award.

- *Steps in the contract administration phase:*

    J. Administration planning

    K. Initiation of work and modifications

    L. Quality assurance

    M. Payment and accounting

    N. Special terms.

Figures 2-1 through 2-3 outline these steps (A through N) and the 71 related functions that make up the three phases of the federal acquisition process. Be aware that each function has a related duty and multiple tasks, even if these are not shown.

    Not every function applies to every acquisition. For example, many contracts are not modified, and few are terminated. Also, the sequencing of functions may vary from contract to contract. For example, some solicitations

---

Phase I: Acquisition Planning

A: Determination of need
- Customer business analysis and strategic planning
- Market research
- Procurement requests

B: Analysis of requirements
- Requirements analysis

C: Extent of competition
- Identifying possible sources
- Limiting competition
- Socioeconomic requirements

D: Source selection planning
- Offer evaluation factors
- Method of acquisition

E: Solicitation terms and conditions
- Pricing arrangements
- Recurring requirements
- Unpriced contracts
- Contract financing
- Obtaining bonds
- Method of payment
- Documenting the source selection plan

FIGURE 2-1. The Federal Acquisition Process: The Acquisition Planning Phase

Phase 2: Contract Formation

F: Solicitation of offers
  - Publicizing proposed acquisitions
  - Subcontracting requirements
  - Oral solicitations
  - Solicitation preparation
  - Inquiries and Freedom of Information Act requests
  - Pre-quote/pre-bid/pre-proposal conferences
  - Amending/canceling solicitations

G: Bid evaluation
  - Receiving bids
  - Bid acceptance periods
  - Late bids
  - Mistakes in bids
  - Price analysis
  - Responsiveness

H: Proposal evaluation
  - Receiving quotations and proposals
  - Evaluating non-price factors
  - Pricing information from offerors
  - Accounting and estimating systems
  - Cost accounting standards
  - Audits
  - Price analysis
  - Cost analysis
  - Evaluating other terms and conditions
  - Award without discussions
  - Communications
  - Establishing the competitive range
  - Negotiation strategy
  - Conducting discussions/negotiation

I: Contract award
  - Responsibility
  - Preparing awards
  - Issuing awards and related notices
  - Debriefing
  - Protests

FIGURE 2-2. The Federal Acquisition Process: The Contract Formation Phase

Phase 3: Contract Administration

J: Administration planning
  - Contract administration planning
  - Post-award orientations

K: Initiation of work and modifications
  - Monitoring subcontract management
  - Contract modification and adjustment
  - Options
  - Task and delivery order contracting

L: Quality assurance
  - Performance management
  - Commercial/simplified acquisition remedies
  - Noncommercial acquisition remedies
  - Documenting past performance

M: Payment and accounting
  - Assignment of claims
  - Administering securities
  - Administering financing terms
  - Allowability of costs
  - Price and fee adjustments
  - Defective pricing
  - Invoices
  - Fraud and exclusion
  - Collecting contractor debts

N: Special terms
  - Administering special terms and conditions
  - Resolving disputes
  - Termination
  - Closeout

FIGURE 2-3. The Federal Acquisition Process: The Contract Administration Phase

may be amended prior to the opening of proposals, but others might not be amended until after the government has begun to evaluate proposals.

39. **What are the COR's performance objectives as a member of the contracting team?**

As a member of the contracting team, it is important for the COR to understand the overall objectives of that team. In the final analysis, the team's performance of the acquisition functions should *not* be judged by:

- How faithfully the team has observed the letter of the applicable laws and regulations (although all acquisitions must comply with those laws and regulations)
- The extent of competition for the requirements (although maximizing competition is a sub-goal of the process)
- Whether the team has obtained a lower price than in prior acquisitions for the same supply or service (although price is an important factor).

The team's performance of the acquisition functions during every step in the acquisition process should be the *only* criterion by which it is judged.

For example, the team may have performed every step of the acquisition process in apparent compliance with the letter of the applicable laws and regulations and may have succeeded in obtaining independently prepared offers from three competitors. Nevertheless, the asking prices might be unacceptably high because:

- Entry was made into the market at the wrong time (e.g., buying produce out of season)
- The specification included unnecessary, restrictive requirements and thereby limited competition to a market segment characterized by premium prices, such as brand name products
- Orders were placed for uneconomic quantities of supplies
- An unnecessarily tight delivery schedule was imposed relative to the delivery terms and conditions that are prevalent in the particular market segment
- The wrong type of contract was used (e.g., a firm fixed price contract for a market that was experiencing or expecting a high rate of inflation during the period of contract performance)
- Warranty requirements were imposed that were in excess of what was customary for that market.

The bottom line: No function of the acquisition process should be viewed as an end in itself. Rather, as you read about each function in the following chapters, *always be mindful of the overall goals of the federal acquisition process.*

STANDARDS OF PERFORMANCE

40. What are standards of performance? Why are they important?

The *standards of performance* found in FAR 1.102-2 apply to all acquisition officials—contracting officers and specialists, purchasing agents, CORs, program managers, technical evaluators, quality assurance specialists, and logisticians. All members of the acquisition team (see FAR 1.102-3) should always have the following standards in mind when performing any specific acquisition-related function, duty, or task:

1. Satisfy the customer in terms of cost, quality, and timeliness of the delivered product or service
2. Minimize administrative operating costs
3. Conduct business with integrity, fairness, and openness
4. Fulfill public policy objectives.

41. What are some strategies that the acquisition team can use to meet these standards of performance?

The acquisition team should:

1. *Shift the focus from "risk avoidance" to "risk management."* The costs of eliminating *all* risk would be prohibitive. The team should use its professional judgment to take action to manage individual risks.
2. *Forecast requirements and develop long-range plans for accomplishing them.* The extent of planning should be commensurate with the size and nature of the acquisition. The team should be flexible in accommodating changes in mission needs.
3. *Team with other participants in the acquisition process.* Participants include representatives of the technical, supply, and procurement communities and their customers and suppliers.
4. *Empower participants to make decisions within their area of responsibility.* Delegate the authority to make decisions (and accountability

for the decisions) to the lowest level possible in the organizational structure—at the working level as opposed to the headquarters level, for example.

5. *Encourage innovation and local adaptation.* Assume that any strategy, practice, policy, or procedure is a permissible exercise of authority if it is in the best interests of the government, and it is *not* prohibited by the FAR, law (statutory or case law), executive order, or other regulation.

6. *Communicate with the commercial sector as early as possible in the acquisition cycle.* Communication can help acquisition officials become aware and take advantage of the production and delivery capabilities available in the commercial marketplace. Maximize the use of commercial products and services in meeting government requirements.

7. *Foster cooperative relationships between the government and its contractors.* Keep the government's overriding responsibility to the taxpayers in mind. Select contractors who have a track record of successful past performance or who demonstrate a current superior ability to perform.

8. *Promote competition.* Competition is beneficial for the following reasons:

   • It helps build and maintain a base of responsible suppliers that can provide better supplies and services at lower cost

   • It encourages those suppliers to innovate and assist the government in accomplishing its mission more effectively and efficiently

   • It broadens the industrial and mobilization base in the event of a need to rapidly build up the armed forces.

ETHICS AND INTEGRITY

The COR must understand and comply with all applicable ethical principles and procurement integrity requirements.

42. What ethical principles apply to the COR, and why are these principles important?

First, it is important to understand the distinction between ethics and compliance. One *should* practice ethical behavior; one *must* act in compliance with established regulations. Because the COR is also the government's representative or liaison with contractors, it is important that his or her actions, actual and perceived, reflect well on government procurement personnel. Merely doing what the law requires may not be sufficient to give the impression of honest and fair conduct. Sensitivity toward the ethics of a given situation is essential for the COR.

Ethical standards are the cornerstone of every business relationship. These standards protect all the parties involved in business transactions and ensure that the parties have a "level playing field" on which to strive for their objectives.

The fundamental objective of all government procurement professionals is *to protect the interests of the federal government by spending its money wisely*. CORs must be prepared to account for the actions they take in pursuit of this objective. Thus, CORs must make ethics and procurement integrity rules a part of their daily professional lives. They must not hesitate to apply established ethical standards to every action.

43. **What general guidance on ethics does the FAR provide?**

FAR 3.101-1 states:

> Government business shall be conducted in a manner above reproach and, except as authorized by statute or regulation, with complete impartiality and with preferential treatment for none.

> Transactions relating to the expenditure of public funds require the highest degree of public trust and an impeccable standard of conduct.

> The general rule is to strictly avoid any conflict of interest or even the appearance of a conflict of interest in government contractor relationships.

44. **What are other useful sources of ethical guidance?**

The COR should refer any questions related to ethics or procurement integrity to his or her CO. Within the COR's agency, the Office of General Counsel for General Law, the Office of the Inspector General, and the personnel office can provide clarification of ethical issues. The Office of Government Ethics (*www.usoge.gov*), which is responsible for compiling and publishing standards of ethical conduct for all executive branch employees, is also a source of information and guidance.

45. What procurement integrity requirements apply to the COR?

Agencies are required by Executive Order 11222 of May 8, 1965, and 5 CFR (Code of Federal Regulations) 735 to prescribe "Standards of Conduct." These agency standards contain:

1. Agency-authorized exceptions to FAR 3.101-2 (see Question 48)

2. Disciplinary measures for persons violating the standards of conduct.

Requirements for employee financial disclosure and restrictions on private employment for former government employees can be found in the Office of Personnel Management regulations and specific agency regulations implementing Public Law 95-521, which amended 18 U.S.C. 207; CORs should be sure to check individual agency regulations.

Remember that public service necessitates trustworthiness. Each employee has a responsibility to the United States government and its citizens to adhere to the laws and principles set forth in the Constitution; laws and ethical principles must be upheld without concern for private gain.

46. What ethical concerns and issues of integrity are relevant to the COR's work?

The COR, as a representative of the government or liaison between the government and the contractor, needs to adhere to ethical principles in his or her conduct. It is in the best interest of the COR and the government for the COR to go beyond mere compliance. The COR should keep in mind that some ethical principles are backed by rules that, if violated, could lead to embarrassment at best; at worst, these violations could be grounds for criminal sanctions.

The primary ethical concerns for a COR are:

- Treating contractors impartially (see the reference to FAR 3.101-1 under Question 43)
- Not accepting gratuities
- Not discussing employment opportunities with contractors
- Avoiding conflicts of interest
- Safeguarding source selection or proprietary information.

47. What is the gratuities clause?

Nearly every contract above the simplified acquisition threshold (currently $150,000) includes at least a reference to the *gratuities clause*, FAR 52.203-3, as prescribed in FAR 3.202. This clause gives the government the right to terminate for default a contractor who offers or gives a gratuity (in the form of entertainment or a gift) to an officer, official, or employee of the government, intending to thereby obtain a contract or favorable treatment. Agency personnel are to report suspected violations of the gratuities clause to the CO or another designated official in accordance with agency procedures.

48. **What else must the COR know about gratuities and gifts?**

FAR 3.101-2 states:

> As a rule, no government employee may solicit or accept, directly or indirectly, any gratuity, gift, favor, entertainment, loan, or anything of monetary value from anyone who:
>
> (a) has or is seeking to obtain government business with the employee's agency,
>
> (b) conducts activities that are regulated by the employee's agency, or
>
> (c) has interests that may be substantially affected by the performance or non-performance of the employee's official duties. Certain limited exceptions are authorized in agency regulations.

There are exceptions for small food items and refreshments, such as soft drinks, coffee, or donuts that are not offered as a part of a meal. However, it is best for the COR to seek advice from government legal counsel or an ethics advisor about specific concerns related to gratuities and gifts.

49. **Why must the COR avoid conflicts of interest?**

Government employees cannot hold financial interests that conflict with the conscientious performance of duty. If a COR suspects a conflict of interest, he or she must notify the CO and offer to disqualify himself or herself from the position of COR.

An employee is prohibited by criminal statute from participating *personally and substantially* in an official capacity in any particular matter in which, to his or her knowledge, he or she, or any person whose interests are imputed to him or her under this statute (e.g., a family member), has a financial interest, if the particular matter will have a direct and predictable effect on that interest. Although this issue is more likely to apply to a member of a source selection evaluation board than a COR, once again, CORs are safest obtaining legal counsel on the details of prohibitions relating to conflicts of interest.

50. What does the Procurement Integrity Act restrict?

Section 27 of Public Law 100-679, the Procurement Integrity Act, has been legally binding in its current form since January 1, 1997. Its four main provisions pertain to:

- A ban against disclosure of procurement information
- A ban against obtaining procurement information
- A requirement for procurement officers to report employment contacts by or with a competing contractor
- A one-year ban for certain personnel against accepting compensation from the contractor.

The Procurement Integrity Act is encapsulated in FAR 3.104.

Participating personally and substantially. "Participating personally and substantially in a federal agency procurement" means active and significant involvement of an individual in any of the following activities directly related to that procurement:

- Drafting, reviewing, or approving the specification or statement of work for the procurement
- Preparing or developing the solicitation
- Evaluating bids or proposals, or selecting a source (i.e., a contractor)
- Negotiating price or terms and conditions of the contract
- Reviewing and approving the award of the contract.

Restrictions on offers of employment. If an agency official who is participating personally and substantially in a federal agency procurement for a contract in excess of the simplified acquisition threshold (currently $150,000) contacts or is contacted by a contractor who is a bidder or offeror in that federal agency procurement regarding possible non-federal employment for that official, the official shall:

1. Promptly report the contact in writing to his supervisor and to the designated agency ethics official (or designee) of his agency

2. Either reject the possibility of non-federal employment or disqualify himself or herself from further personal and substantial participation in that federal agency procurement until the agency authorizes him or her to resume participation in such procurement, on the grounds that:

   (a) The contractor no longer is a bidder or offeror in that federal agency procurement

   or

   (b) All discussions with the bidder or offeror regarding possible non-federal employment have been terminated without an agreement or arrangement for employment.

Post-employment restrictions. Any former agency official may not accept compensation from a contractor as an employee, officer, director, or consultant within a period of one year after serving as a member of a selection board or as the chief of a financial or technical evaluation team for a procurement in which that contractor was selected for award of a contract in excess of $10 million.

Release of proprietary information. The Procurement Integrity Act also prohibits any person who is given authorized or unauthorized access to proprietary or source selection information regarding a procurement from disclosing such information to any person other than one authorized by the head of an agency or a CO.

51. How is the Procurement Integrity Act enforced, and what penalties can be imposed for violating it?

The Procurement Integrity Act can be enforced through contractual action or by penalties of an administrative, civil, or criminal nature. Penalties can include:

- Criminal punishment, including fines and/or five years in prison
- Civil penalty of $50,000, plus twice the amount of the illegal compensation offered or received
- Organizational penalty of $500,000, plus twice the amount of the illegal compensation offered or received.

52. What can the COR or other government officials do if they are concerned that they may have violated the Procurement Integrity Act?

Officials or former officials in doubt as to whether they may have violated the Procurement Integrity Act may request advice from the appropriate agency ethics official. To find out who this is, the COR should consult his or her agency's Office of Counsel or the Inspector General's Office, or ask the CO for a counsel reference. The request for an advisory opinion should be in writing and must be signed and dated. It should contain specifics about the procurement, the requestor's role in it, and the contractor involved. The ethics official will issue an opinion within 30 days or as soon thereafter as practicable and will rely on the information provided by the requestor unless there is reason to believe the information is fraudulent, misleading, or otherwise incorrect.

CHAPTER 3

Planning for the Acquisition

The COR's duties at the beginning of the procurement process include determining the government's needs, planning for the procurement, researching the marketplace, coordinating funding documents, developing competition strategies, and defining the requirements.

The COR leads the technical team members in these efforts and must work closely with the contracting office team members to ensure that a complete, accurate, and effective acquisition is developed in terms of its technical requirements, price, and delivery. In many respects, these initial duties constitute the "translation phase," i.e., the process of translating technical requirements into contractual requirements.

These initial efforts include:

- Developing the acquisition plan
- Conducting market research
- Coordinating funding information
- Considering competition requirements
- Developing the work package, which includes the:
    - Purchase request
    - Requirements document
    - Surveillance plan
    - Government cost estimate

- – Evaluation factors
- – Concurrence and approval documentation
- Considering government property issues
- Considering service contract issues.

These efforts will result in a complete technical work package that will be forwarded to and coordinated with the CO. This coordination could include responding to questions; providing missing or deficient information; possibly preparing justifications for sole source or otherwise limited competition; or getting approvals for funding commitments, government cost estimates, and other documents related to the technical requirements as required. The COR will most likely be responsible for overall coordination, but he or she will also need to rely on other program or budget personnel to perform some coordination duties and to provide information as necessary. After the CO accepts the work package, action to initiate the procurement will begin at the contracting office.

After the CO has started the procurement process, the COR will frequently need to provide technical assistance to the contracting office team as the process moves forward. (The COR's technical assistance duties will be covered in Chapter 4.)

KEY TERMS

Several key terms will be helpful to the COR when he or she is involved in developing the acquisition plan, conducting market research, identifying competition requirements, and developing the work package, purchase request, and requirements document.

FAR 2.101 defines a *commercial item*, in part, as:

Any item, other than real property, that is of a type customarily used for nongovernmental purposes and that

(1) Has been sold, leased, or licensed to the general public, or

(2) Has been offered for sale, lease, or license to the general public.

This definition goes on to provide guidance regarding the determination of a commercial item in various circumstances.

A *commerciality determination* is a review of the requirements for a particular acquisition to determine if the government's need could be met by an item or service customarily available in the marketplace. This determination will be based on the government's market research and will be made without asking prospective offerors to provide more than the minimum information necessary about their products relative to the requirement. The CO may ask the COR to conduct this review.

If:	Then:
The item or service customarily available in the marketplace *could* meet the requirement	The method established by FAR Part 12, Acquisition of Commercial Items, should be used to solicit offers and award contracts.
The government requirement *cannot* be met by an item or service customarily available in the marketplace	The method outlined in FAR Part 12 should *not* be used.

Nondevelopmental items (NDI) are items that do not have to be developed for the current requirement. For example, an NDI may:

- Have been previously developed and used exclusively for governmental purposes
- Require only minor modification of an item customarily available in the commercial marketplace
- Be an item that has already been produced but is not yet in use.

DEVELOPING THE ACQUISITION PLAN

53. What is the acquisition plan?

The *acquisition plan* is the product of effective teamwork on the part of the entire team—the program manager, the CO, and the appropriate functional experts (e.g., project officer, program director, engineer in charge of the items being acquired). As prepared by program managers in partnership with contract specialists and other members of the acquisition team, acquisition plans are designed to:

- Satisfy the government's needs in the most effective, economical, and timely manner

- Encourage or require offerors to supply and use commercial items or, to the extent commercial items are not suitable, other nondevelopmental items to the maximum extent practicable
- Employ strategies for acquiring services that implement performance-based contracting methods (or provide rationale for not using those methods)
- Provide for full and open competition through the use of competitive procedures that are tailored to reflect the circumstances of the acquisition and are consistent with the need to fulfill the government's requirements efficiently.

54. **What acquisition background information and objectives should the COR provide when he or she assists in preparing the acquisition plan?**

In addition to the "statement of need,"[1] the COR should compile information on:

- The findings of market research
- Cost concerns (the overall cost estimate as well as any critical cost factors)
- Delivery or performance period requirements
- Tradeoffs (among cost/schedule/performance requirements)
- Risks associated with technical requirements or delivery
- Sources (and their unique or outstanding capabilities, if applicable)
- Competition (or lack thereof)
- Budgeting and funding
- Product or service descriptions
- Priorities, allocations, and allotments (this information would identify any critical materials or facilities that might have to be provided on a priority basis, e.g., material for an urgent government requirement)
- Make or buy (should the contractor make the needed item or buy it from a subcontractor?)

---

[1] The *statement of need* is a general overview of the circumstances and requirements that initially created the need to acquire supplies or services by contract. This information, compiled by the program office, is the technical genesis (i.e., the "what, why, and when" relative to the technical requirements) of the acquisition plan.

- Testing and evaluation requirements of supply items prior to full production, usually referred to as first article or prototype unit items
- Government-furnished property (is it better for the government to furnish or not to furnish property?)
- Environmental and energy conservation considerations
- Security considerations
- Any other relevant considerations.

The COR will need to perform the following tasks to update or prepare the acquisition plan and provide funding coordination as necessary:

1. Assist in identifying acquisition-related information
2. Perform market research
3. Assist in preparing the acquisition plan
4. Coordinate funding information with the contracting office.

55. How does the COR assist in identifying acquisition-related needs from program and project plans?

The COR is responsible for:

- Providing technical details about supplies and services to be procured
- Providing technical input for the development of acquisition strategies (e.g., decisions related to contract type or whether to provide government property)
- Making decisions on whether to use advance notices or call conferences to clarify complex technical details prior to issuance of the solicitation
- Technically researching alternative techniques to enhance competition
- Creating program baselines (milestones, cost, and performance).

56. What sources of information can assist the COR in identifying these acquisition-related needs?

The COR can consult the following sources to identify the government's acquisition-related needs:

- Changes in agency policies or regulations
- Documents related to budget, plans, and programs
- Projections from data on the currently expiring contract (if applicable) or on previously completed contracts

- Surveys of requiring activities and other program planners
- Changes in contract requirements.

The COR may also obtain this information by participating in meetings to plan agency missions.

CONDUCTING MARKET RESEARCH

57. What is market research, and why is it important? How are market data classified?

The COR needs to perform *market research* for all procurements to identify what products or services may be available to satisfy the government's needs and to obtain a greater understanding of the marketplace before he or she makes procurement-related decisions. The program office has overall responsibility for conducting market research that is focused on the technical aspects of the procurement. Usually the COR, assisted by other program personnel as necessary, needs to gather data early in the process, giving consideration to:

- Historical data
- Industry data
- Data related to the competitive nature of the requirement.

For purposes of market research, historical data may include relevant acquisition histories and agency-wide past performance file data. In collecting historical data, the COR may find and include information on:

- Current suppliers of the required products or services
- Potential suppliers
- Previous procurement strategies, acquisition plans, and lead times
- Problems and issues in the award and administration of previous contracts
- A contractor's past performance, including:
  - Quality of products or services provided
  - Timeliness of performance
  - Cost control
  - Past performance of key personnel.

Industry data or trends will affect how a requirements document or performance schedule may be developed for the procurement. The COR needs to gather and document data on the following industry developments and trends when compiling the work package:

- The existence of new or upgraded products and services
- The existence of products and services capable of being modified to meet government needs
- Trends in technology, price, supply, and demand
- Practices of commercial firms, including information on terms, conditions, the availability of buyer financing, maintenance of contract deliverables, and warranties
- Production and delivery lead times
- The availability of other qualified sources that can provide or offer:
  - Commercial items
  - Commercial practices that can be modified to fit the government's requirements
  - Commercial items that can be modified to meet the government's needs (i.e., a nondevelopmental item; see Key Terms earlier in this chapter for further information)
  - Better warranty, buyer financing, or discount terms
  - Laws and regulations unique to the government's requirement
  - Possible industry-wide provisions for distribution and support capabilities of local suppliers
  - Information not generally available to the public.

58. How does the COR perform market research?

To collect market data, the COR may:

- Contact commercial experts
- Use other recent market research information
- Consult the government-wide point of entry (GPE), *www.fedbizopps.gov*
- Query databases or conduct on-line communication
- Obtain source lists from other agencies or associations
- Review company catalogs and product literature
- Hold presolicitation conferences.

COORDINATING FUNDING INFORMATION

59. How does the COR coordinate funding information with the contracting office before solicitation to determine if funds are available for the government to enter into a contract?

The COR should coordinate funding information between the fiscal officer in the program office and the CO. These coordination duties include responding to any questions or providing missing or deficient information as required until the CO is satisfied that all issues related to contract funding have been resolved. The CO must be certain that adequate funding exists prior to awarding the contract. Specifically, these duties might include obtaining the independent government cost estimate (IGCE; see Question 72) from the project officer (or program manager); getting funding documents from the program fiscal officer, including applicable accounting and appropriation data; and forwarding all this information to the CO.

The program fiscal officer must commit (or reserve) funds in an amount determined by the IGCE (included in the work package) to ensure that adequate funds are available later when the CO obligates (or spends) the funds by signing the contract at the time of award. The COR may, of course, be required to coordinate adjustments in the funding if the original IGCE and the final award amount differ.

The COR should follow these steps to ensure that the funding process is properly executed:

1. Identify the type of funding to be provided and select the matching contract clause:
   - Multi-year (funding expires at the end of number of years specified, e.g., 5 years)
   - Annual (funding expires at the end of the year in which funds are appropriated)
   - No-year (generally used to refer to funds that have no expiration date specified).

2. Determine the date by which funds must be obligated; that is, determine when the funds will expire and if funds will be available prior to contract award.

3. Prior to initiating the procurement action, determine if the amount of funds provided is sufficient, based on the independent government cost estimate and the anticipated award amount.

CONSIDERING COMPETITION REQUIREMENTS

While conducting market research, contracting and program officials need to be aggressive in collecting competitive data by:

- Finding out the competitive history of a procurement
- Identifying and using required sources of supply
- Obtaining competitive sources for the new procurement.

The COR may recommend to the CO the data-gathering strategy or strategies that would be optimal in terms of the mission and the market and that would yield the maximum number of responsible offers. Any selected method or strategy should:

- Consider industry-wide performance capabilities
- Not rule out the availability of commercial items or nondevelopmental items.

60. What are required supply sources?

Although the government purchases many of the items and services it needs on the open market, there are statutory and regulatory sources that have priority over other sources and *must be used* prior to soliciting commercial sources.

The following sources are listed in the required order of priority for supply requirements:

1. Agency inventories
2. Excess from other agencies
3. Federal Prison Industries, Inc. (UNICOR)
4. Products available from the Committee for Purchase From People Who Are Blind or Severely Disabled
5. Stock programs:
   - General Services Administration
   - Defense Logistics Agency
   - Department of Veterans Affairs
   - Military inventory control points
6. Mandatory Federal Supply Schedules
7. Optional use Federal Supply Schedules
8. Commercial sources (including educational and nonprofit institutions).

For *service* requirements, sources must be consulted in this order:

1. Services on the Procurement List maintained by the Committee for Purchase from People Who Are Blind or Severely Disabled
2. Mandatory Federal Supply Schedules
3. Optional use Federal Supply Schedules
4. Federal Prison Industries, Inc. (UNICOR) or commercial sources (including educational and nonprofit institutions).

61. What are the three types of competition?

The Competition in Contracting Act (CICA) established three types of competition:

*   Full and open competition
*   Full and open competition after exclusion of sources
*   Other than full and open competition.

In *full and open competition,* all responsible sources are permitted to compete. The term *responsible sources*, in this context, means that the potential contractor meets the standards of responsibility set forth in FAR 9.104. In everyday terms, it simply means that the prospective contractor has the capacity and capability, in all respects, to perform the contract.

The method of *full and open competition after exclusion of sources* has two different applications. The head of an agency can elect full and open competition after excluding certain sources in order to obtain and maintain alternate sources. Also, sources may be excluded in order to use small business set-asides; when sources are excluded for this reason, the decision to do so may be made by the CO and does not have to be authorized by the head of the agency.

The method of *other than full and open competition* requires one of the following exceptions to support its use, but by statute a CO cannot use other than full and open competition if the underlying reason for its use is lack of advanced acquisition planning or the possibility of losing expiring funds.

62. What are the exceptions to full and open competition?

The Competition in Contracting Act (CICA) permits contracting without providing for full and open competition when the following conditions exist:

1. Only one responsible source is available to provide services or supplies.
2. Unusual and compelling urgency.

3. Industrial mobilization (e.g., the need to maintain a facility or a producer in case of a national emergency).

4. International agreements such as the North American Free Trade Agreement (NAFTA); foreign military sales are also covered by this exception.

5. The procurement is expressly authorized or required by statute (i.e., procurement from a certain source, such as the Federal Prisons Industries, government printing, or qualified nonprofit agencies for the blind or other severely handicapped persons, is expressly authorized/required).

6. National security concerns (i.e., circumstances in which simply publicizing the procurement would compromise classified information).

7. Public interest concerns (e.g., a situation in which the head of an agency determines that it would be best to use other than competitive procedures in a particular procurement). (A recent relevant example involved cleanup of hazardous waste that endangered public health. The type of environmental hazard posed by the waste necessitated the use of one particular source, with specialized skills and facilities, for the cleanup. This situation was similar to one in which only one responsible source was available to perform contract work. Because significant public health and safety risks were involved, this exception was used so that congressional review and approval would be a part of the approval process.)

DEVELOPING THE WORK PACKAGE

63. What are work packages?

Work packages are prepared by the office needing the supply or service to describe its requirement. As stated at the beginning of this chapter, these packages include:

- The purchase request
- The requirements document
- The surveillance plan
- The government cost estimate
- Evaluation factors
- Concurrence and approval documentation
- Any other attachments necessary to support the acquisition of the government requirement.

A complete work package must include information on the desired/required time of delivery or the desired performance period and place of performance. Signed and approved work packages are submitted to the CO. Once the CO has received the signed work package from the appropriate officials, the CO initiates the procurement process.

64. **What tasks does the COR perform to develop a work package?**

The COR, assisted by other program personnel as necessary:

1. Prepares the purchase request (PR)
2. Responds to PR deficiencies
3. Prepares the requirements document
4. Prepares the surveillance plan
5. Prepares the government cost estimate
6. Prepares the evaluation factors
7. Obtains concurrence and approval for documents as required.

65. **What information should be included in the purchase request?**

The following information should be included in the purchase request (PR):

- The goals and objectives of the procurement
- A commerciality determination (see Key Terms earlier in this chapter for more information)
- A listing of supply or service sources
- The quantity of supplies needed
- Evaluation factors (for the evaluation of contractors' offers)
  - Price-related factors
  - Non-price-related factors
- Packaging and marking instructions
  - Any other special instructions
- Delivery and shipment requirements
  - Date by which the government needs the item or service
  - Address to which items should be delivered
- Contract administration information

- Any special requirements
  - Identity (i.e., name, phone number) of the COR, if unique technical qualifications are involved
  - Any special provisions and clauses
- Signatures from officials authorized and required to sign the form.

66. What if the CO finds elements of the PR missing or deficient?

The COR must respond to any requests from the CO regarding missing or deficient elements of the PR and provide corrections or supplementary information necessary to achieve acceptance of the PR by the CO.

67. What is a requirements document?

A *requirements document* is a written description of the government's needs, including definition of the necessary physical characteristics and functions of the supplies or services that must be delivered or accomplished to meet those needs. The requirements document establishes the expectations for the contractor so that during and after contract performance, the government can evaluate the contractor's performance.

Providing an adequate description of the government's needs is one of the most important duties of the COR and the technical personnel, and is an area where the CO's knowledge and ability can be of assistance. A well-written requirements document should contain:

- Clear and precise requirements that allow the government to structure sound proposal evaluation criteria.

- Clear and explicit description of these requirements. Precise descriptions of the government's needs will reduce the likelihood that offerors will misinterpret the requirements; thus, good descriptions enhance the quality of the offers submitted.

A well-written requirements document should also help prevent delays, save administrative effort, and reduce the chances of protests by unsuccessful offerors.

Agencies may select from existing requirements documents, modify or combine existing requirements documents, or create new requirements documents to meet agency needs, consistent with the following order of precedence:

1. Documents mandated for use by law

2. Performance-oriented documents

3. Detailed design-oriented documents

4. Standards, specifications, and related publications issued by the government outside the Defense or federal series for the non-repetitive acquisition of items (see FAR 11.101).

68. **What is a product description, and what are the different types of product descriptions?**

The *product description* comprises the actual documents used for a requirements document. Types of product descriptions include:

- *Commercial item description.* An indexed, simplified product description that describes (by functional or performance characteristics) the available, acceptable commercial product that will satisfy the government's needs.

- *Specification.* A description of the technical requirements for a material product or service that includes the criteria for determining whether these requirements are met. Specifications state only actual minimum needs of the government and are designed to promote full and open competition. A specification can be written in many different ways; specifications may dictate:

  - *Performance.* A performance specification expresses requirements for the output, function, or operation of a commodity.

  - *Functionality.* A functionality specification states only the end result to be achieved.

  - *Design.* A design specification specifies the exact dimensions, materials, composition, physical and chemical requirements, and other details about the product to be provided or the service to be performed.

  See Figure 3-1 for additional information on performance and design criteria.

- *Non-government voluntary standard.* A standard for products supplied to the government established by the private sector and available for public use. Voluntary standards do not include the private standards of individual firms.

- *Purchase description.* A statement of the essential physical characteristics and functions required to meet the government's minimum needs, or a statement of work (SOW) outlining the services to be provided under a contract.

Performance Criteria	The preferred method of describing agency needs is stating requirements in terms of the *final outcome* and allowing the contractor to achieve that outcome *without specific direction*. This method employs *performance criteria*.
Example	When the government required a heavier-than-air flying machine, it stated the following performance criteria: • Quick and easy assembly and disassembly of the aircraft for transportation in army wagons • The aircraft should be capable of being assembled and put in operating condition in about one hour • The aircraft must be able to carry two persons with a combined weight of 350 pounds plus sufficient fuel for a flight of 125 miles.
Pros and Cons	Performance criteria are preferred because the liability for performance is placed on the *contractor*. The use of performance criteria also allows greater competition because there is greater flexibility in design parameters. However, requirements using performance criteria are *harder to write* and the contractor's performance is *harder to monitor and inspect* when performance criteria are used for evaluation.
Design Criteria	*Design criteria* are employed when the product description describes in *explicit detail* how the contractor is to perform or manufacture a product.
Example	The government could have specified the type of material to be used in building the heavier-than-air flying machine, or its wingspan, weight, dimensions, or other specific characteristics.
Pros and Cons	Design criteria place maximum liability on the *government* for results because any flaw in the design is the fault of the government. Product descriptions employing design criteria are *easier to write*, and it is easier to *perform objective surveillance* when design criteria have been established.

FIGURE 3-1.   Performance versus Design Criteria

69.   What must the COR do to encourage government offices to provide the appropriate information when determining the government's needs?

A COR needs to ensure that government offices do all of the following when determining the government's needs:

• State requirements in terms the market can satisfy
• Promote full and open competition

- Include restrictive provisions in the specification or statement of work only to the extent needed to satisfy the minimum needs of the agency or as authorized by law
- State requirements in terms of functions to be performed, performance parameters required of the contract deliverables, or essential physical characteristics of a supply item (rather than design characteristics)
- Define requirements that enable offerors to supply commercial items or nondevelopmental items (NDI) if suitable commercial items are not available
- Provide firms offering commercial or other items an opportunity to compete to meet agency requirements
- Require prime contractors and subcontractors to incorporate commercial items or NDI as components of the required items
- Require the offeror to comply with federal, state, and local environmental laws and regulations
- Modify requirements when appropriate so that commercial items (or if commercial items are not available, NDI) can satisfy the requirement
- To the extent practicable, obtain feedback from potential offerors on similar potential or current requirements given to them by other government agencies for other contract work.

70. What should be avoided, and what must be included, when creating a requirements document?

Figure 3-2 lists potential inadequacies in requirements documents.

71. What is a surveillance plan, and what is the COR's role in developing it?

A *surveillance plan*, which is generally developed by the COR, provides a systematic, structured method for the COR to evaluate services and products that contractors are required to furnish. At a minimum, the surveillance plan:

- Outlines how the government will monitor a contractor's performance
- Is structured according to the surveillance plan format specified in agency policy, as well as the agency's quality control and quality assurance procedures
- Includes award/fee plans, as appropriate.

A requirements document should yield the best market response in terms of competition, quality, timeliness, price, and fulfillment of the actual functional need. In particular, the use of commercial or nondevelopmental items should be encouraged. The following should be avoided when writing a requirements document:

- Specification of design characteristics (e.g., describing *how* a service is to be performed) for requirements that can, with equal or greater validity and reliability, be cast in terms of needed functions, performance, or essential physical characteristics
- Use of fixed minimum performance requirements rather than performance targets, when market research data suggest that the government is likely to benefit by providing offerors the flexibility to propose price or performance tradeoffs
- Failure to provide sufficient detail regarding needed items for a potential offeror of commercial items; the offeror may then not know which of its commercial products or services to offer the government
- Specification of a particular brand name, product, or a feature of a product that is peculiar to one manufacturer, thereby unnecessarily precluding consideration of a product manufactured by another company
- Other restrictive or impractical requirements with regard to the market's capabilities
- Nonessential or obsolete requirements
- Ambiguous or vague terms
- Unclear division of responsibilities between the government and the offeror
- Omission of needed information or requirements that are too loosely worded to screen out inadequate products or services (i.e., failure to include all minimum essential requirements in the specification or the statement of work)
- Assignment of supporting functions that contractors can do at lower cost to the government
- Failure to use metric measurements where warranted
- Failure to require contractors and subcontractors at all levels to buy commercial or other nondevelopmental components for contract deliverables to the maximum extent practicable
- Combination of requirements into a single acquisition too broad for the agency or a prospective contractor to manage effectively
- Requirements that can be restated to promote the use of environmentally preferable and energy-efficient products and services (e.g., promoting energy conservation, elimination or reduction of ozone-depleting substances usage, use of recovered material content).

FIGURE 3-2. Potential Inadequacies in Requirements Documents

72. What is an independent government cost estimate?

An *independent government cost estimate* (IGCE) is a detailed assessment of the cost to the government for services or supplies to be acquired from a contractor. This estimate is:

- Generally developed by the COR or other government technical experts

- An internal government estimate of the price a contractor should propose based on the specification or statement of work (SOW)
- Confidential information that should not be discussed or shared with the contractor.

Government cost estimates are simple when the requirements are for products or services that are commercially available because pricing for these are based on an average of commercial prices. Cost estimates for more complex requirements or noncommercial items require a detailed breakdown. The COR should ensure that the government cost estimate:

- Describes program needs (i.e., technical objectives of the acquisition)
- Identifies sub-objectives for each task and the project office that will complete each task
- Identifies and sequences tasks to organize the overall objectives for each sub-objective
- Identifies resources needed
- Identifies the length of time each task should take
- Accurately reflects all available data on the project
- Lists probable line items and the probable quantity, cost, and procurement milestones for each
- Describes and is based on factual information that is representative of potential offers.

73. What are evaluation factors, and what is the COR's role in preparing them?

Some awards can be made on the basis of price alone. Other, more complex contracts will be awarded on the basis of price and other non-price factors, i.e., technical factors.

The COR should prepare a list of significant technical factors and subfactors that are directly related to the government's technical requirements and that will be used to evaluate the contractors' offers. An example of an evaluation factor might be:

Significant technical factor: Quality of work
Subfactors: Work appearance
            Thoroughness and accuracy of work
            Engineering competence

The particular requirements of each acquisition will determine appropriate evaluation factors. Acquisition circumstances can also determine which evaluation factors and procedures should be used. The CO may fashion suitable evaluation procedures in accordance with relevant parts of the FAR, such as:

- FAR Part 13, when using simplified acquisition procedures
- FAR Part 12, when contracting for commercial items
- FAR Part 14, when using sealed bidding
- FAR Part 15, when negotiating competitive acquisitions.

The COR should remember that all evaluation factors and subfactors are used to determine if the offeror can meet the government's needs and if the offer is the most advantageous to the government. Evaluation factors should be designed to ensure complete and impartial evaluation of all offers received.

74. What are the two general types of evaluation factors?

Evaluation factors can be based on *price-related factors* and *nonprice-related factors.*

Price-related factors help the government realistically determine the lowest overall cost at which it can obtain commercial supplies or services. Typical price-related factors included in a solicitation, e.g., an invitation for bids (IFB) used in sealed bidding, might be:

- The cost of government-furnished property
- Options
- The cost of leasing needed items versus purchasing them
- Transportation costs
- Other costs.

The cost of government-furnished property. When contractors possess government property, they are required to use that property to the maximum practical extent. At the same time, agencies are required to eliminate any competitive advantage that might arise from using such property. Accordingly, solicitations that provide for government-furnished property will include the following:

- A description of the evaluation procedures to be followed

- Whether a rental equivalent evaluation factor will be used
- Whether rent charges will be applied in lieu of a rental equivalent evaluation factor
- Other costs or savings to be evaluated
- A requirement that the offeror disclose:
  - All government property the offeror proposes to use
  - Whether property offered in the solicitation is already in its possession
  - Any other information regarding the government property.

Options. An option indicates a unilateral right in a contract by which, for a specified time, the government may:

- Elect to purchase additional supplies or services called for by the contract
- Elect to extend the term of the contract.

Solicitations containing option provisions:

- State whether the option will be included in the evaluation. (Options should be evaluated if the government reasonably intends to exercise them.)
- Inform offerors at the time of award of the government's plan to exercise the option.
- Allow option quantities to be offered with no price limitation.
- Allow offerors to submit varying prices for options.
- Require, in limited situations, that option prices be no higher than prices for the initial requirement.

Lease versus purchase. Generally, the government's decision to either lease or purchase needed items is a matter of economics. Purchasing is preferred if long-range leasing costs will exceed the purchase price. Leasing is appropriate in circumstances when doing so will benefit the government. Additionally, agency policy, acquisition histories, or market research may affect the decision to buy or lease supplies.

Typical reasons for soliciting for *purchase only* include:

- The requirement does not lend itself to leasing (e.g., when services, perishables, weapons, or spare parts are needed).

- Property will be provided to other contractors as government-furnished property.
- The product has a long expected life and will not need upgrading (e.g., desks, chairs).
- The product has a short shelf life.
- The products will be used in a secure area (unless security can be ensured under a lease).

Typical reasons for soliciting a *lease only* or a *lease with option to buy* include:

- One-time use of the item or items and no future need for them
- Urgency
- The products are needed only on a limited, intermittent basis (e.g., cranes)
- The particular goods needed are available from the market only through a lease
- Maintenance by the original equipment manufacturer is offered only when the equipment is leased
- Prices are expected to decline rapidly or technology is expected to improve rapidly during the period of need
- Continued need for the goods is not known beyond the period of performance.

However, when the relative economic advantages of lease versus purchase are unknown or minimal, and when market research discloses that the industry offers both options, prices for both lease and purchase should be solicited. The solicitation will advise offerors that the government's award decision will be based upon the most advantageous offer received, considering:

- Prices for a new purchase
- Cumulative lease prices for the estimated period of use
- Net overall prices in leases with options to purchase or own
- Transportation and installation costs.

Transportation costs. The COR must inform the CO if he or she wants offerors to submit offers that address shipping requirements for the products to be delivered. Shipping options include:

- Free on board (F.O.B.) at origin, with the cost of shipping and risk of loss borne by the buyer (the government)
- F.O.B. destination, with the cost of shipping and risk of loss borne by the seller (the contractor)
- Both bases—prospective contractors may quote both F.O.B. origin and F.O.B. destination costs.

Generally, F.O.B. at origin offers may be more advantageous to the government when lower freight rates are available to the government for shipment to final destinations. When offers on both bases are permitted, the solicitation will advise the offerors that the two F.O.B. offers will be evaluated on the basis of the lowest overall cost to the government.

Other costs. Other price-related factors that may be applicable to some procurements include:

- Energy conservation and efficiency criteria
- Estimated quantities of goods needed (for indefinite delivery contracts)
- Life cycle costs (or modified life cycle costs)
- Select life cycle costs for equipment with an expected life greater than one year if there are sufficient data (derived from market research) to develop and apply the life cycle cost formula
- Cost factors to consider when additional supplies and services are needed to support the purchase, such as:
  - Installation
  - Maintenance
  - Warranty protection or repair
  - Training
  - Technical manuals
  - Spare parts
  - Supplemental supplies.

When preparing a list of factors that can be used in evaluating government requirements, the COR needs to consider *non-price-related factors* and a methodology for applying them. Such factors may include:

- The contractor's past performance

- The contractor's understanding of the government's requirements
- The contractor's technical approach to performing the work
- The contractor's experience in performing similar work
- The qualifications of engineering personnel or other technical personnel
- The quality of the facilities to be used for performing the work
- The contractor's quality assurance programs and plans
- The contractor's management capabilities to perform the proposed work
- The contractor's scheduling and delivery-related controls
- The contractor's subcontracting and make-or-buy plans
- The contractor's environmental objectives, including its consideration of environmentally preferred products
- The contractor's cost realism and other relevant factors.

The COR should also consider that some non-price-related factors may:

- Exclude some offerors
- Dilute the relative importance of the requirements
- Be unnecessary, inconsistent, irrational, arbitrary, and not pertinent to the requirement
- Have been overlooked or omitted
- Be described in ambiguous terms
- Overemphasize subfactors in evaluating the requirement, i.e., be overly restrictive by concentrating on minute details that are not actually relevant.

75. **What two steps should the COR take before submitting the work package to the CO?**

The COR must:

1. *Ensure that the work package is current, accurate, and complete.* The work package should:
   - Be sufficient to proceed with contract action; it should contain all required documents, information, and approvals from the program office.

- Be written in terms that accurately reflect the market's capabilities (lead-times, production, delivery, and cost) and procurement lead-times.
- Be designed to obtain maximum competition.
- Ensure that quality assurance requirements are met.
- Satisfy the government's needs in the most effective, economical, and timely manner.
- Include past performance data as an evaluation factor. (Note: Section 1091 of the Federal Acquisition Streamlining Act states: "Past contract performance of an offeror is one of the relevant factors that a contracting official of an executive agency should consider in awarding a contract.")
- Encourage or require offerors to supply and use materials or, to the extent that commercial items are not suitable, other non-developmental items to the maximum extent practicable.

2. *Secure all necessary authorizations.* To prevent delays in the procurement cycle, the COR should obtain concurrence and approval for documents in the work package as specified by agency policies. The approvals are necessary to ensure that:
   - Funding requirements have been made and certified
   - Justifications for restrictive requirements have been included
   - A source list considering small businesses, 8(a) firms, and other socioeconomic programs has been included with the purchase request package.

The following officials or offices may be required to provide concurrence or approval of the work package:
- Agency head or higher authority
- CO or head of the contracting activity
- Competition advocate, acting also as the commercial items advocate
- Designated officials from requirements/user organizations
- Legal counsel
- Accounting, budgeting, or finance office
- Small business/minority business officer.

GOVERNMENT PROPERTY CONSIDERATIONS

During development of the work package, the COR has the initial responsibility for recommending whether to provide government property to the contractor. Later, during contract administration, the COR may be given responsibility for administering government property, or a property administrator and plant clearance officer may be assigned to the contract. However, even if a property administrator and/or a plant clearance officer are assigned, the COR still may or may not be responsible for overall monitoring of the contract, including government property administration.[2]

According to government policy, contractors are ordinarily required to furnish all property necessary to perform government contracts. Government property may be provided when its use is necessary to achieve:

- Significant economy by using the government's significant buying power to obtain price discounts
- Standardization through the government providing all materials and production facilities
- Expedited production
- Increased competition
- Security objectives that might otherwise be too expensive for contractors, especially small businesses
- Other objectives that are considered to be in the best interest of the government.

When contractors request government property during administration of the contract, the COR must evaluate the request and provide appropriate recommendations to the CO. The COR should refer to FAR Subpart 45.3, *Authorizing the Use and Rental of Government Property*, and FAR 45.102, *Policy*, for guidance on providing government property.

76. What is government property?

The term *government property* means all property owned or leased by the government under the terms of a contract. Government property includes both government-furnished property and contractor-acquired property.

---

[2]This depends on the specific responsibilities assigned by his or her letter of designation; see Chapter 1 for more details about the letter of designation.

Government property includes material, equipment, special tooling, special test equipment, and real property. Government property does *not* include intellectual property and software.

The term *property* denotes all tangible property, real and personal, and may include:

- *Equipment.* A tangible item that is functionally complete for its intended purpose, durable, nonexpendable, and needed for the performance of the contract. Equipment is not intended for sale, and it does not ordinarily lose its identity or become a component part of another article when put into use. Equipment does *not* include material, real property, special test equipment, or special tooling.

- *Material.* Property that may be consumed or expended during the performance of the contract, component parts of a higher assembly, or items that lose their individual identity through incorporation into an end item. Material does *not* include equipment, special tooling, special test equipment, or real property.

- *Special tooling.* Jigs, dies, fixtures, molds, patterns, taps, gauges, and all components of these items, including foundations and similar improvements necessary for installing special test equipment. Special tooling does *not* include material, special test equipment, real property, equipment, machine tools, or similar capital items.

- *Special test equipment.* Either single or multipurpose integrated test units engineered, designed, fabricated, or modified to accomplish special-purpose testing in performing a contract.

- *Plant equipment.* Personal property of a capital nature (including equipment, machine tools, test equipment, furniture, vehicles, and accessory and auxiliary items) for use in manufacturing supplies, in performing services, or for any administrative or general plant purpose. It does *not* include special tooling or special test equipment.

Government-furnished property (GFP) means property in the possession of, or directly acquired by, the government and subsequently furnished to the contractor for performance of a contract. It includes, but is not limited to, spares and property furnished for repair, maintenance, overhaul, or modification. It also includes contractor-acquired property if that property is a deliverable under a cost contract when accepted by the government for continued use under the contract.

Contractor-acquired property means property acquired, fabricated, or otherwise provided by the contractor for performing a contract and to which the government has title.

A *property administrator* is an authorized representative of the CO assigned to administer the contract requirements and obligations relating to government property. However, the person assigned as the COR under the contract may be asked to provide preaward guidance on government property.

A *plant clearance officer* is an authorized representative of the CO, appointed in accordance with agency procedures, responsible for screening, redistributing, and disposing of contractor inventory from a contractor's plant or work site.

77. What are the COR's roles on the contract with regard to government property?

The COR will need to perform the following tasks:

1. Identify what, if any, government property will be needed for proposed procurements.

2. Notify the CO of the use of government property. The contractor may use government property for only the specific contract intended, unless otherwise provided for and approved by the CO. The contractor may not modify, cannibalize, or make alterations to government property unless the contract specifically identifies the modifications, alterations, or improvements as work to be performed.

78. How does the COR determine if government property should be used on the proposed procurement and what government property should be used?

The COR should:

- Consider recommendations from other government officials
- Review acquisition histories of similar procurements
- Review reports on existing property inventory.

Once the determination is made that the use of government property is required, the COR should determine whether the government property for the proposed procurement will be:

- Furnished by the government to the contractor for use under the government contract

- Purchased by the government for the contractor to use under the government contract
- Acquired by the contractor for use under the government contract.

The COR should also identify the date that government-furnished property will be available and reserve the property in the agency inventory system. The COR should specify any special restrictions or conditions applicable to the government property, including:

- Whether the property is to be provided "as is"
- Security issues and other special handling, if needed
- Minimum skills needed to operate the government property.

79. How does the COR notify the CO of the use of government property, and what property-related issues should the COR consider in his or her notification?

The COR should submit a written document to the CO that lists all relevant factors necessary for justifying the use of government property as an integral part of the procurement. This document should also address issues specific to the type of government property needed, including:

1. *Government-furnished property issues*
   These issues may include:
   - Government liability for performance of GFP
   - Administrative costs and logistics support costs for GFP
   - Cost of modifying GFP
   - Opportunity costs of GFP (i.e., other ways the government might use the property)
   - Potential impact on the total contract price if GFP is proposed
   - Reductions in direct costs, indirect costs, and fee with GFP
   - Economic benefits of standardization through GFP
   - Estimated residual value of the items
   - Amount offered by the contractor for the right to retain the items
   - Effect on future competition and contract pricing.

2. *Contractor-acquired property issues*
   These issues may include:

   - Potential performance problems if contractor-acquired property is not delivered
   - Ownership of the contractor-acquired property
   - Use of contractor-acquired property on other contracts
   - Administrative costs and maintenance costs for contractor-acquired property
   - Government liability for storage of contractor-acquired property.

The COR needs to inform the CO of the availability of government property before a solicitation is issued. If government property is not available, the CO must have time to consider including a requirement for contractor-acquired property in the solicitation.

80. **What government property issues may arise after a solicitation has been issued?**

After the solicitation is issued, the CO may ask the COR to provide assistance when:

- A comparison with offers based on contractor-acquired property needs to be made
- An offeror has proposed different terms and conditions than those solicited with respect to GFP
- The contractor has submitted a postaward request for property not covered by the contract.

When government property is involved, it is imperative that the COR read the pertinent property clause of the contract. The COR must understand the rights and obligations of the government and contractor and be particularly aware of whether any deviations are authorized in the contract. Accurate COR files regarding delivery of property, changes, accountability, and condition of the property are essential in any dispute over GFP.

See Chapter 6, Administration of Government Property, for a discussion of COR responsibilities after contract award.

SPECIAL CONSIDERATIONS WHEN CONTRACTING FOR SERVICES

Acquiring contract services is a unique process and requires that the COR and other program officials understand the different types of service contracts that may be used, as well as those that may not be used. To avoid creating or entering into an illegal personal services contract, it is essential that the government contract team be aware of the distinction between personal and nonpersonal services as the team crafts the requirements document. It can be difficult to determine the difference between personal and nonpersonal services; the decision is a subjective one.

The FAR also authorizes a specific category of service contracts known as advisory and assistance services, which are services of a purely advisory nature relating to the support or improvement of agency policy development, decision making, management and administration, or research and development activities.

FAR Part 37 *requires the use of performance-based acquisitions for services to the maximum extent practicable* and prescribes policies and procedures for the use of performance-based acquisition methods. The COR and other program officials will need to thoroughly analyze their requirements to determine the applicability of performance-based acquisition procedures. These individuals serve as the principal technical experts and are usually the most familiar with the requirement; they are therefore best able to identify potential technical tradeoffs and determine whether the requirement can be met using a commercial solution.

If performance-based procedures are determined to be applicable, the COR and other program officials will primarily be involved with assisting the CO and other members of the acquisition team in developing the performance-based work statement and establishing measurable performance standards. The key to using performance-based methodologies is describing requirements as *outcomes* rather than in terms of *how* to accomplish the requirement. A performance-based work statement must be carefully structured to ensure that the requirement is articulated in this manner.

Although not all acquisitions for services can be conducted in a performance-based manner, the vast majority can. Those cases in which performance-based strategies are not employed should become the exception.

Another aspect of service contracting that CORs and program officials are likely to encounter relates to the current trend in the government to "contract out" a large amount of government work. These service contract efforts are classified and governed by the commercial activities (CA) program. The Office of Management and Budget's (OMB) Circular A-76 prescribes policy for this program; this circular is further discussed under Questions 95 through 99.

The COR will need to perform the following tasks to properly prepare a requirements document to acquire contractor services or to prepare the statement of work (SOW) under the CA program:

1. Distinguish requirements for services from requirements for supplies and assist the CO with Service Contract Act information as necessary

2. Determine whether the services are personal or non-personal

3. Determine whether the services are of the advisory and assistance type

4. Determine the applicability of performance-based acquisition procedures and assist the CO as necessary.

5. Review the procedures and requirements of the CA program and assist the CO as required.

81. What are the differences between requirements for services and requirements for supplies?

The COR will need to correctly determine if the requirement asks the contractor to perform services (which may include obtaining supplies) or merely to deliver products.

A service contract is a contract that directly engages the time and effort of a contractor whose primary purpose is to perform an identifiable task rather than to furnish an end item of supply. A service contract may be either a nonpersonal or personal contract. It can also cover services performed by either professional or non-professional personnel, whether on an individual or organizational basis.

Service contracts govern the following activities:

- Maintenance, overhaul, repair, servicing, rehabilitation, salvage, or modernization of supplies, systems, or equipment

- Routine, recurring maintenance of real property

- Housekeeping and base services

- Advisory and assistance services

- Operation of government-owned equipment, facilities, and systems

- Communications services
- Architect-engineering
- Transportation and related services
- Research and development.

The FAR states that program officials are responsible for accurately describing the need to be filled or problem to be resolved through service contracting in a manner that ensures full understanding and responsive performance by contractors. The program officials should obtain assistance from contracting officials as needed.

82. What is the Service Contract Act?

The Service Contract Act (SCA) of 1965 provides for minimum wages and fringe benefits as well as other conditions of work for contractors under certain types of service contracts. Whether or not the SCA applies to a specific service contract will be determined by the definitions and exceptions given in the act or implementing regulations.

83. When does the Service Contract Act apply, and when does it not apply?

The SCA is applicable if:

- The amount of the contract exceeds $2,500
- The principal purpose of the contract is to furnish services
- The contract is to be performed to a significant or substantial extent by other than executive, administrative, or professional employees
- The contract is to be performed primarily in the United States
- The contract is not otherwise exempted.

The SCA is not applicable to:

- Construction contracts (the Davis-Bacon Act applies for these contracts because labor categories and conditions for construction contracts differ from those for service contracts)
- Supply contracts (the Walsh-Healey Act applies for these contracts because labor categories and conditions for supply contracts are also different from those for service contracts)
- Carriage of freight or personnel by vessel, airplane, bus, truck, express, railway line, or oil or gas pipeline where published tariff rates are in effect

- Radio, telephone, telegraph, and cable services subject to the Communications Act of 1934
- Public utility services
- Employment contracts
- Other types of contracts that are exempted by the Department of Labor (DOL).

84. What are wage determinations?

Wage determinations are made by the Secretary of Labor to establish wage rates that a contractor must pay its employees during performance of a contract. These rates are to equal the prevailing wage rates paid in the locality in which the contract is to be performed.

A CO contemplating a service contract in excess of $2,500 must request a wage determination from the Department of Labor. There are two types of wage determinations: prevailing rates and the collective bargaining agreement (CBA).

A prevailing rates wage determination will list the minimum wages and benefits to be paid to the categories of service employees listed. If the classification of a service employee is not listed in the wage determination, but that individual is performing on the subject contract, the contractor must comply with the Fair Labor Standards Act (the national minimum wage).

If the incumbent contractor has a CBA with an employee union, the CBA becomes the wage determination if the contract is awarded to that contractor or if an option is exercised. The CBA automatically becomes the wage determination unless it is determined that the CBA was not reached at arms-length negotiations or the wage rates set by it vary significantly from average local pay for similar work.

85. What is the COR's role in making wage determinations?

The COR may be required to:

- Provide the skill classifications required by the contract technical requirements and the number of service employees in each skill class to the CO
- Assist in identifying the wage rates that would be paid to the members of each class if employed by the federal agency

- Provide the CO with information regarding places of performance if some contractor service employees will be working in different locations
- Assist in updating wage determinations when the contract has provisions for adjusting the contract price to reflect changes in wage rates. Some typical examples are:
  - Contract modifications that change the scope of work whereby labor requirements are affected significantly
  - Exercise of options or other such extensions of contract performance
  - Multiple-year contracts.

86. How does the COR determine whether services are personal or nonpersonal?

The FAR provides the following definitions of personal and nonpersonal service contracts:

- *Nonpersonal service contract*: A contract under which the personnel rendering the services are not subject, either by the contract's terms or by the manner of its administration, to the supervision and control usually prevailing in relationships between the government and its employees. (FAR 37.101.)
- *Personal service contract:* A contract that, by its express terms or as administered, makes the contractor personnel appear, in effect, to be government employees. An employer-employee relationship under a service contract occurs when, as a result of the contract's terms or the manner of its administration during performance, contractor personnel are subject to the relatively continuous supervision and control of a government officer or employee. Giving an order for a specific article or service, with the right to reject the finished product or results, is *not* the type of supervision or control that converts an individual who is an independent contractor (such as a contractor employee) into a government employee. (FAR 37.104.)

Nonpersonal service contracts are proper under general contracting authority. However, personal service contracts must be specifically authorized by statute. The government is normally required to obtain its employees by direct hire under competitive appointment or other procedures required by the civil service laws. Obtaining personal services by contract, rather than by direct hire, circumvents those laws unless Congress has specifically authorized acquisition of the services by contract.

87. What general guidance should the COR follow in making the determination of whether service contracts are personal or nonpersonal?

Each contract arrangement must be judged in the light of its own facts and circumstances, with the key question always being: "Will the government exercise relatively continuous supervision and control over the contractor personnel performing the contract?" The sporadic, unauthorized supervision of only one of a large number of contractor employees might reasonably be considered irrelevant, and the services provided by the contractor would still be considered nonpersonal. However, relatively continuous government supervision of a substantial number of contractor employees would have to be taken into account in determining whether the services are personal or nonpersonal.

Certain elements can be used as a guide in assessing whether or not a proposed contract is personal in nature. If the following conditions apply, an improper personal services contract might exist:

- Contractor employees are performing contract work at the government site

- Principal tools and equipment have been furnished by the government

- Services are applied directly to the integral effort of agencies or an organizational subpart in furtherance of the assigned function or mission

- Comparable services, meeting comparable needs, are performed in the same or similar agencies using civil service personnel

- The need for the type of service provided can reasonably be expected to last beyond one year

- The inherent nature of the service, or the manner in which it is provided, reasonably requires direct or indirect government direction or supervision of contractor employees to:
  - Adequately protect the government's interest
  - Retain control of the function involved
  - Retain full personal responsibility for a function that should be the responsibility of a duly authorized federal officer or employee.

88. What are advisory and assistance services, and how are they classified?

FAR 2.101 provides the following definition of this term:

Advisory and assistance services are those services provided under contract by nongovernmental sources to support or improve:

Organizational policy development; decision-making; management and administration; program and/or project management and administration; or research and development activities. It can also mean the furnishing of professional advice or assistance rendered to improve the effectiveness of Federal management processes or procedures (including those of an engineering and technical nature).

Advisory and assistance services can be classified as follows:

- *Management and professional support services.* These services support or contribute to the improved organization of program management, logistics management, project monitoring and reporting, data collection, budgeting, accounting, and administrative/technical support for conferences and training programs.

- *Studies, analyses, and evaluations.* These provide organized, analytical assessments/evaluations in support of policy development, decision-making, management, or administration.

- *Engineering and technical services.* These offer support to the program office by providing such services as systems engineering and technical direction to ensure effective operation and maintenance of a major system, as defined by OMB Circular No. A-109.

89. When should advisory and assistance services be used, and in what situations can they not be used?

FAR 37.203 provides the following policy guidance:

The acquisition of advisory and assistance services is a legitimate way to improve government services and operations. Accordingly, advisory and assistance services may be used at all organizational levels to help managers achieve maximum effectiveness or economy in their operations.

- Agencies may contract for advisory and assistance services when essential to the agency's mission to:
  (1) Obtain outside points of view to avoid too-limited judgment on critical issues
  (2) Obtain advice regarding developments in industry, university, or foundation research

(3) Obtain the opinions, special knowledge, or skills of noted experts

(4) Enhance the understanding of, and develop alternative solutions to, complex issues

(5) Support and improve the operation of organizations

(6) Ensure the more efficient or effective operation of managerial or hardware systems.

- Advisory and assistance services shall not be used to:

(1) Perform work of a policy, decision-making, or managerial nature that is the direct responsibility of agency officials

(2) Bypass or undermine personnel ceilings, pay limitations, or competitive employment procedures

(3) Contract on a preferential basis to former government employees

(4) Create any circumstances which specifically aid in influencing or enacting legislation

(5) Obtain professional or technical advice that is readily available within the agency or another federal agency.

90. What is performance-based acquisition (PBA)?

FAR Section 2.101 defines performance-based acquisition (PBA) as follows: "PBA means an acquisition structured around the results to be achieved as opposed to the manner by which the work is to be performed."

Another working definition might be: PBA involves acquisition strategies, methods, and techniques that describe and communicate measurable outcomes rather than direct performance processes. It is structured around defining a service requirement in terms of performance objectives and providing contractors the latitude to determine how to meet those objectives. Simply put, it is a method for acquiring *what is required* and placing the responsibility for *how it is accomplished* on the contractor.

91. What are the elements of a PBA?

To be considered performance-based, an acquisition should contain, at a minimum, the following elements:

1. *Performance work statement*—describes the requirement in terms of measurable outcomes rather than prescriptive methods.

2. *Measurable performance standards*—to determine whether performance outcomes have been met, defines what is considered acceptable performance.

3. *Remedies*—procedures that address how to manage performance that does not meet performance standards. While not mandatory, incentives should be used where appropriate to encourage performance that will exceed performance standards. Remedies and incentives complement each other.

4. *Performance assessment plan*—describes how contractor performance will be measured and assessed against performance standards. This is often referred to as a quality assurance plan or quality assurance surveillance plan.

92. What are the overall objectives of PBA?

By describing requirements in terms of performance outcomes, agencies can help achieve the following objectives:

- *Maximize performance*: PBA enables a contractor to deliver the required service by following its own best practices. The use of incentives further motivates contractors to furnish the best performance of which they are capable.

- *Maximize competition and innovation*: Encouraging innovation from the supplier base by using performance requirements maximizes opportunities for competitive alternatives in lieu of government-directed solutions.

- *Encourage and promote the use of commercial services*: The vast majority of service requirements are commercial in nature. Use of FAR Part 12 (Acquisition of Commercial Items) procedures minimizes the reporting burden and reduces the use of government-unique contract clauses and similar requirements, which can help attract a broader industry base.

- *Shift the risk*: Much of the risk is shifted from the government to industry because contractors become responsible for achieving the objectives in the work statement through the use of their own best practices and processes.

- *Achieve savings*: Experience in both government and industry has demonstrated that use of performance requirements results in cost savings.

93. What are some examples of performance standards?

The following are just a few examples of general performance standards that might be adapted to specific requirements:

- Response times, delivery times, timeliness—meeting deadlines or due dates, adherence to schedule

- Error rates—number of mistakes/errors allowed in meeting the performance standard

- Accuracy rates—similar to error rates, but most often stated in terms of percentages

- Completion milestone rates—"x" percent complete at a given date

- Cost control—keeping within the estimated cost or target cost (applies in cost-reimbursement contract arrangements).

94. What are some of the different types of incentives that can be used in PBA?

Incentives are an essential part of PBA and can be monetary, non-monetary, positive, or negative. They can be based on cost, schedule, or quality of performance. Regardless of the final composition and structure of the incentives, the goal is to encourage and motivate the best-quality performance.

Some different types of incentives are:

- *Cost-based incentives.* Performance incentives are designed to relate profit or fee to results achieved by the contractor in relation to identified cost-based targets.

- *Award-fee contract arrangements.* Using evaluation factors established in an award fee plan, award-fee contracts are a tool for subjectively assessing contractor performance for a given evaluation period. (See Questions 137 and 140 for further details regarding these types of contracts.)

- *Schedule incentives.* Schedule incentives focus on getting a contractor to exceed delivery expectations. They can be defined in terms of calendar days or months, attaining or exceeding milestones, or meeting rapid-response or urgent requirements.

- *Past performance.* Past performance information can affect decisions to exercise options or to make future contract awards. Thus, past performance assessments are a quick way to motivate improved performance or to reinforce exceptional performance.

THE COMMERCIAL ACTIVITIES PROGRAM

95. What is the commercial activities (CA) program?

The Office of Management and Budget's (OMB) Circular A-76, "Performance of Commercial Activities," sets the policies and procedures that executive branch agencies must use in identifying commercial-type activities and determining whether these activities are best provided by the private sector, by government employees, or by another agency through a fee-for-service agreement. The term typically used to describe this process is "competitive sourcing."

OMB Circular A-76 states:

> *The longstanding policy of the federal government has been to rely on the private sector for needed commercial services. To ensure that the American people receive maximum value for their tax dollars, commercial activities should be subject to the forces of competition.*

The Federal Activities Inventory Reform (FAIR) Act of 1998 (P.L. 105-270) requires executive agencies to make an annual accounting of the *commercial activities* performed by federal employees and submit them to OMB. OMB Circular A-76 also requires that agencies account for inherently governmental activities performed by federal employees.

The agency lists that result from these requirements are referred to as "FAIR Act inventories."

After OMB reviews and approves an agency's inventory, the agency must post it on its public website. It is important to remember that the inventory reflects *activities*, which are not the same as *positions*. One single employee may perform *both* inherently governmental and commercial activities.

96. What is a commercial activity?

OMB Circular A-76 defines a *commercial activity* as:

> *A recurring service that could be performed by the private sector and is resourced, performed, and controlled by the agency through performance by government personnel, a contract, or a fee-for-service agreement. A commercial activity is not so intimately related to the public interest as to mandate performance by government personnel. Commercial activities may be found within, or throughout, organizations that perform inherently governmental activities or classified work.*

Examples of commercial activities include:

- Automated data processing
- Training
- Food services
- Facilities/grounds/utilities maintenance
- Mail and file
- Architecture and civil engineering
- Library services
- Motor pool/vehicle maintenance
- Accounts management.

97. What is an inherently governmental activity?

An *inherently governmental activity* is defined as:

An activity that is so intimately related to the public interest as to mandate performance by government employees. These activities require the exercise of substantial discretion in applying government authority and/or in making decisions for the government.

Inherently governmental activities normally fall into two categories:

(1) The exercise of *sovereign government authority*

(2) The establishment of procedures and processes related to the oversight of monetary transactions or entitlements.

An inherently governmental activity involves:

- Binding the United States to take or not take some action by contract, policy, regulation, authorization, order, or otherwise;

- Determining, protecting, and advancing economic, political, territorial, property, or other interests by military or diplomatic action, civil or criminal judicial proceedings, contract management, or otherwise;

- Significantly affecting the life, liberty, or property of private persons; or

- Exerting ultimate control over the acquisition, use, or disposition of United States property (real or personal, tangible or intangible), including establishing policies or procedures for the collection, control, or disbursement of appropriated and other federal funds.

While inherently governmental activities require the exercise of substantial discretion, not every exercise of discretion is evidence that an activity is inherently governmental. Rather, the use of discretion is deemed inherently governmental if it commits the government to a course of action when two or more alternative courses of action exist and decision making is not already limited or guided by existing policies, procedures, directions, orders, and other guidance that (1) identify specified ranges of acceptable decisions or conduct and (2) subject the discretionary authority to final approval or regular oversight by agency officials.

98. What is the commercial activities competitive process and who are the officials responsible for its execution?

Once an agency decides that it wants to compete a function, the first decision is whether to conduct a streamlined competition or a standard competition. If 65 or fewer full time equivalent (FTE) positions are involved, the agency has the option of conducting a streamlined competition. If more than 65 FTE are involved, the agency must conduct a standard competition. The agency will then need to consult with any affected employees and their unions.

Streamlined competition

In a streamlined competition, an agency determines an estimated contract price for performing the work by a private contractor. To accomplish this, the agency may solicit proposals from prospective contractors or conduct more informal market research.

The agency also determines how much it costs to perform the function in-house, with government employees. The agency can either cost the existing organization or develop a plan to streamline the organization (called a "most efficient organization," or MEO) and base its in-house cost estimate on that plan.

After the costs for both the public and private sectors are compared, the organization that costs the least, wins. A streamlined competition must be completed—a decision made to keep the work in-house or contract it out—within 90 days from the date it was publicly announced.

Standard competition

In a standard competition, an agency selects a service provider based on formal offers submitted in response to an agency contract solicitation. The government submits its own offer along with those submitted by prospective private contractors.

In a standard competition, the government organization develops an MEO based on the staffing plan that will form the basis for the agency's offer in the competition. The MEO typically involves streamlining of the existing organization and is designed to place the government in the best competitive position against the private sector offerors.

A standard competition must be completed within 12 months of the date that it was publicly announced. The Competitive Sourcing Official (CSO) can extend this deadline by an additional six months; as in a streamlined competition, this deadline may be extended even further with OMB's prior written approval.

In a standard competition, unlike a streamlined competition, there is a *conversion differential*, which is added to the costs of the non-incumbent competitors. The conversion differential is the lesser of 10 percent of the MEO's personnel-related costs or $10 million over all the performance periods stated in the solicitation. This is intended to preclude moving work from one provider to another where estimated savings are marginal and captures non-quantifiable costs related to a conversion, such as disruption and decreased productivity.

Winning the competition

OMB Circular A-76 provides that an agency may choose from several different procedures for determining the winner of a competition, and two of these give an agency leeway to take non-cost factors into account. However, cost will in all cases continue to be an important factor, often the most important factor, in selection decisions.

OMB Circular A-76 requires the CSO to appoint competition officials for every standard competition and, as appropriate, for streamlined competitions. These officials include:

- The CSO is responsible for implementation of the Circular within the agency. This person is typically a senior official in the agency.

- The agency tender official (ATO) is responsible for developing the agency offer (the MEO submitted in response to a solicitation for a standard competition) and represents the government team's offer during source selection.

- The human resources advisor (HRA) is a human resources expert who is responsible for assisting the ATO in human resource-related matters related to the agency bid.

- The performance work statement (PWS) team leader develops the PWS and quality assurance surveillance plan (QASP), determines if the government will furnish property, and assists the CO in developing the solicitation.

- The source selection authority (SSA) is responsible for determining the winner.

- The CO is responsible for issuance of the solicitation and the source selection evaluation, and also serves as a member of the PWS team.

99. What is the COR's role in commercial activities?

The COR will most likely initially be involved with the PWS team leader in developing the PWS and the QASP. Later, the COR may be required to assist the CO in developing the source selection criteria for the solicitation and subsequently may be involved in the source selection evaluation process. The COR will need to work closely with the CO to understand the unique aspects of CA acquisitions in order to comply with the somewhat different procedures that apply.

CHAPTER 4

Preaward Technical Assistance

This chapter relates to an important period in the contracting process: the processing of the requirement from the technical requiring office to the contracting office, that is, the *technical to contractual translation period*. The COR's roles are that of primary technical point of contact, coordinator, and technical expert, and he or she provides information and advice to the CO as necessary. The COR's objective is to facilitate an effective and expeditious processing of the program office requirements through the contracting office actions to award.

The COR provides technical assistance during the three contracting phases:

- *Presolicitation.* The initial development of the purchase request (PR) by the technical requiring office and the coordination of it with the contracting office. The COR's tasks include:
  - The development of various requirement documents
  - The coordination of documents requiring approval
  - The provision of a suggested sources list
  - The development of the technical evaluation plan
  - The provision of financing and bond needs assessment.
- *Solicitation.* The acceptance of the PR and all contractual actions up to the receipt of offers (bids or proposals), i.e., the development of the solicitation. The COR's tasks include:
  - Assisting the CO in determining the method of procurement and selecting the contract type

- Providing preaward inquiry and other responses
- Participating in prebid and preproposal conferences.
- *Evaluation and source selection.* The receipt, processing, and evaluation of offers and all other contractual actions required up to the award decision by the CO. The COR's tasks include:
  - The technical evaluation of proposals
  - Past performance survey technical assistance
  - Technical responsibility determination
  - Negotiation technical support
  - Participation in debriefings and protests.

PRESOLICITATION TECHNICAL ASSISTANCE

100. What does the presolicitation phase of the contracting process involve?

During the *presolicitation phase* of the contracting process, the technical requiring office develops the purchase request (PR) as a part of the work package that will be forwarded to the contracting office. Chapter 3 provides a discussion of the PR and a listing of information that should be included in the PR, such as determinations, descriptions, justifications, and other documents that may be required to complete the particular acquisition (see Question 65). The contracting office will process the PR, as well as other documents included in the work package, and after all necessary documentation has been satisfactorily provided, accept the work package. Acceptance of the work package ends the presolicitation phase.

101. What tasks will the COR need to perform in providing technical assistance during the presolicitation phase?

The COR:

1. Develops determinations,[1] descriptions, justifications, and other documents as applicable to the requirement
2. Develops and coordinates funding documents and other documents that require approval

---

[1] In Chapter 3 and later in this chapter, various types of *determinations* are discussed. For example, there are determinations associated with commercial items (commerciality determination), government property (whether to furnish it and what type to furnish), and the types of services to be acquired (advisory and assistance, personal versus nonpersonal).

3. Provides a suggested sources list

4. Provides the technical evaluation plan

5. Assists the CO with financing and bond needs assessment.

102. What is an "inherently governmental function"?

An *inherently governmental function* (IGF) is a performance that is so intimately related to the public interest that government employees *must* execute it.

103. How do inherently governmental functions relate to the COR's duties?

The COR must ensure that IGFs are *not* included in the requirement. The COR should prepare a written determination indicating that none of the functions to be performed under the contract are "inherently governmental." This written determination is required for all new contracts and should address the conditions and information that restrict the discretionary authority, decision-making responsibility, or accountability of government officials using contractor services or work products.

104. What is a statement of work?

The *statement of work* (SOW) serves as the foundation for the request for proposals (RFP) or invitation for bids (IFB) and the resultant contract. It concisely explains what is to be accomplished by the contractor in terms of results so that the government can effectively monitor and evaluate the progress of the project.

The SOW in large part determines the quality of contractor performance. It lists and defines the following:

- Services to be supplied by the contractor
- Tasks to be accomplished by the contractor
- Conditions under which the work is to be performed
- Methods by which the government intends to judge the delivered services.

105. What is the role of the SOW in the contract?

The SOW becomes a part of the contract and is thereafter legally binding upon the contractor and the government. It provides an objective measure of contractor performance so that both the government and the contractor will know when increments of work are completed and payments justified.

106.   Why is it important to prepare a good SOW?

The degree to which requirements can be clearly defined in the SOW will generally dictate whether the sealed bidding or the negotiated acquisition method will be chosen, as well as the type of contract (e.g., fixed price, cost reimbursement) to be awarded.

When released in a solicitation document, the SOW may affect the number of contractors who are willing and able to respond to the solicitation. If the SOW is not definitive, some contractors may not respond, either because of uncertainty about the risks involved or because they do not understand the relationship of the requirement to their own particular capabilities. On the other hand, if the SOW is too restrictive, competent contractors may decline to respond because they believe that the government will inhibit their creativity or their opportunity to propose alternatives.

The clarity and explicitness of the requirements presented in the SOW will invariably enhance the quality of the proposals submitted. A definitive SOW is likely to produce definitive proposals, thus reducing the time needed for proposal evaluation.

During the proposal evaluation and contractor selection process, the SOW plays a significant role. Clear and precise requirements allow the government to establish conclusive baselines on which sound technical evaluation criteria can be structured. Delays and administrative effort in evaluation can thus be reduced.

107.   How does the SOW relate to measuring contractor performance?

The SOW becomes the standard for measuring the contractor's performance. When a question arises regarding the work to be performed, the SOW is the baseline document for resolving the question. Language in the work statement that defines the limits of the contractor's efforts is critical. If the limits on the contractor's work are unclear, it will be difficult to determine if there has been an increase in the scope of the work. Negotiation of cost and schedule modifications will be impaired, if not made impossible.

108.   What is a work summary?

The *work summary* is a brief summary of the work necessary to fulfill the requirement. The COR prepares this for the CO, who uses it as the governmentwide point of entry (GPE) synopsis to publicize the requirement.

109. How and when does the COR write a justification for other than full and open competition?

A *justification for other than full and open competition* (JOFOC) must be prepared if the government cannot allow or obtain full or open competition for an acquisition. The JOFOC should explain in detail why it is impossible or impracticable to obtain full and open competition for the acquisition. The JOFOC is required for all noncompetitive contract actions, including modifications for work outside the scope of the contract.

110. What are the exceptions to full and open competition?

Seven statutory exceptions permit contracting without providing for full and open competition. (See Chapter 3, Question 62, for details.) The COR will need to review these exceptions, determine their applicability to the requirement, and then develop the JOFOC for CO review and approval.

111. What presolicitation documents may require approval by program office officials or the CO?

These documents include:

- *Funding/requisition document.* This document provides the funds citation, i.e., the accounting and appropriation data applicable to the funds the program office intends to use for the acquisition and the certification of funding availability. The funds citation is required for all new contracts, delivery/task orders, and any modifications that add money to the contract.

- *COR nomination form.* An individual one level above the prospective COR (for example, the COR's technical supervisor, the project officer, or the program manager, depending on the COR's position or rank) prepares this memorandum, which indicates the COR's training and experience. This form is required for new contracts. If the COR will not be formally named until after the contract is awarded, it is not necessary to submit the nomination form prior to that time.

- *Contract security classification specification.* This document is used to convey the security classification requirements to the contractor. It identifies the classified areas in the contract and the specific items of information requiring classified protection.

- *Shipping instructions.* The office requesting the product will indicate to the CO whether special shipping instructions are required.
- *Special provisions and instructions.* Documentation may be provided for new contract actions or modifications. Examples include:
  - Proposed payment provisions other than the usual fixed-price or cost-reimbursement arrangements
  - Suggested contract clauses that are not described in the FAR (e.g., a listing of key personnel or personal financial disclosure statements relating to conflict of interest documentation, if applicable)
  - Any other information that should be provided to the CO.

112. **What is a suggested sources list?**

Sources are firms that are capable of providing a product or service that meets the government's requirements. The COR compiles a list of suggested sources from the following resources:

- Recommendations from technical experts
- Past contracts for similar products and services
- Sources' responses to the government's requirements as listed on the GPE
- Government agencies' Office of Small and Disadvantaged Business Utilization
- Market research.

The Technical Evaluation Plan

113. **What is a technical evaluation plan, and what does it include?**

A *technical evaluation plan* is required for all new contracts that will be competitively negotiated. The plan is used to determine which proposal will receive the award on a technical basis and includes:

- A listing of people who will compose the technical evaluation panel (TEP). The COR will assemble a list of individuals who have been determined to be technically competent. This list will be approved by the CO, and in most instances, the panel will be chaired by the COR. The list of TEP members should be included with the work package.

- The criteria to be used for evaluating a contractor. Evaluation factors and methods must be *reliable* (that is, technically competent individuals would evaluate the same proposal consistently using the evaluation factors independently from one another) and *valid* (the factors are in fact predictive of the contractor's ability to satisfy the government's actual needs). Members of the TEP will be given a list of these criteria.

114. When is a technical evaluation plan not required?

If the contract will be awarded based solely on the lowest price, then the evaluation criteria and the technical evaluation plan are *not* required.

115. What steps does the COR take in developing the technical evaluation plan?

The COR:

1. Researches evaluation factors from prior or comparable acquisitions and looks for any problems with the factors and the validity of the factors in practice.

2. Identifies applicable evaluation factors.

   - When contracting for commercial items, the COR may limit evaluation factors to:
     - Past performance
     - Technical capability (i.e., how well proposed products meet the government's requirements)
     - Price (e.g., purchase price and relevant price-related factors).

   - When contracting for noncommercial items, the COR should consider the following factors:
     - Price (e.g., purchase price and relevant price-related factors)
     - Past performance
     - Quality (by using factors such as past performance, technical excellence, management capability, personnel qualifications, prior experience, and schedule compliance to evaluate the contractor's work)
     - Environmental objectives, such as promoting waste reduction and energy efficiency.

3. Determines the relative importance of each evaluation factor and significant subfactors, if any. (See Chapter 3, Questions 73 and 74, for further information on evaluation factors.) The COR then selects the evaluation method (e.g., adjective ratings, numerical scores, ranking) and defines the relative importance, technically speaking, of each evaluation factor, as appropriate. The COR also must prepare and include a written rationale for the rating/scoring methodology.

   Numerical weighting of the factors and subfactors is *not* mandated (or encouraged) by the FAR. However, the FAR affirms that numerical weighting can be used—and does not necessarily have to be disclosed in the RFP. COs may disclose numerical weights "on a case by case basis" in the solicitation. Although the FAR is silent on this practice, disclosing weights generally is *not* a good practice. The General Accounting Office (GAO) has repeatedly ruled that source selection authorities have discretion to overrule numerical scores when numerical weights are not disclosed in the solicitation.

4. Drafts the minimum criteria for acceptable award (i.e., "go/no-go" factors).

5. Accurately recognizes and diagnoses problems with proposed factors, such as:

   • Omissions (e.g., missing standards)

   • Vagueness or ambiguity

   • No apparent relationship to the SOW

   • Inconsistency with the SOW.

6. Provides data to assist the contracting office in determining whether to solicit on the basis of:

   • Tradeoffs or

   • Award to the lowest-priced, technically acceptable offer. For example, the COR should consider tradeoffs between price and non-price factors when:

     – Soliciting cost-type contracts

     – Using performance or functional specifications that will open the door to a variety of technical approaches, each characterized by different strengths and weaknesses

> – There is no clear-cut means of determining the technical acceptability of marginal offers.

7. Identifies TEP members and briefs them on their roles and responsibilities.

8. Determines the importance of the non-price factors relative to price. Relative importance is a function of the business and technical risks inherent in the work. The higher the risks, the greater the emphasis on non-price evaluation factors. The COR should expressly state whether non-price evaluation factors (taken as a whole) are significantly more important than, approximately equal in importance to, or significantly less important than cost or price. When a solicitation indicates that price will be considered but does not indicate the relative importance of price and technical factors, they are considered approximately equal in weight.

Government Financing

116. What general criteria must the CO apply in determining whether to provide for government financing in the initial solicitation?

The CO must make a determination whether to provide for government financing in the initial solicitation. In making this determination, the CO must apply FAR Part 32 criteria and consider financing provisions and clauses when otherwise responsible firms would be unable to compete. For example, include financing provisions and clauses when:

- Contractors would not be able to bill for the first delivery of products, or other performance milestones, for a substantial amount of time— normally six months or more (four months for small business concerns)

- Otherwise responsible firms in the market are likely to have an actual financial need or may not be able to obtain private financing for the work.

117. What are the criteria for providing government financing for non-commercial contracts?

Unless otherwise authorized by agency regulation, contract financing may be provided in contracts for noncommercial items. The contracting officer must:

- Provide government financing only to the extent actually needed for prompt and efficient performance

- Administer contract financing so as to aid, not impede, the acquisition
- Avoid any undue risk of monetary loss to the government through the financing
- Include the form of contract financing deemed to be in the government's best interest in the solicitation
- Monitor the contractor's use of the contract financing provided and the contractor's financial status.

118. What are the criteria for providing government financing for commercial contracts?

Commercial interim payments and commercial advance payments may be made under the following circumstances:

- The contract item financed is a commercial supply or service.
- The contract price exceeds the simplified acquisition threshold.
- The CO determines that government financing is appropriate or customary in the commercial marketplace.
- Authorizing this form of contract financing is in the best interest of the government.
- Adequate security is obtained.
- Prior to any performance of work under the contract, the aggregate of commercial advance payments will not exceed 15 percent of the contract price.
- The contract is awarded on the basis of competitive procedures or, if only one offer is solicited, the financing is expected to be substantially more advantageous to the offeror than the offeror's normal method of customer financing.
- The contracting officer obtains concurrence from the payment office concerning liquidation provisions when required by FAR 32.206(e).

119. What methods of government financing are available?

The available methods of government financing include:

- *Advance payments*, which are advances of money by the government to a prime contractor before, in anticipation of, and for the purpose of complete performance under a contract. Advance payments are

expected to be liquidated from payments due to the contractor incidental to performance of the contract. They differ from progress and partial
payments in that they are not based on contractor performance (that is,
they are more like an upfront loan to the contractor).

- *Progress payments*, based on costs incurred as work under the contract
  progresses, or based on a percentage or stage of completion of the contract work.

- *Loan guarantees* by Federal Reserve banks for contracts related to
  national defense.

- *Partial payments* for accepted supplies and services, based on
  performance.

- *Performance-based payments*, measured by objective, quantifiable
  methods; defined events; or other measures of result.

120. What methods of payment may the CO select?

The CO must select an available method of payment and related clauses
that will minimize the government's overhead for making contract payments, while preserving opportunities for small business concerns to compete for federal contracts. Payment alternatives include:

- Electronic Funds Transfer (EFT), Central Contractor Registration
  (CCR)

- EFT other than CCR

- Governmentwide commercial purchase card

- Payment by a third party.

121. How does the CO determine whether to require bonds for a contract?

The CO will also be required to determine whether to require bonds in
accordance with FAR Part 28. The Miller Act (40 U.S.C. 270a–270f)
specifically mandates performance and payment bonds for all construction
contracts exceeding $150,000 unless waived (see FAR 28.102-1). For other
contracts, the CO must identify and review data from acquisition histories
and the market in terms of performance risks, and he or she must especially
consider any government financing being provided when considering bond
requirements.

122. What types of bonds are available for the CO's consideration?

The CO may consider the following bond types (see FAR Part 28 for descriptions of bonds and other financial protections):

- Performance bond
- Annual performance bond
- Payment bond
- Annual bid bond
- Advance payment bond
- Patent infringement bond
- Some combination of these bonds.

123. What is the COR's role in financing and bond needs assessment?

The CO will identify and obtain independent information on the contractor's financial status from auditors, the Small Business Administration (SBA), and other sources such as sureties, commercial underwriting institutions, and banks. The CO must make a critical determination regarding the financial risk associated with each requirement. A major element of this risk determination is the contractor's responsibility.

The COR must evaluate the contractor's responsibility; that is, he or she must verify that the contractor has adequate production capability and a satisfactory past performance record. The COR makes a technical assessment of these factors and advises the CO of his or her findings. Based on this assistance, the CO will then agree to provide financing for, and require bonds only from, firms that are otherwise responsible and have a valid need for financial assistance.

When communicating with the CO about financing and bond determinations, the COR should use the opportunity to acquire knowledge of the different types of financing and bond determinations and the associated risks of each type for future contract monitoring duties.

SOLICITATION TECHNICAL ASSISTANCE

The solicitation phase of the contract is the period of time between acceptance of the PR and receipt of offers (bids or proposals). During this phase, many plans, decisions, and preparations must be made by the CO and the other members of the acquisition team, particularly the COR, to permit development of an adequate solicitation that will completely and accurately convey the government's requirements to the marketplace. This effort is the critical part of the technical-to-contractual translation that must take place, and it requires significant involvement by the COR.

124. What tasks will the COR need to perform to provide technical assistance during solicitation?

The COR must:

1. Assist in determining the method of procurement, i.e., simplified acquisition, sealed bidding, or negotiations
2. Assist in selecting the contract type
3. Refer preaward inquiries to the CO and provide technical responses and advice on other issues to the CO as requested
4. Participate in prebid and preproposal conferences as requested.

125. What is a market survey and why is it conducted?

Once the government identifies its legitimate needs and is considering the use of a contract to satisfy those needs, a *market survey* is performed, ideally through a joint effort of the requiring activity and the contracting office, to determine:

- Whether sources for needed services or products are available
- Whether commercial items can be used
- What customary trade practices apply
- Potential costs, possible tradeoffs, and methods to promote conservation.

See Chapter 3, Conducting Market Research, for further details.

126. What are the available methods of soliciting offers?

Offers can be solicited in the form of a *simplified acquisition*, which is the use of simplified acquisition procedures prescribed by FAR Part 13; *sealed bidding*, when there is ample competition, the specifications are clear and not unnecessarily restrictive, and lowest price can determine the award (refer to FAR Part 14); or *negotiations*, when there may be a need to hold discussions to establish the best value for the government (refer to FAR Part 15).

Sealed Bidding

127. What is the advantage of sealed bidding?

The appearance of fairness has always been associated with sealed bidding. Contractors respond to an invitation for bid (IFB) by submitting sealed offers not to be opened until a public formal bid opening. Late bids are usually unacceptable. The lowest evaluated offer from a responsible bidder that conforms to all the terms and conditions of the solicitation will receive the award.

128. When is sealed bidding used as a solicitation method?

Select sealed bidding when *all* of the following conditions exist:

- There is a reasonable expectation of receiving more than one sealed offer.
- There is sufficient lead-time for the sealed bidding process.
- Final award can be made on price and price-related factors alone.
- Award can be made without discussing offers with offerors other than to resolve minor informalities or irregularities.

129. What evaluation factors are used in sealed bidding?

In sealed bidding, only price and price-related factors (e.g., transportation costs) can be considered. For example, an offer with a price that incorporates delivery to the government (F.O.B. destination) can be compared to an offer with a price not including delivery (F.O.B. origin, i.e., contractor's plant) by adding estimated transportation costs to the F.O.B. origin offer for evaluation purposes.

130. What types of contracts may be used with sealed bidding?

Only a firm fixed price (FFP) or a fixed price with economic price adjustment (FP/EPA) contract may be used with sealed bidding. (See Fixed Price Contracts later in this chapter for more information about these contract types.)

Negotiation

131. What are the advantages of negotiation as a solicitation method?

Negotiation is a more flexible method than the other two solicitation methods (sealed bidding and simplified acquisition) because negotiations allow the government and the contractor to discuss the contractor's proposal, and contractors can revise their proposals during these discussions. While sealed bidding is limited to only two contract types (firm fixed price and fixed price with economic price adjustment), any contract type may be used with negotiation. Finally, negotiation can help the government and the contractor arrive at a fair and reasonable price through an analysis of price and costs that drive the price.

132. **What criteria are used in selecting negotiation as a solicitation method?**

The CO should select negotiation (i.e., competitive proposals under FAR Part 15) if *any* of the following conditions exist:

- The government does not reasonably expect to receive more than one sealed bid.

- Time does not permit the solicitation, submission, and evaluation of sealed bids.

- Award will in part be made on other than price and price-related factors.

- Discussions with offerors are necessary and cannot be limited to questions of technical acceptability.

133. **What evaluation factors are used in a negotiated procurement?**

Unlike sealed bidding, in which price and price-related factors alone can be used, in negotiated solicitations offerors' other attributes, such as quality of work, management, delivery, technical approach, and subcontracting plans, may also be considered. The specific factors being considered and the relative importance of each must be stated in the solicitation, and the evaluation, whether formal or informal, must be in accord with this statement. "Best value" dictates that the contractor in line for award will not necessarily be the lowest priced.

An informal evaluation of the chosen factors may last a few days. A formal evaluation usually lasts weeks, and a source selection authority of high rank is usually involved. Some individuals who eventually become CORs may be involved in either an informal or a formal source selection process. The knowledge of what decisions were made, and why, during the negotiation and source selection phases will help the COR immensely during contract administration.

Memoranda documenting these evaluation and negotiation actions are a part of the contract file and should be made available upon request.

Contract Type Selection

134. What role does the COR play in assisting in contract type selection?

The COR must identify the factors in the requirement that are the most uncertain or unpredictable, determine the potential risks entailed by those uncertainties, and assist the CO in selecting the type of contract that will:

- Minimize the potential risks (in terms of cost and performance) inherent in the requirement and the expected cost of contract administration (both to the government and industry), taken together
- Have the greatest likelihood of motivating contractors to perform at optimal levels
- Provide a reasonable allocation of risk between the government and the contractor
- Conform to FAR Part 16 and agency requirements and limitations on the use of the different contract types.

The COR's responsibilities will differ significantly according to contract type. For this reason, it is important to know the distinguishing characteristics of the two basic types of contracts:

- Fixed price
- Cost reimbursement.

The administration of a fixed price contract is very different from the administration of a cost reimbursement contract. In a *fixed price contract* the government holds the contractor accountable for results, whereas in a *cost reimbursement contract* the "best effort" of the contractor may be all the government gets from the contractor.

135. How do the quality of requirement definition and the level of potential risk help determine the contract type that will be used?

Figure 4-1 illustrates the correlation between requirement definition and contract type. If the requirement is well-defined and the unknowns (risks) will be minimal (as in routine production-type contracts), the appropriate contract type will be firm fixed price (FFP), wherein the contractor accepts 100 percent of the risk. On the other hand, if the requirement is not well-defined and the unknowns are significant (as in research and development type contracts), the appropriate contract type will be cost plus fixed fee (CPFF), under which the government must take on 100 percent of the risk.

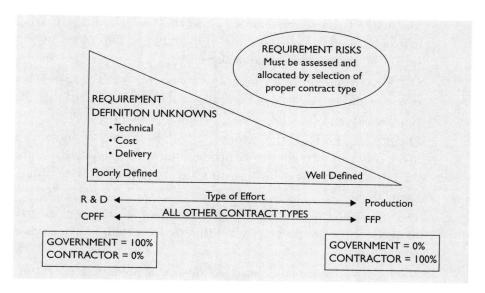

FIGURE 4-1. Contract Type versus Risk

In between these extremes, requirement definition falls somewhere between well-defined and very poorly defined, and the appropriate type of contract must be subjectively determined and subsequently negotiated with the contractor. Remember, when determining the appropriate method of procurement, with sealed bidding the requirement must be well-defined, and the only types of contracts allowed by the FAR in a sealed bidding situation are firm fixed price and fixed price with economic price adjustment. All other types of contracts, including firm fixed price contracts and fixed price contracts with economic price adjustment, must be negotiated. The various contract types are discussed later in this chapter.

136. How does the COR help conduct a risk analysis?

The COR, using his or her insight and expertise regarding the contract's specific technical requirements, assists the CO in identifying the potential technical and business risks of the acquisition. The COR and CO must account for:

- *Risks inherent in the requirement*, given the:
  - Type of requirements documents involved (e.g., commercial item description, design, performance, or functional requirements)
  - Nature and complexity of the requirement

- Maturity of the requirement (e.g., extent to which the market is experienced in providing the deliverable; extent of change to specifications from prior acquisitions)
- Quantity required (e.g., magnitude needed relative to market capacity and the degree of certainty at the time of award that the required quantity will be available or likely to be produced)
- Quality required and the extent to which performance incentives are likely to motivate the contractor to optimize performance when quality is critical in meeting the requiring activity's functional need
- Delivery schedule (e.g., routine versus urgent requirement, degree of certainty at the time of award that delivery will be made when required)
- Period of performance or length of the anticipated production run
- Stability of the technology (e.g., prospects for technological innovation during the life of the contract that might lead the government to modify or terminate the contract).

- *Risks inherent in doing business with prospective contractors*, given:
  - The probable level of competition for the contract
  - The adequacy of the contractors' accounting, estimating, and other management control systems
  - The contractors' relative capability and experience (e.g., technological, organizational)
  - The contractors' performance records
  - The probable changes in the general level of business (boom, decline, or constant) over the life of the contract
  - The probable extent and nature of subcontracting
  - Terms of concurrent contracts, if any.

- *Market risks*, including:
  - Availability of the type and number of resources necessary for the work
  - Trends in prices for labor, energy, raw materials, semi-finished goods, equipment, and other critical components.

- Any other risks (e.g., adverse economic conditions, national emergencies).

Fixed Price Contracts

137. What are the types of fixed price contracts and what is the role of risk in each?

Contracts in the *fixed price* family include:

Firm fixed price (FFP). The contractor assumes all risks. This type of contract is the norm when contracting for commercial products and services in price-competitive markets or establishing production contracts for mature hardware.

- Contemplate award of an FFP contract when the total cost of performance can be estimated with a high degree of accuracy and confidence.

Fixed price with economic price adjustment (FP/EPA). The government assumes part of the risk of market fluctuations.

- Contemplate award of an FP/EPA contract when market prices for critical categories of labor or materials:
  - Are likely to be unstable over the life of the contract
  - Are at risk because of industry-wide contingencies beyond the contractor's control
  - Are significant to the overall price
  - Can be severed and covered separately in the contract.

Fixed price incentive (FPI). The government shares part of the cost risk up to the ceiling price (the maximum amount the government will pay), after which the contractor assumes all risks.

- Contemplate award of an FPI contract when:
  - FAR Part 12 does not apply (i.e., it is not a commercial item contract)
  - The expected cost of performance is moderately uncertain
  - Actual costs will probably not exceed a specified ceiling price (i.e., the ceiling price covers the most probable risks inherent in the nature of the work)
  - The government needs a firm commitment from the contractor to deliver the supplies or services with that ceiling price
  - The contract price is high enough to justify the additional costs of administering the FPI terms and conditions.

The FPI contract provides for adjustment of profit and establishment of final price through the use of a formula (or sharing ratio) based on the relationship of final total cost to target cost and profit agreed to by the parties at the time of award. After performance of the contract work is completed, the contractor and the government, using the previously established formula, agree on the final cost of the contract, taking into account any deviation from the target cost. The formula can link price not only to costs, but also to other objective indicators of performance (e.g., performance benchmarks or standards, such as the quality level of services to be provided). Only contemplate such links when:

- A mathematical relationship can be established between the price and the indicators of performance
- Establishing such relationships is likely to have a meaningful impact on the contractor's management of the work
- The expected performance benefits are of sufficient magnitude to justify the additional costs of administering the FPI terms and conditions.

Fixed price award fee (FPAF). This is a type of incentive contract in that an additional amount (award) of fee may be added to the base amount of fee, based on judgmental measures of productivity (i.e., if the contractor performs especially well). Of course, if the contractor does not perform above the established criteria, the award would be smaller, or the contractor might not even receive an additional award. The award amount will be decided by the government based on a subjective evaluation of the contractor's performance against the established performance criteria. Such contracts are especially suitable when contracting for services. See Exhibit 4-1, Sample Award Fee Plan, at the end of this chapter.

- Contemplate award of a FPAF contract when:
  - FAR Part 12 does not apply (or, if it applies, the award fee would be based solely on factors other than cost)
  - Performance indicators (i.e., inspection and acceptance criteria) are inherently judgmental (e.g., what is "clean"?), with a corresponding possibility that the end user will not be fully satisfied
  - Judgmental standards can be fairly applied by an award-fee panel
  - Expected benefits are likely to exceed the expected costs of conducting award-fee evaluations
  - The potential fee is large enough to both provide a meaningful incentive and justify the additional costs of administering the award fee terms and conditions.

Firm fixed price/level of effort (FFP/LOE). Such a contract requires the contractor to demonstrate a specified effort, over a stated period of time, in return for a fixed dollar amount. This contract type is used for investigations or studies for which the government can only explain the work to be performed in general terms.

- Contemplate award of an FFP/LOE contract when:
  - FAR Part 12 does not apply
  - The work required cannot otherwise be clearly defined
  - The required level of effort is identified and agreed upon in advance
  - There is reasonable assurance that the intended result cannot be achieved by expending less than the stipulated effort
  - The contract price is $150,000 or less (unless otherwise approved by the chief of the contracting office).

138. **What is the COR's role in monitoring fixed price contracts?**

Because fixed price contracts place maximum risk on the contractor, the COR's monitoring duties are minimal. However, acceptable contract performance is still a fundamental responsibility that rests primarily with the COR.

To that end, in the event the COR has reason to suspect that delivery or ordered material will not meet stated specifications, the COR must contact the contractor to learn more about the situation, and the contractor must respond to the COR's concerns. The COR should then notify the CO of the situation and must continue to monitor progress under the contract to ensure that delivery will be made as specified, in terms of both quality and timeliness. In the event that the contractor fails to make sufficient progress on the contract and thus endangers timely contract completion, the COR should immediately contact the CO again so he or she can determine what action is to be taken.

Cost Reimbursement Contracts

139. **When are cost reimbursement contracts typically used, and what is the risk involved?**

Under *cost reimbursement* contracts, the government assumes the risk for all allowable costs incurred up to a pre-established limitation on costs. Cost reimbursement contracts are typically established for research, preliminary exploration or study, or development and testing. Contemplate award of a cost reimbursement contract when the resources that will be required to perform the work (e.g., labor hours, labor mix, material requirements) are highly uncertain at the time of award.

140. What are the types of cost reimbursement contracts?

Contracts in the *cost reimbursement* family include:

Cost plus fixed fee (CPFF). The contractor is reimbursed all allowable, allocable, and reasonable costs and is paid a predetermined fee regardless of actual costs incurred.

- Contemplate award of a CPFF contract when relating fee to measures of performance (e.g., to actual costs) would be unworkable or, compared to the cost of administering an award fee or incentive contract, of marginal utility.

Cost plus incentive fee (CPIF). This contract type establishes a formula to relate fee to objective measures of performance (e.g., actual costs; delivery dates; performance benchmarks; or standards, such as the quality levels of services to be provided).

- Contemplate award of a CPIF contract when:
  - A mathematical relationship can be established between the fee and critical aspects of performance
  - The potential fee is large enough to provide a meaningful incentive to the contractor and to justify the additional costs of administering the incentive fee terms and conditions.

Cost plus award fee (CPAF). An additional award fee may be added to a base fee, based on judgmental measures of productivity. See Exhibit 4-1, Sample Award Fee Plan, at the end of this chapter.

- Contemplate award of a CPAF contract when:
  - Objective incentive targets are not feasible for critical aspects of performance
  - Judgmental standards of performance can be fairly applied by an award-fee panel
  - The potential fee is large enough both to provide a meaningful incentive to the contractor and to justify the additional costs of administering the award fee terms and conditions.

Cost (no fee) and cost sharing. The contractor works without a fee or shares the cost of performance with the government.

- Contemplate award of a cost or cost sharing contract when the contractor:
  - Expects substantial compensating benefits for absorbing part of the costs or forgoing the fee (such as being able to develop commercial markets for products that result from federal research)
  - Is a nonprofit entity.

141. What is the COR's role in monitoring cost reimbursement contracts?

Since cost reimbursement contracts place maximum risk on the government, the COR's monitoring duties are extensive and critical. Not only does the COR have to monitor the contractor for acceptable performance, but the CO also relies primarily on the COR to track and guide the contractor's activities in order to conserve funds. Therefore, the COR's careful review of the contractor's billings under a cost reimbursement type contract is particularly important.

The COR needs to closely monitor and guide the contractor's effort in order to prevent the waste of taxpayers' funds and to obtain the services or products needed within budget. Inefficient or misguided performance by the contractor can mean that the government will have to curtail or forgo needed services or rob other programs to provide additional funding. Either alternative has an adverse program impact.

142. What is the allowable cost and payment clause?

Cost reimbursement type contracts contain a clause entitled "allowable cost and payment." This clause:

- Obligates the government to pay the contractor the "allowable" costs of performing the contract
- Entitles the contractor to submit periodic invoices claiming such costs as the work progresses
- Promises timely payment of such invoices.

143. What is an allowable cost?

An *allowable* cost:

- Is reasonable

- Is allocable
- Is authorized by FAR Part 31 and by the terms of the contract
- Follows accounting rules for cost accounting standards or generally acceptable accounting principles.

144. What are reasonable costs?

The FAR defines a *reasonable* cost as follows: "A cost is reasonable if, in its nature and amount, it does not exceed that which would be incurred by a prudent person in the conduct of competitive business." The CO has the ultimate responsibility for determining whether a particular cost is reasonable; however, the COR generally has technical experience related to the work that is being performed under the contract and can certainly assist the CO in determining reasonableness. Accordingly, to support the CO, invoices are routed to the COR for review, with respect to the reasonableness and allocability of costs claimed for reimbursement.

145. What are allocable costs?

A cost is properly *allocable* to a contract if it is incurred specifically for the contract or is incurred for another activity that also benefits the contract. With regard to the allocability of costs claimed, the COR must look for any direct costs that appear to have no connection with the contract work. If the COR cannot understand why the contractor would need materials or effort billed for to perform the contract, then the costs may have been charged to the contract in error.

146. What funding clauses are related to the cost-reimbursement contract?

FAR 32.704 provides for the use of two clauses regarding payment and funding of cost reimbursement contracts:

- *Limitation of cost clause.* This clause is used when a contract is fully funded. It states the parties' agreement that performance of the contract will not cost the government more than the estimated cost specified in the contract. The contractor is required only to make his "best effort" to fulfill the requirements of the contract. If the estimated cost figure is reached and the contract requirements are not fulfilled, the government must make a decision about whether or not to provide additional funding and proceed with the project.

- *Limitation of funds clause.* This clause is used in contracts to be funded incrementally. The clause is a risk-mitigation factor for the government. It provides that the amount of funds obligated to a contract at any given time represents the limit of the government's obligation under the contract. If there is no progress or unsatisfactory progress in performance, the government is under no obligation to provide additional funding.

Other Contract Types

147. What are time-and-materials and labor, hour contracts, and what are the risks involved in using these contracts?

In a *time-and-materials* (T&M) contract, the government assumes all risks except for fluctuations in per-hour wage rates and indirect costs. *Labor-hour* (LH) contracts are fixed on a per-hour basis with regard to the amount the contractor will be paid per hour. There is a "ceiling price," but it functions more like the "limitation of costs" provision of a cost reimbursement contract.

The government uses T&M contracts in much the same way that private citizens acquire car repair services. The contractor will be paid the cost of material and the cost of labor by the hour. The government insists that it be charged only for the cost of materials, without additional charges for overhead and profit. This is meant to discourage the contractor from attempting to make a higher profit through repair by replacement, that is, making the repairs by furnishing new materials (and charging overhead and profit on them) rather than troubleshooting, determining the malfunction, and using labor hours at the fixed rates to make the repairs. However, when the contractor loads the labor hours, care must be taken that the work is not slowed for the same goal of higher profits. Therefore, T&M and LH contracts demand the ultimate in COR monitoring responsibilities.

- Contemplate award of a T&M or LH contract when the resources that will be required to perform the work (e.g., labor hours, labor mix, material requirements) are highly uncertain at the time of award. Also contemplate a T&M or LH contract when the expected cost of the work is too low to justify an audit of the contracting firm's indirect expenses.

T&M or LH contracts are often used in lieu of cost reimbursement contracts for markets in which price competition typically occurs on the basis of per-hour rates (e.g., repair services).

148. What are indefinite delivery contracts?

There are three types of *indefinite delivery* contracts:

1. *Definite quantity.* Provides for delivery of a definite quantity of specific supplies or services for a fixed period, with deliveries or performance to be scheduled at designated locations upon order (task order or delivery order).

2. *Indefinite quantity.* Provides for an indefinite quantity, within stated limits, of supplies or services for which the government places orders for individual requirements during a fixed period. Quantity limits (a minimum and a maximum) may be stated as number of units or as dollar values. The contract requires the government to order (and the contractor to furnish) at least a stated minimum quantity of supplies or services, but not to exceed the stated maximum.

3. *Requirements.* A contract that establishes what goods or services will be bought if and when they are needed by the government. The government must use a requirements contract if it has a need that can be satisfied by using it.

149. What is a letter contract?

A *letter contract* is a written preliminary contractual instrument that authorizes the contractor to immediately begin manufacturing supplies or performing services.

A letter contract may be used when:

- The government's interests demand that the contractor be given a binding commitment so that work can start immediately and

- Negotiating a definitive contract is not possible in sufficient time to fulfill the requirement.

The FAR states that a letter contract should be as complete and definite as possible under the circumstances. Each letter contract should contain a negotiated definitization schedule, including:

- Dates for submission of the contractor's price proposal

- A date for the start of negotiations

- A target date for definitization, which must be within 180 days after the date of the letter contract or before completion of 40 percent of the work to be performed, whichever occurs first.

Preaward Inquiries, Technical Advice, and Confidentiality

150. What is the COR's role in fielding preaward inquiries and providing technical responses and advice on other issues to the CO?

Communication with interested parties regarding a solicitation may be conducted only by the CO or others having authority to do so. The COR does not have this authority. However, the CO often queries the COR regarding technical details, technical clarifications, delivery or performance schedules, and other issues that can result in amendment or cancellation of the solicitation.

151. What information may not be given to bidders prior to the opening of a sealed bid?

In sealed bidding, information that may *not* be imparted to bidders prior to the public bid opening includes:

- Information on a firm's responsibility or proprietary data
- Identity and number of bids
- Bid prices or lists of bid prices
- Rankings of bids
- Other information that, if disclosed to a competing contractor, would jeopardize the integrity of the procurement (e.g., the government's estimate for the procurement).

152. In a negotiated procurement, what information may not be given to the contractor prior to an award?

When acquiring supplies or services by negotiation, information that may *not* be imparted to the contractor includes:

- Source selection or technical evaluation plans
- Identity and number of offerors
- Proposed costs or prices submitted by offerors
- Information on a firm's responsibility or proprietary data
- Other information that, if disclosed to a competing contractor, would jeopardize the integrity of the procurement (e.g., a unique or innovative technical approach that has been proposed by one of the offerors).

153. What is the COR's role regarding inquiries or requests for information from contractors?

The COR must refer *all* inquiries to the CO promptly and be prepared to respond completely and effectively to all requests for technical information, advice, or recommendations. Some of these responses may necessitate revisions to the requirements document. For example, an error or omission in the government specification or statement of work might be discovered by one of the offerors and would have to be corrected.

The COR must be aware that these inquiries from interested contractors may come from friends or previous acquaintances from previous contracts, and these individuals may be quite upset that the COR refuses to tell them anything about the solicitation. The COR must remember, however, that the integrity of the contracting system *must* be maintained.

The Prebid or Preproposal Conference

154. What is a prebid or preproposal conference?

The CO may decide that a *prebid* or *preproposal conference* would be beneficial for the contracting parties so that they may discuss the requirement (e.g., to clarify complex technical requirements). The CO usually considers the following factors in determining whether to hold a prebid or preproposal conference:

- Contractor inquiries suggest that key terms and conditions in the contract are vague, ambiguous, or unattractive to industry (e.g., the government specifies that progress payments will not be provided for a requirement that has significant startup costs involved; thus, the contractor will have full capital investment responsibility and risk).

- Contractors do not appear to have a reliable or valid understanding of the contract requirements.

- A significant amount of money is at risk.

- A complex requirement or technical evaluation factor must be explained.

- Contractors need to physically inspect work sites.

155. What steps does the CO take in planning and conducting the pre-bid or preproposal conference?

The CO will generally perform the following steps, as appropriate, to plan and conduct the conference:

1. Develop an *agenda*, including:
   - A briefing on the solicitation
   - A presentation of prepared responses to questions submitted in advance
   - Questions and answers from the floor.

2. Prepare and mail conference *invitations* to all prospective offerors that received a copy of the solicitation. The invitation should include:
   - Notice of time and place
   - A copy of the agenda
   - A request that questions be submitted in writing, in advance, if possible. (Technical questions will be forwarded to the COR for response.)

3. Conduct a *meeting* with all involved government personnel (the COR and other technical personnel, as necessary) to ensure that roles and responsibilities are clearly understood. The CO will remind these individuals of the limits on providing information to the offerors at the conference.

4. Conduct the *conference*. The CO will inform attendees that remarks and explanations made at the conference will not qualify the terms of the solicitation and that the terms of the solicitation and specifications remain unchanged unless the solicitation is amended in writing.

5. Prepare *consolidated responses* to all questions raised at the conference, and, if necessary, amend the solicitation as required.

156. What is the COR's role in planning the conference?

The COR is responsible for participating and responding as necessary to all questions and requests from the CO related to the conference described above.

EVALUATION AND SOURCE SELECTION TECHNICAL ASSISTANCE

The *evaluation and source selection phase* of the contract relates to the period from receipt of offers up to the award decision by the CO. The effort involved during this phase necessitates *significant* and *critical* support from the COR in the areas of technical interpretation, analysis, and evaluation to ensure that the award ultimately made is the most advantageous to the government in all respects.

Note: When contracting by sealed bidding, bids are evaluated to determine which offer provides the lowest evaluated price, and award is usually made to that bidder. When using negotiation, however, the process is more complicated in that award will be based on *both* price and technical factors. The following discussion refers to the negotiation process *only*. Figure 4-2, The Negotiation Process, provides an overall perspective on this process.

157. What tasks does the COR perform during the evaluation and source selection phase?

The COR:

1. Assists the CO in the receipt, processing, and evaluation of proposals

2. Provides past performance survey assistance

3. Assists the CO in evaluating other terms and conditions and in determining the responsibility of potential contractors

4. Participates in fact-finding sessions, negotiation preparations, and discussions with offerors

5. Gathers facts, prepares technical documentation, and participates in debriefings and protests by functioning as a technical expert witness for the government

6. Reviews and provides advice on the acceptability of unsolicited proposals.

158. How does the COR provide assistance to the CO in receiving, processing, and evaluating proposals?

The CO will initially review all proposals upon receipt to identify all variances from the RFP terms and conditions. These variances often

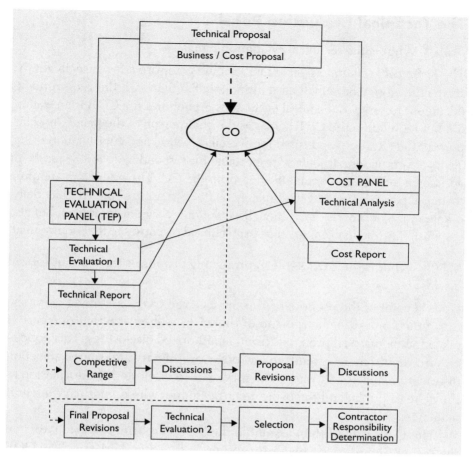

FIGURE 4-2. The Negotiation Process

require, and can be resolved by, technical review and interpretation by the COR or others in the program office. These initial reviews can sometimes result in proposals being immediately excluded from further consideration (e.g., excluded from the competitive range due to technical or other deficiencies). More often, these reviews serve to identify issues that require attention during discussions with the offeror. The CO will then forward all remaining proposals to the technical evaluation panel for evaluation, in accordance with the technical evaluation plan discussed earlier in this chapter.

The Technical Evaluation Panel

159. What is the technical evaluation panel?

The *technical evaluation panel* (TEP) should comprise a few, usually four to six, technical personnel who are intimately familiar with the requirements document to serve as technical evaluators. Sometimes the COR is an evaluator, but more often the COR serves as the chairperson of the panel. As chairperson, the COR is responsible for overall direction and coordination of the TEP's efforts and is particularly responsible for responding to any requests for additional information or clarification from the CO. The evaluators are often technical personnel who will ultimately be the end users of the contract deliverables; members of the TEP, then, have not only a significant role in, but also responsibility for, determining the best technical responses to the requirement.

160. What is the COR's role in protecting proposals from unauthorized disclosures?

Upon receipt of the proposals from the CO, the COR (assuming he or she is to function as the chairperson of the TEP) will ensure that due care is taken to safeguard all proposals from unauthorized disclosures. This nondisclosure requirement extends to any other proprietary and source selection information. The COR must remember not to disclose this information to the general public and to government personnel who do not have a legitimate need to know.

The COR should then assemble the TEP and brief the evaluators on the technical evaluation plan procedures, process, and criteria. The COR should also ensure that there are no conflicts of interest with the offerors.

161. What does the CO expect from the TEP evaluation?

Overall, the CO expects information sufficient to:

- Determine the technical acceptability of proposed deliverables
- Determine the need for communications or fact-finding
- Determine the need for amending or canceling the RFP
- Present and support negotiation objectives (i.e., areas of discussion)
- Support the CO's determination of the competitive range
- Conduct assessments of technical acceptability and tradeoff analyses (if any) based solely on requirements documents and non-price evaluation factors in the solicitation

- Provide constructive information to offerors regarding their technical proposals for debriefings

- Sustain the government's position on ratings and scoring in protest forums.

Specifically, the CO hopes to obtain:

- An overall comparative assessment of each proposal's potential for award

- Initial ratings or analysis of how each proposal fares against the solicitation's factors and, if any, subfactors. *Remember*: The evaluation must be based solely on the factors and subfactors specified in the RFP!

- Added details on the proposal's specific deficiencies and relative strengths

- If necessary for cost or price analysis (or cost realism analysis), an analysis of proposed labor mix and hours, material mix and quantities, proposed special tooling and facilities, proposed scrap and spoilage factors, tasks, and schedule

- Consideration of any need for fact-finding or communications to clarify offerors' proposals and, if necessary, specifics on what must be asked of the offeror

- Consideration of any need to amend or cancel the RFP and, if necessary, the nature of any such amendment

- A list of recommended negotiation objectives

- Signatures required by agency policy.

162. What can the COR expect when the CO briefs the TEP?

The CO will likely brief the TEP to stress the following points:

- The importance of evaluating the contractors' proposals against factors and subfactors set forth in the RFP

- The essentiality of having no contact with any offerors or conducting any onsite visits unless approved by the CO

- The necessity and criticality of safeguarding source selection and proprietary information.

Any additional instructions applicable to the evaluators will also be given during the briefing.

163. What report does the TEP provide the CO?

The TEP will perform its technical evaluation and forward the results to the CO in a *technical evaluation report*. This report should provide the CO not only with numerical scores of each proposal, reached by consensus, but also with a consensus narrative explanation for each score. The report should address any deficiencies in proposals or any other issues relating to the evaluation. Finally—and most importantly—the report should advise the CO of which proposals are rated highest; this advice will be the basis for the CO's determination of which proposals will be included for further consideration.

164. What is a technical cost analysis?

The CO may request that the TEP perform a *technical cost analysis* of the proposed types and quantities of materials or labor, for example, set forth in the proposals. The TEP may be better-suited to perform the cost analysis because, generally, cost/price analysts are not technically knowledgeable regarding appropriate labor categories, types and quantities of materials, and other relevant factors such as work processes, special tooling, equipment proposed, and the reasonableness of scrap and spoilage. The technical analysis will determine the need for and reasonableness of the proposed resources, assuming reasonable economy and efficiency. At a minimum, the technical analysis should examine the types and quantities of material proposed and the need for the types and quantities of labor hours and the labor mix. Any other data that may be pertinent to an assessment of the offeror's ability to accomplish the technical requirements or to the cost or price analysis of the service or product being proposed should also be included in the analysis.

The CO may also develop "should cost" positions on the offeror's plans for performing the work; he or she will likely request technical assistance in this area.

165. What is a tradeoff analysis?

A tradeoff process is appropriate when it may be in the best interest of the government to consider award to other than the lowest-priced offeror or other than the highest technically rated offeror. The solicitation should state whether all evaluation factors other than cost or price, when combined, are significantly more important than, approximately equal to, or significantly less important than cost or price.

When using this process, a *tradeoff analysis* must be performed to determine the best overall offer, which permits tradeoffs among cost or price and non-cost factors and allows the government to accept other than the lowest-priced proposal, based on the factors and criteria being used. The perceived benefits of the higher-priced proposal must merit the additional cost, and the rationale for the tradeoffs must be documented in the file by the CO.

The CO, assisted by technical and pricing personnel, performs the tradeoff analysis and must ensure that the scoring or ratings are reliable and valid and that they are based solely on RFP evaluation factors and the agreed-upon methodology from the non-price evaluation factors. Proposals should *not* be scored or rated against each other. To support the scoring or ratings, the COR should provide the following documentation:

- The basis for evaluation of proposals
- Analysis of the proposals' strengths and weaknesses against each technical evaluation factor and subfactor
- A summary, matrix, or quantitative rating or score of each technical proposal in relation to the best possible score
- A summary of findings.

166. What are negotiation objectives?

As stated earlier, the TEP should also include in its report any recommended technical *negotiation objectives* to better meet the government's requirements. These objectives are derived from the technical evaluation and provide the CO with insight about which areas of each proposal need to be negotiated to serve the government's interests. For example, one proposal might have a great, even unique, technical approach, but the offeror's proposed price is too high. The CO's objective should then be to try to negotiate a lower price and still benefit from the better technical approach. Or the opposite could be true: A proposal might have a low price, but the offeror's technical approach is lacking in some respect. In this case, the CO would identify the proposal's deficiencies during negotiation and give the offeror an opportunity to improve its technical proposal.

Evaluating Past Performance

167. What is past performance, and how is it used to evaluate contractors?

Refer to FAR 42.15 for policies and responsibilities for recording and maintaining contractor performance information.

The Federal Acquisition Streamlining Act (FASA) was signed into law by President Clinton on October 13, 1994 (P.L. 103-355). Congress acknowledged that it is both appropriate and relevant for the government to consider a contractor's *past performance* in evaluating whether that contractor should receive future work. Section 1091 of FASA states:

- Past contract performance of an offeror is one of the relevant factors that a contracting official of an executive agency should consider in awarding a contract.

- It is appropriate for a contracting official to consider past contract performance of an offeror as an indicator of the likelihood that the offeror will successfully perform a contract to be awarded by that official.

FASA requires the administrator of the Office of Federal Procurement Policy (OFPP) to "establish policies and procedures that encourage the consideration of the offerors' past performance in the selection of contractors." Specifically, the act requires the establishment of:

- Standards for evaluating past performance with respect to cost (when appropriate), schedule (i.e., how well the contractor has adhered to the delivery schedule for past contracts), compliance with technical or functional specifications, and other relevant performance factors that facilitate consistent and fair evaluation by all executive agencies

- Policies for the collection and maintenance of information on past contract performance

- Policies for ensuring that offerors are afforded an opportunity to submit relevant information on past contract performance, including performance under contracts entered into by the executive agency concerned, by other agencies, by state and local governments, and by commercial customers, and that such information is considered by the government

- A period for which past performance information may be maintained.

OFPP's *Past Performance Guide* states:

> To select a high quality contractor, commercial firms rely on information about a contractor's past performance as a major part of the evaluation process. The government, on the other hand, for large contracts attempts to select a quality contractor by analyzing elaborate proposals describing how the work will be done and the

management systems that will be used to ensure good performance. The current practice allows offerors that can write outstanding proposals, but may not perform accordingly, to continue to "win" contracts when other competing offerors have significantly better performance records, and therefore offer a higher probability of meeting the contract requirements.

Settling for inexpensive mediocrity hardly seems in the taxpayers' best interest if an agency determines that it can get better overall value by doing business with a higher-priced supplier with an excellent track record.

When the government demands high quality services as a requirement for future business opportunities, as does the private sector, competition will intensify and result in higher-quality service by contractors.

168. What should the source selection team take into account when evaluating past performance?

The source selection team, which includes the COR, should consider the following aspects of contract performance when evaluating an offeror's past performance:

- Quality of products or services offered in the past
- Timeliness of performance
- Cost control
- Business practices
- Customer (end user) satisfaction
- Past performance of key personnel.

169. What should the COR know about conducting past performance surveys?

Survey questions, answered by past customers, are designed to collect consistent (from one offeror to the next), reliable, and valid data for applying the past performance evaluation factors (price and non-price) stated in the solicitation.

The COR will be required to assist the CO in conducting the surveys. The COR must be careful not to disclose any source selection information relating to other offerors' proposals to the respondents of the surveys—he or she must discuss only the proposal of the particular offeror whose past performance is being evaluated. Before using past performance information to evaluate an offeror, the CO should provide the offeror with an opportunity to discuss information obtained from customers, but the CO must *never* reveal the names of individuals who provided the past performance information.

When developing an overall judgment of an offeror's past performance, the CO and the COR should consider the following factors:

- The number and severity of an offeror's deficiencies, in relation to the offeror's overall work record

- The age and relevance of past performance information

- Potential bias on the part of any given customer (e.g., whether the customer is a potential competitor of the offeror for other requirements)

- The extent to which poor performance by an offeror on a past contract may have been as much or more the fault of the customer as it was the offeror's

- Differences in requirements between the current solicitation and contracts with the customer (e.g., differences in the level of technical and performance risk)

- The extent to which the offeror has taken measures to correct past problems (e.g., are ratings improving with time?)

- Survey-related bias (e.g., the "halo" effect—a situation in which the individual making the past performance evaluation knows the offeror did not perform well but gives the offeror a good rating because of favoritism).

The CO will provide sufficient documentation for the file to demonstrate that the government's evaluation of past performance was fair, impartial, and reasonable given available data.

170. What is the COR's role in conducting the past performance survey?

The COR is a key figure in this initial past performance survey of offerors. Many of the performance factors being evaluated will directly relate to the technical aspects of the requirement. For example, the contractor's demonstrated ability to perform a critical and complex engineering task in the past may serve as assurance that the risk of unsuccessful performance on the current contract is minimal.

In Chapter 6, we will discuss the COR's responsibilities for rating and documenting the contractor's performance during the contract administration monitoring phase of the contract. In May 2000, OFPP revised its past performance guide to encourage increased attention to contractor performance on current (in-process) contracts; OFPP made this change to ensure that past performance data will be readily available for source selection teams. In other words, the new guide attempts to strike a balance between after-the-fact reporting of contractor performance for use in source selection and the use of performance information to improve current contractor performance during the life of the contract. In using past and current performance information, two benefits for the government arise: better current performance resulting from the active dialogue between the contractor and the government, and increased ability to select high-quality contractors for new contracts because contractors know the performance assessments will be used in future award decisions.

Evaluating Contractor Responsibility

171. What is the COR's role in providing assistance to the CO on other terms and conditions and responsibility evaluation?

In the process of developing prenegotiation positions on terms and conditions other than price, the CO will require the technical assistance of the COR. The positions developed will address significant variances between the requirements of the solicitation and what the offerors are providing in their proposals. The potential impact on price of each variance and all potential tradeoffs must be identified. For example, if an offeror proposes a type of material of lesser quality than required by the solicitation, the government would need to negotiate a lower price for the material, provided, of course, that the lower quality of material was acceptable to the government.

Variances can occur in areas such as contract type, lease versus purchase, financing, government property, and many other terms and conditions, such as:

- The requirements documents
- Quality assurance requirements
- Time, place, and method of delivery or performance
- Bonding or insurance requirements
- Patents or rights in data
- Warranty requirements.

172. How is contractor responsibility determined?

The CO and the contracting team, including the COR, must determine that the contractor who is selected for award is qualified and eligible to receive the award. In making this determination, the contractor's *responsibility* must be considered.

The contracting team must determine that the contractor being considered has:

- Met, or can meet at the time of award, any special standards that apply to the procurement. (When it is necessary to ensure adequate contract performance for a particular acquisition, the CO may develop special standards of responsibility associated with unusual expertise or specialized facilities, for example. These special standards are set forth in the solicitation, identified as such, and apply to all offerors.) The CO, along with the COR and other specialists, as required, must then determine the offerors' compliance with these special standards; otherwise, the offerors are deemed nonresponsible.

- Adequate financial resources to perform or the ability to obtain the needed resources.

- The ability to comply with the delivery or performance schedule.

- A satisfactory performance record.

- A satisfactory record of integrity.

- The necessary organization, experience, accounting and operational controls, and technical skills, or the ability to obtain them.

- The necessary production, construction, and technical facilities or equipment, or the ability to obtain them.

- Met all other qualification requirements. This means that the contractor is otherwise qualified and eligible to receive an award (e.g., not suspended or debarred from receiving government contracts because of fraud or criminal conduct).

The Preaward Survey

173. What is a preaward survey?

A *preaward survey* is an evaluation by a surveying activity of a prospective contractor's capability to perform a proposed contract. (A "surveying activity" is usually the contract administration office, but if there is no designated contract administration office, it would be another organization designated by the agency to conduct preaward surveys.)

174. When is a preaward survey typically conducted?

A preaward survey is normally required *only* when the information on hand or readily available to the CO, including information from commercial sources, is not sufficient to make a determination regarding contractor responsibility. Also, if the contemplated contract will have a fixed price at or below the simplified acquisition threshold (currently $100,000) or will involve the acquisition of commercial items, the CO should *not* request a preaward survey unless circumstances justify its cost. The surveying activity should always ascertain whether the prospective contractor is debarred, suspended, or otherwise ineligible before beginning a preaward survey.

175. What is the COR's role in conducting a preaward survey?

The COR will be required to perform as the principal technical expert on the contracting team during the evaluation of other terms and conditions and the determination of responsibility, as requested. If the CO requests a preaward survey, the COR will serve as a key member of that team as well.

Remember, a little effort invested in preaward evaluations and determinations is quite likely to pay huge dividends later during postaward performance and monitoring. Finding out during performance that the chosen contractor does not possess the required capabilities will at least create extensive delays and expenses for the government, and could require that the contract be terminated due to the contractor's default.

Negotiations and Discussions

176. What are negotiations, and what are discussions?

Negotiations are exchanges, in either a competitive (multiple offers) or sole source (a single offer) environment between the government and offerors, that are undertaken with the intent of allowing the offeror to revise its proposal. These negotiations may include bargaining. Bargaining may involve persuasion, alteration of assumptions and position, and give-and-take on the part of both parties, and, it may apply to price, schedule, technical requirements, type of contract, or other terms of a proposed contract. When negotiations are conducted in a competitive acquisition, they take place after establishment of the competitive range (the most highly rated proposals based on proposal evaluation and subjective determination by the CO) and are called *discussions*.

177. What is the objective of discussions?

The primary objective of discussions is to persuade offerors to revise their proposals in ways that will optimize the government's ability to obtain best value, based on the requirement and the evaluation factors set forth in the solicitation.

For each offeror still being considered for award, the CO must prepare to discuss the offeror's significant weaknesses, deficiencies, and other aspects of the offeror's proposal (e.g., cost, price, technical approach, past performance, terms and conditions) that could be altered or explained to materially enhance the proposal's potential for award.

When conducting discussions with offerors, the contracting team should first establish negotiation priorities and potential tradeoffs or concessions. The team will:

- Rank the issues of concern (these could be technical or price problems, or problem areas or tradeoffs in the offerors' proposals)
- Determine the negotiation range for the government's position on each issue (i.e., distinguish positions that are relatively "firm" from "give" positions)
- Compare the government's positions to the offerors' anticipated positions
- Identify potential tradeoffs
- Determine how each issue should be addressed.

178. What is the COR's role in developing a negotiating strategy?

The COR will be required to participate in all activities necessary to support the CO in ensuring that an effective negotiation strategy is developed that will accomplish the government's objectives.

Debriefings

179. What are debriefings? When are they conducted? What is the COR's role in them?

Debriefings are exchanges of information between the CO and the offeror regarding the offeror's status relative to the proposal evaluation, discussion, and source selection (award) process.

Debriefings may be conducted either preaward or postaward by the CO with assistance from the COR and others (e.g., legal counsel), as may be required or requested by the CO. Debriefings must be requested by the offeror and conducted in conformance with FAR requirements, which include the request for a debriefing being submitted in writing and within prescribed time limits. *Preaward debriefings* occur when an offeror is notified by the CO that it has been excluded from the competitive range or is no longer eligible for consideration otherwise (e.g., the contracting team has found that the offeror was suspended from participating in government contracts due to criminal conduct and had failed to report that information when submitting its offer.) If the offeror desires a debriefing, it must be requested in writing within three days of receiving notice that it has been excluded from the competitive range. *Postaward debriefings* occur when an offeror is notified that it did not receive the award. If the offeror desires a debriefing, it must be requested within three days after notification of award. The CO will request technical support from the COR both in preparation for and conduct of the actual debriefing.

For preaward debriefings, the CO will:

- Present the agency's evaluation of significant elements in the offeror's proposal (i.e., the strengths and weaknesses of its proposal that resulted in its not being one of the most highly rated proposals)
- Provide a summary of the rationale supporting the offeror's elimination from the competitive range, or provide evidence for exclusion otherwise
- Provide reasonable responses to relevant questions about whether source selection procedures contained in the solicitation, applicable regulations, and other applicable authorities were followed in eliminating the offeror from the competitive range.

For postaward debriefings, the CO will:

- Provide the overall evaluated cost and technical rating of the successful offeror and the offeror being debriefed
- Provide the offeror being debriefed the overall ranking of all offerors when any ranking was developed by the agency during the source selection
- Provide a summary of the rationale for the basis of award
- If the acquisition is for commercial items, identify the make and model of the items being provided by the successful offeror

- Provide reasonable responses to relevant questions about whether source selection procedures contained in the solicitation, applicable regulations, and other applicable authorities were followed in making the award
- Not disclose any information exempt from release under the Freedom of Information Act (FOIA), including:
  - Trade secrets
  - Privileged or confidential manufacturing processes and techniques
  - Commercial and financial information that is privileged or confidential, including cost breakdowns, profit, indirect cost rates, and similar information
  - The names of individuals providing reference information about an offeror's past performance
- Not provide point-by-point comparisons of the debriefed offeror's proposal with those of other offerors.

Protests

180. What is a protest?

A *protest* is an objection, written by an interested party, to any of the following:

- A solicitation (or other request by an agency for offers) for a contract for the procurement of property or services
- The cancellation of the solicitation or other request
- An award or proposed award of the contract
- A termination or cancellation of an award, if the written objection contains an allegation that the termination or cancellation is based in whole or in part on improprieties concerning the award of the contract.

181. What is an interested party?

An *interested party* is an actual or prospective bidder or offeror whose direct economic interest would be affected by the award of a contract or by the failure to award a contract. This means that the complaining party must show that it has, in some manner, been adversely affected by the government decision that serves as the basis for the protest.

182. What are the methods by which a bidder may file a protest?

There are two methods by which an individual can file a protest:

1. Filing a protest with the CO is called an *agency protest*. The CO will review the protest and make a determination as to its validity.
2. Filing a protest with the General Accounting Office (GAO) is called a *formal protest*.

The protest must be filed in writing and must name the contracting agency and the contract or solicitation, and it must provide a detailed statement of the legal and factual grounds for the protest and provide information establishing that the protester is an interested party for the purpose of filing a protest.

The protest must also be timely. Protests against alleged improprieties (e.g., the government's making restrictive specifications) must be filed prior to bid opening or proposal closing. Other protests must be filed within ten calendar days from the date the basis for the protest is known or should have been known. For example, if an agency protest is denied, a protest to GAO would have to be filed within ten days. In negotiated procurements for which an offeror requested a debriefing, the offeror has ten calendar days, dating from the debriefing, to file a protest.

183. What is the formal protest process?

After a GAO protest has been filed, GAO will notify the CO and will request the submission of a protest report. The COR may be required to assist the CO in preparing this report. In addition, if GAO decides to hold hearings, the COR may be required to attend them to support the contracting agency's position. GAO has 100 calendar days to make a decision on a protest unless the "express" option is requested by either party, in which case GAO has 65 calendar days to make its decision (or recommendation).

184. What may GAO recommend when a protest is filed?

GAO may recommend that the contracting agency:

- Issue a new solicitation
- Award a contract consistent with statute or regulation
- Re-compete the contract
- Terminate the contract

- Refrain from exercising options (to purchase additional quantities or extend the period of performance) under the contract
- Follow other GAO recommendations to promote compliance.

185. **What is the COR's role in the event of a protest?**

The COR must gather facts, document the situation, and be prepared to support the government's position and participate in the debriefing and protest processes as required. The COR's documentation skills will be put to the test because of the intense legal scrutiny and potential ramifications from both a contractual remedy and cost standpoint; that is, the COR's documentation usually has significant bearing on whether the government wins or loses the litigation.

Unsolicited Proposals

186. **What are unsolicited proposals?**

An *unsolicited proposal* is a written proposal that is submitted to an agency on the initiative of the offeror for the purpose of obtaining a contract with the government. It is not in response to a request for proposals or any other government-initiated solicitation or program.

Unsolicited proposals allow unique and innovative ideas or approaches that have been developed outside the government to be made available to government agencies for use in the accomplishment of their missions. These proposals are offered with the intent that the government will enter into a contract with the offeror for research and development or other efforts supporting the government's mission, and they often represent a substantial investment of time and effort by the offeror.

187. **What criteria must an unsolicited proposal meet to be valid?**

A valid unsolicited proposal must:

- Be innovative and unique
- Be independently originated and developed by the offeror
- Be prepared without government supervision, endorsement, or direction, or direct government involvement
- Include sufficient detail to permit the determination that government support could be worthwhile and the proposed work could benefit the agency's research and development or other mission responsibilities

- Not be an advance proposal for a known agency requirement that could be acquired by competitive methods.

188. What qualities are considered in the evaluation of an unsolicited proposal?

An evaluation of the proposal is required to determine if the proposal contains:

- Unique, innovative, and meritorious methods, approaches, or concepts
- Overall scientific, technical, or socioeconomic merits
- A potential contribution to the agency's specific mission.

The CO also considers the offeror's capabilities, related experience, facilities, and techniques.

189. What is the basis for rejection of an unsolicited proposal?

Unsolicited proposals must be rejected if:

- The services or supplies proposed are available to the government without restriction from another source
- The proposal closely resembles a pending competitive acquisition requirement
- The proposal does not relate to the government's mission
- The proposal does not demonstrate an innovative and unique method, approach, or concept, or is otherwise not deemed a meritorious proposal.

190. When may a CO accept an unsolicited proposal on a sole source basis?

The CO may commence negotiations on a sole source basis only when:

- An unsolicited proposal has received a favorable comprehensive evaluation
- A justification and approval for negotiation of the proposal on a sole source basis has been obtained from the program (technical) office
- The program office sponsoring the contract furnishes the necessary funds

- The CO has complied with synopsis requirements (FAR Part 5, the policies and procedures for publicizing contract opportunities and award information) because the acceptance and final negotiation of the unsolicited proposal constitutes a sole source contract award.

191. What is the COR's role when an unsolicited proposal is received?

The COR will be responsible for the technical coordination and evaluation of the unsolicited proposal; he or she will provide technical advice on whether the unsolicited proposal should be accepted or rejected. The CO is responsible for determining the contractual acceptability of the unsolicited proposal and may also have to coordinate with other members of the acquisition team (such as the cost or price analyst, legal counsel, or small business representatives) depending on the particulars of the specific unsolicited proposal.

EXHIBIT 4-1. Sample Award Fee Plan

The following example of an award fee plan should not be used as a template. This is just a sample plan; the specifics of your actual requirement will determine what is included in your plan.

1. **Contractual award fee requirements.** The resulting contract shall provide that the total fee earned by the contractor shall be determined on a quarterly basis (or other period of time agreed upon by both parties) based on evaluation of the contractor's performance.

   The performance criteria used for development of the recommended award fee are:

   a. **Performance of work**

      (1) **Quality.** Assess contractor's compliance with contract specifications, considering services not completed and those that required re-performance.

      (2) **Timeliness.** Monitor compliance with scheduled requirements and response to unscheduled tasks.

      (3) **Technical data requirements.** Assess the quality, accuracy, and timeliness of data required by contract specifications.

   b. **Management**

      (1) **Cost control.** Assess the contractor's ability to control costs on scheduled and unscheduled tasks.

      (2) **Performance to cost estimate.** Compare the contractor's total actual costs to the contractual estimated costs.

      (3) **Government property.** Assess the contractor's control, inventory, care, maintenance, and utilization of government property.

   c. **Inspection system**

      (1) **System implementation and maintenance.** Assess the contractor's compliance with its own inspection system. Assess the method by which the contractor monitors its overall inspection system. Evaluate the contractor's ability to change or modify its system when problems arise.

      (2) **Corrective actions.** Assess the contractor's ability to correct actions within time frames established in the contract.

      (3) **Documentation and records.** Assess the contractor's requirement to document and maintain records on the inspections system.

2. **Numerical ratings.** Each evaluation factor will be assigned a numerical rating for each rating period.

Rating	Numerical Equivalent	Rating Description
Excellent	90–100	Performance in all areas is well above average
Very Good	70–89	Performance in most areas is well above average; all areas are above average
Average	60–69	Performance in all areas meets the requirements
Marginal	50–59	Performance in some areas meets the minimum requirements
Sub-Marginal	0–49	Performance does not meet minimum requirements.

3. **Contractor fee evaluation worksheet.**

The relative weights of the performance elements are as follows:

Criteria	Rating	Item Factor	Evaluation Rating	Category Factor	Factored Rating
Performance of Work					
1. Quality	————	x .50 =			
2. Timeliness	————	x .40 =			
3. Technical data requirements	————	x .10 =			
		Total		x .50 =	————
Management					
1. Cost control		x .30 =			
2. Performance to cost estimate	————	x .50 =			
3. Government property	————	x .20 =			
		Total		x .20 =	————
Inspection System					
1. System implementation and maintenance	————	x .50 =			
2. Corrective action	————	x .30 =			
3. Documentation and records	————	x .20 =			
		Total		x .30 =	————
		Total Weighted Rating			————

AWARD FEE CONVERSION CHART

Total Weighted Rating Fee	% of Award Fee	Total Weighted Rating	% of Award
100	100	85	50
99	97	84	47
98	93	83	43
97	90	82	40
96	87	81	37
95	83	80	33
94	80	79	30
93	77	78	27
92	73	77	23
91	70	76	20
90	67	75	17

Total Weighted Rating Fee	% of Award Fee	Total Weighted Rating	% of Award
89	63	74	13
88	60	73	10
87	57	72	7
86	53	71	3
		70-0	0

Planning for Contract Administration

Now that the contract has been awarded, the contracting team must begin the process of ensuring that the government will get what it needs, when it needs it, at a fair and reasonable price; in other words, the contracting team must administer the contract effectively and efficiently.

Every successful undertaking has as its beginning good, thorough planning, and the intent of this chapter is to prepare the COR, as a member of the contracting team, to perform all of his or her contract administration duties in an exemplary manner. Following the award of the contract, the COR truly begins to function as the "eyes and ears" of the CO.

Postaward planning is undertaken to:

- Ensure that the supplies or services to be provided are exactly what was contracted for
- Assign and communicate contract roles and responsibilities for both parties, the government acquisition team and the contractor
- Identify the required level of contract administration, monitoring, and inspection.

The three primary areas of concern for the COR during postaward planning are:

Postaward orientation. Promptly after award of the contract, the CO is responsible for postaward orientation involving both parties to the contract, i.e., the government acquisition team and the contractor. The COR's duties include preparation for and participation in the CO's preliminary briefing of the government team to ensure a united front on all contract issues and concerns. The COR will then provide technical expertise during the actual postaward orientation conference.

The COR workplan. The COR accepts, rejects, or clarifies delegated duties in the letter of designation, establishes necessary files, and, of course, develops the COR workplan itself. The COR workplan is often referred to as the *contract administration plan.* It establishes a plan for monitoring contract performance and serves as a baseline for project management, scheduling, and successful contract completion.

Task order contracting. The information on task order contracting provided in this chapter focuses on the popular indefinite delivery, indefinite quantity (IDIQ) contracts with which the COR is likely to be involved, as well as the ordering officer and task monitor responsibilities and issues usually associated with these contracts.

POSTAWARD ORIENTATION

192. What are the major goals of the postaward orientation period?

The three major goals of postaward orientation, in general, are:

1. *To achieve clear and mutual understanding of the contractual requirements*

   This is the primary goal of orientation. The following two goals are intended to clarify both sides' (the contractor's and the government contracting team's) understanding of the contract requirements.

2. *To understand what the contractor is planning to do*

   Finding out what the contractor plans to do before it is done is important in preventing the misapplication of contractor effort. Misapplication of contractor effort wastes project funds and could delay successful project accomplishment. Therefore, a review of the contractor's performance plans at the postaward orientation meeting is essential.

   Some contracts break down the contract job into component steps or phases and require that the contractor submit for technical approval a plan for each phase prior to commencing effort on that phase. Some contracts may also require the contractor to submit, at the end of each contract phase, a report on the work done to date as a prelude to the effort for the next phase. The COR is the representative for receipt and technical approval of such reports when the contract requires them.

It is not enough for the COR merely to stay informed regarding what the contractor has accomplished at any point in time. Without an overall plan for the work against which actual accomplishments may be compared, it will not be possible for the COR to know whether a contractor has fallen behind; the COR would not be aware that a problem exists and would be unable to determine the cause of delay and to develop a solution in a timely manner.

If the contractor's written plans are sufficiently detailed, the COR should be able to detect elements of planned performance that may threaten successful contract completion.

3. *To answer contractor questions and resolve potential problems*

During the orientation, the contractor may have technical questions, and the COR will need to provide technical clarification. In some cases, there may be disagreements between the government and the contractor about what is required or how to implement the requirements. During the orientation, if a disagreement occurs, the COR should delve into the reasons behind the contractor's position and include the contractor's reasoning in the orientation report. If disagreement with the contractor lends an emotionally charged atmosphere to the orientation, the COR, in consultation with the CO, should consider deferring resolution of the disagreement, promising the contractor prompt resolution, if that is possible. If the problem requires joint contractor/government problem-solving, the COR should set up a time for a separate meeting with only those individuals who need to attend.

It is important that the COR resolve each issue that arises in a fair and equitable manner, as quickly as possible. It is best to resolve all problems before the contractor begins any work on the contract, although this is not always practical. In seeking mutual agreement between the government and the contractor, the CO may hold further discussions with the contractor's top management or may consider a contract modification.

As covered briefly in Chapter 1, the COR has several major responsibilities during the contract administration phase. These responsibilities are first defined and planned at the postaward orientation conference.

The Postaward Orientation Conference

193. What is the postaward orientation conference or start of work meeting?

A *postaward orientation conference* is a planned, structured discussion between the government and the contractor that focuses on:

- Understanding the technical aspects of the contract
- Identifying and resolving oversights
- Preventing problems
- Averting misunderstandings
- Deciding how to solve problems that may occur later
- Reaching agreement on common issues, as discussed earlier in Goal 3 of Question 192, regarding resolution of points of disagreement.

Some agencies refer to this conference as a *start of work meeting*.

194. What is the purpose of the postaward orientation conference?

The conference is useful for postaward administration planning. Although the FAR does not require postaward orientation conferences for all contracts, it does provide some fundamental guidelines for determining the need for a formal orientation. The FAR states that postaward orientations should be held when it is determined that the contractor does not or may not have a clear understanding of the scope of the contract, its technical requirements, or the rights and obligations of the parties in any area of the contract.

COs use postaward orientation conferences to:

- Ensure that both parties have a clear and mutual understanding of all contract requirements (this is especially important when dealing with contractors who are inexperienced in furnishing deliverables to the government)
- Identify and resolve potential problems
- Furnish notices and other data to the contractor
- Otherwise set the stage for a good working relationship under the contract.

A successful postaward orientation conference is characterized by the following accomplishments:

- The contractor is informed of the postaward rights, duties, and milestones of both parties that could affect performance
- All potential issues (e.g., disagreements about technical requirements) are identified and resolved
- The resolution of each issue is fully documented in a postaward report
- The CO is notified of any issues that were not resolved after subsequent effort
- The contractor is advised of procedures, including rebuttal rights, for documenting performance in the agency past performance file.

195. What tasks will the COR need to perform during the postaward orientation period?

The COR must:

1. Prepare for the CO's preliminary meeting (or briefing)
2. Participate in the CO's preliminary meeting
3. Participate in the postaward orientation conference
4. Review a report of the postaward orientation conference
5. Complete assigned action items.

The Preliminary Meeting

196. What is the preliminary meeting prior to the postaward orientation conference?

Before the postaward orientation conference with the contractor, the CO will usually call a meeting of the government acquisition team to ensure the widest input on possible points of discussion during the orientation itself. One of the objectives of this meeting is to make sure the government team discusses its own issues and plans a coordinated and cohesive presentation—a united government front—on all issues that will arise during the actual conference. The government can do serious harm to its contractual interests by displaying a divided or confused position on the actual requirements of the contract at the conference. Contractors could easily use this lack of unity to their advantage, for example, by not adequately performing some aspect of the contract and then claiming that the government's lack of clarity created confusion and thus caused the problem.

If these preliminary discussions make clear the need for a possible change to the contract or to the government's normal method of operations, the CO will obtain agreement that a change should be made from appropriate government personnel prior to the conference. The CO will also communicate with the government acquisition team to coordinate and finalize how potential problems will be handled.

197. What are typical agenda items for the preliminary meeting?

The agenda of the preliminary meeting should be based on the requirements and constraints of the specific contract, with the goal of averting future problems. Agenda items may include the following:

- Discussion of the type and complexity of the effort
- Clarification of specifications and requirements
- Discussion of any special technical directions
- Discussion of the urgency of delivery or performance schedules
- Discussion of any incentive features of the contract
- Explanation of allowable and non-allowable costs
- Discussion of formal procedures for contract changes and modifications
- Discussion of the extent and nature of subcontracting
- Discussion of prime contractor versus subcontractor responsibilities
- Clarification of subcontractor reporting requirements
- Discussion of the transfer of government-furnished property (GFP)
- Discussion of special security or Privacy Act requirements.

198. What does the COR need to do to prepare for the preliminary meeting?

The COR will need to do the following to be prepared for the preliminary meeting:

- Review the contract.
- Prepare a significant milestone memorandum for the CO. (For more information about the significant milestone memorandum, see the section entitled The Significant Milestone Memorandum later in this chapter.)
- Develop a discussion paper for the CO.

Reviewing the Contract

199. Why does the COR need to read and understand the contract?

Now that the contract has been awarded by the CO, the contracting office will send the COR a copy of the contract. One of the COR's first duties is to become intimately familiar with all contract elements related to technical requirements and delivery. The COR must pay particular attention to elements such as special clauses (e.g., those regarding government property or government financing), the statement of work (SOW) schedule, and performance standards in order to effectively carry out his or her monitoring responsibilities. In other words, the COR must know exactly what the contract obligates the contractor to do in order to be able to compare those standards to what the contractor actually does during performance of the contract requirements. This awareness will enable the COR, during contract performance monitoring, to detect any differences (i.e., non-conformances) and to take action to correct or resolve them.

200. What are the most important items in the contract for the COR to review?

Figure 5-1 lists items in the contract that the COR should review carefully because they commonly come up for discussion at postaward orientation sessions.

• Special contract clauses	• Waivers and deviations
• Critical milestones	• Drawing/design approval
• The contractor's quality control procedures	• Manuals (these could be attached to the contract or incorporated by reference)
• The contractor's reporting requirements	• Pre-production samples (discussed in or referenced by the contract)
• Environmental, safety, and health provisions	• Inspection and acceptance provisions
• Description of the roles of the *government's* contract management team members	• Interpretation of specifications
	• Description of laboratory facilities
	• Production requirements
• Description of the roles of the *contractor's* contract management team members	• Documentation of production planning

FIGURE 5-1. Items the COR Must Look for
When Reviewing the Contract

201. What is the uniform contract format?

The use of a *uniform contract format* (UCF) facilitates preparation of the solicitation and contract as well as reference to and use of the contract by all parties involved. The UCF outlines the distinct sections of a contract for all federal contracts no matter the agency and keeps the sections in the same sequence so that contractors who may supply or perform for various agencies do not have to learn anew where to find information in the contract.

FAR 15.204 identifies the contents of each of the sections in the UCF. The content of some sections will vary depending on the method of procurement, i.e., sealed bidding versus negotiation; the type of solicitation and the relevant contract clauses would have to be tailored to each method.

Note that according to the FAR, Part IV of the UCF is included in the solicitation, but upon award, the CO must not actually include Part IV in the resulting contract. The CO must, however, retain Part IV in the contract file. Section K (of Part IV) must be incorporated by reference in the contract.

The FAR also identifies instances when the UCF need not be used (e.g., construction or architect-engineer contracts).

Figure 5-2 highlights sections of the UCF that are generally of interest to the COR.

The Significant Milestone Memorandum

202. How does the COR help the CO track progress on the contract?

The COR should develop a memorandum to the CO outlining the significant milestones applicable to the contract requirements and the corresponding due dates for each milestone. This memorandum will be used by the COR to monitor progress in performance and will act as an early warning device if work progresses slowly or the contractor fails to perform as required by the contract. Important milestones that should be included in the memorandum are:

- Reports or drafts due
- Presentations given
- Deliveries due
- Tests conducted
- Other similar events (e.g., completion of designated or periodic phases).

The COR should discuss these milestones with the CO to ensure mutual understanding, to acknowledge the limits of the COR's responsibilities, and

Contract Section	Examples of Information That Might Be Included in Each Section of the UCF
Part I: The Schedule	
A Solicitation/contract form	
B Supplies or services and prices/costs	
C Description/specifications/ work statement	SOW Scope ➤ Reference documents _____ Requirements
D Packaging and marking	
E Inspection and acceptance	
F Deliveries or performance	Contract delivery dates ➤ Contract line items _____ Performance time frame
G Contract administration data	
H Special contract requirements	Security clearances ➤ Geographic location _____ Unique requirements
Part II: Contract Clauses	
I Contract clauses	➤ Clauses required by regulation or law that _____ pertain to this procurement
Part III: List of Documents and Exhibits	
J List of attachments	➤ List contains: _____ Security form Data orders Contract data requirements list (CDRL) SOW Specification Financial data sheet Exhibits
Part IV: Representations and Instructions	
K Representations, certifications, and other statements of offerors	
L Instructions, conditions, and notices to offerors	Type of contract Solicitation ➤ Definitions Property requirements
M Evaluation factors of award	➤ How the proposal will be evaluated _____

FIGURE 5-2.   Sections of the UCF Relevant to the COR

to ensure his or her familiarity with the technical and administrative aspects of the contract requirements. This communication process should be maintained throughout the contract performance period. The COR's filing responsibilities regarding these efforts will be discussed later in this chapter.

The Discussion Paper

203. How does the COR prepare a discussion paper?

The COR will need to develop a discussion paper for the CO's preliminary briefing. The three steps in developing this paper are:

1. *Prioritizing all performance issues*

   CORs should focus on communication, teamwork, and proaction—elements instrumental to the success of the project. All issues of concern should be addressed and prioritized based on potential risk to the contractor or the government. Although the COR is not required to use it, the Potential Risk Worksheet (see Figure 5-3) may help the COR assess various areas and degrees of potential risk.

#	Describe the issue	Will the contract price need to be revised?	Will this create a change in the delivery or performance schedule?	Will the technical requirements have to be modified?	Are there other resources that must be added?	Rank the impact of the issue upon contract performance: High Moderate Little/None
1						
2						
3						
4						
5						
6						
7						
8						
9						
10						

FIGURE 5-3. Potential Risk Worksheet

The COR should consider the following elements of contract performance when identifying priorities:

- Work requirements (description of the contract performance requirements)
- Technical performance issues
- Interpretation of specifications
- Testing requirements
- Reports (e.g., progress reports, test reports, work completion reports)
- Approval processes
- Data requirements and manuals
- Facility and equipment availability/adequacy
- Technical direction limitations
- Key personnel provisions
- Subcontracting operations
- Overtime policy and approvals
- Property management
- Transportation and shipping.

Problems with any of these elements might affect the quality of the product provided or work performed, cause delays in contractor delivery, or increase the scope of work and the contract cost. All of these elements of contract performance should be reviewed and discussed at the orientation to ensure that the contractor has a complete understanding of the requirements.

The orientation must be an interactive process in which everyone involved in managing the contract has the opportunity to clarify any unclear issues. The clarification process, however, sometimes results in a need to change the requirements. If this occurs, both the contractor and the government are advised that a formal change must be processed using contract modification procedures.

2. *Selecting the issues that pose the greatest risk to performance*

Using the Potential Risk Worksheet, the COR should be able to determine those issues most detrimental to successful contract completion. The more "yes" answers on the worksheet, the greater the negative impact of an issue or issues upon contract performance. The COR should focus his or her attention on issues posing the greatest risk—those that impact cost, delivery/schedule, technical requirements, and resources.

3. *Developing solutions or other recommendations*

   Identifying the issues that present the greatest risk to contract performance is only half the battle. The COR also needs to consider solutions to these potential problems. The COR should not attend the CO's preliminary briefing with only a list of problems; the COR may be the best person to develop solutions to these problems. At a minimum, the COR should address the following questions for each issue selected as posing a risk to performance:

   • What are the recommendations for resolving the issue?

   • What resources are needed to resolve the issue?

   • What will be the contractor's reaction to the issue?

   Presenting a complete listing of significant issues and risks and solutions to possible problems to the CO results in a more productive preliminary briefing. It is critical that the contract administration team address these issues and resolutions before the team meets with the contractor. *A unified government team is a major goal of postaward orientation.* Waiting until the postaward orientation conference to raise these issues for the first time indicates that the government team is not united or fully apprised of the important issues.

Conduct of the Preliminary Meeting

204. Who attends the preliminary meeting?

The CO generally invites government representatives who interact with the contractor during performance to attend the preliminary briefing. These individuals include the:

• COR

• Program manager

• Project inspector

• Quality assurance specialist

• Other appropriate subject matter experts, such as a nuclear containment scientist or an environmental engineer.

205. Who is the chairperson for the preliminary meeting?

The CO chairs the preliminary meeting. The CO may provide an agenda or a postaward orientation checklist (see Exhibit 5-1, Postaward Orientation Checklist, at the end of this chapter), which is used to focus the discussions on the contract and issues impacting performance. At a minimum, the CO will provide guidance on the procedures for responding to questions at the postaward orientation conference.

206. What usually takes place at the postaward orientation conference, and what should the COR prepare before the conference?

Agenda items at the postaward orientation conference may include:

- *Questions.* The COR needs to know *before the conference* how questions will be handled later at the postaward orientation conference. Because the COR will be handling the questions during the conference, the CO must decide at the preliminary meeting (and inform the COR of his or her decision) whether or not questions will be allowed at any time or if they must be held until the end of the conference.

- *Presentations.* The COR may be asked to make presentations on elements of the contract that he or she is to monitor. Possible presentation topics include:

  - Clarification of technical issues
  - Security requirements
  - Labor policies
  - Environmental considerations
  - Safety considerations
  - Procedures for using government facilities
  - Payment procedures
  - Obtaining government property provided by the contract
  - First article testing procedures[1]
  - Monitoring methods

---

[1] *First article* is defined by the FAR (2.101) as "a pre-production model, initial production sample or test sample, first lot, pilot lot, or pilot models." *First article testing* is defined as "testing and evaluating the first article for conformance with specified contract requirements before or in the initial stage of production."

- Acceptance procedures
- Issuing task orders
- The chain of command for making changes or responding to inquiries
- The past performance file.

Because contracts vary so much, presentations need to be structured to fit the particular contract. For example, every agency generally has established payment procedures. If the COR is working with a first-time contractor, a payment procedures presentation at the postaward orientation conference will probably be necessary. If the COR is hesitant to make a presentation, the CO should be made aware of the COR's concerns at the preliminary briefing. The COR must be prepared to make any presentations requested by the CO.

- *Presentation of the discussion paper.* The COR presents the discussion paper, which focuses on the high and moderate risk issues potentially affecting contract performance. Depending on how the CO is conducting the conference, the COR will either present points from the paper at the time the particular issue is raised by the CO or will present the paper as the starting-off point for the conference. The COR should discuss the risks and solutions addressed in the paper and allow a thorough discussion. (Although the CO is the official responsible for making final decisions, the COR may be asked to take the lead in resolving problems or may be required to prepare a technical assessment of each problem.)

- *Presentation regarding the agency past performance file.* Statutory requirements have recently been enacted for the documentation of a contractor's performance in an agency past performance file. The inclusion of adverse information in the file could result in the contractor not receiving future contracts; this point must be addressed at the preliminary meeting and brought to the contractor's attention during the conference. Any presentation made about documenting past performance files must include a discussion of the contractor's rebuttal rights. The COR may be the official charged with preparing the information for the file, and if so, is the person most likely to make the presentation.

- *Discussion of performance-based service contracting.* The performance-based service contracting requirement may also be discussed. As the government moves away from basing acceptance of the contractor's performance under the contract on design requirements and moves closer to performance-based measurements, some partnering between the government and the contractor is necessary to ensure acceptable contract deliverables (i.e., supplies, services, or both). If the assigned contract is a performance-based service contract, a presentation is needed to cover monitoring and acceptance of deliverables. If monitoring and acceptance are the COR's responsibility under the contract, the COR needs to be fully prepared to discuss both.

- *Discussion of task order contracting, if applicable.* Task order contracting has recently become more common. In lieu of awarding all the work to one contractor, the contract may provide for issuing task orders competitively to a group of selected contractors. If the assigned contract includes this competitive task order provision, the COR may have to make a presentation to explain the procedures to all contractors. Task order contracting will be discussed later in this chapter in the section entitled Task Order Contracting.

207. In what instances may a CO decide not to hold a postaward orientation conference?

At the end of the preliminary briefing, the CO may choose not to hold a postaward orientation conference. The CO might decide that the information gathered at the briefing indicates that the necessary information can simply be conveyed to the contractor by letter, especially if the contractor has done business with the agency on other contracts and has a good history of performance.

A letter can also be used when relatively little information needs to be conveyed to the contractor. The CO may even decide to contact the contractor by telephone and hold a one-on-one discussion.

The COR may be asked to prepare a technical document or other presentation document for the CO to use if he or she chooses one of these alternatives. See Figure 5-4 for an example of a Post-award Orientation Letter.

The Postaward Orientation Conference

208. What is the COR's role at the postaward orientation conference?

The CO is usually the chairperson for the postaward orientation conference. Sometimes, however, the CO may direct the COR to chair the

TO: Gary Green, Project Manager, XYZ Power Co.

FROM: Al Jones, Contracting Officer

SUBJECT: Contract No. 104230-01-C-1234

To avoid any potential difficulties, I am writing to point out a requirement of the subject contract that has led to problems in other contracts. Also, I would like to clarify the contract completion date and identify the government personnel who will play a role in contract administration.

To install the four pieces of equipment required in contract line item #4, you will need to have a power outage in the west wing of Building 569, a heavily populated office building. Please note that paragraph 2.a(1) of the statement of work requires that this power outage take place on Sunday, a federal holiday, between the hours of midnight and 6:00 a.m. In addition, paragraph 2.a(5) of the statement of work requires that you provide me with seven calendar days' notice of your need for this outage. (Send the original notice of the need for a power outage to Mr. Howard Smith; see below.) Such notice is necessary because we have computers on-line 24 hours a day in that wing of the building as well as other operations that cannot be disrupted.

Because performance time is expressed in the contract as 120 calendar days after contract award, I want to affirm the date for contract completion as January 30, 2004.

Mr. Howard Smith is my representative for the technical aspects of this contract. Accordingly, he is referred to as the Contracting Officer's Representative (COR). He is not authorized to make any changes to the contract as written. He does have the authority to inspect and accept the equipment for the government.

You will receive any change to the contract, if required, as an official modification signed by me or another government official.

FIGURE 5-4.   Postaward Orientation Letter

conference. (See Exhibit 5-2, Suggested Procedure for Chairing the Postaward Orientation Conference, at the end of this chapter.) Even if the COR will act as conference chairperson, he or she is still generally responsible for:

- *Providing guidance in areas of expertise.* The COR should come to the conference prepared to provide guidance and make presentations on any assigned area of expertise or topic. At a minimum, any presentation the COR makes should be consistent with the terms and conditions of the contract. Presentations may include an overview of the subject area being discussed, recent changes in applicable regulations, discussion of any relevant procedures or processes, and an opportunity for the contractor to provide input.

If discussion with the contractor of a certain contract element is needed, the COR should be careful not to bind the government in any way that alters the contract during these discussions. Any contract areas disputed by the contractor must be recorded and resolved by the CO, as the CO is the only official who can change or alter a contract. Discussions with the contractor can be used to establish a procedure or process that will ensure compliance with a specific contract term (e.g., first article test procedures).

- *Developing and distributing handouts.* Handouts are permitted at the conference. Some handouts are required, such as Department of Labor posters and notices. Other handouts are developed specifically for the postaward orientation for the purpose of providing guidance and clarification on contract requirements. The COR will need to be careful that any information contained in handouts complies with the terms and conditions of the contract.

  Handouts can include:
  - Listings of relevant FAR provisions and clauses
  - Explanations of security procedures
  - Maps
  - Listings of government-furnished materials
  - Telephone listings of government personnel
  - Work schedules.

- *Responding to questions.* The chairperson (the CO) will give directions as to when questions can be asked. The CO generally makes this decision earlier, at the preliminary briefing. The COR's responses to questions should be accurate and complete. Again, the COR is urged to exercise caution when responding to any question to ensure that the contract terms and conditions are not changed.

- *Identifying further action items.* Issues that cannot be resolved at the conference must be identified and recorded by the COR. Whenever possible, a date should be established for resolution of the issues. All participants should be made aware at the conference of any specific follow-up actions they are personally responsible for completing. For milestones that require the contractor's input, it is best to reach agreement on the milestones at the conference. The CO incorporates the action items and due dates in the conference report.

209. What is the postaward orientation conference report?

The *postaward orientation conference report* should, at a minimum, include the following key elements:

- The names and affiliations of all participants
- The main points discussed and all agreements reached
- Areas requiring resolution
- Names of participants assigned responsibility for further actions
- Completion dates for the actions.

The report should contain all the information necessary to document the events of the conference. All participants, including the CO, the COR, the contractor, and others, as appropriate, should receive a copy of the report for review. Any omissions, deficiencies, or disagreements with the content of the report need to be thoroughly documented and submitted to the CO.

210. Why is it important to resolve identified problems before the contractor begins work?

The COR should select the best solution to any problems and seek agreement. It is important that the COR resolve each issue in a fair and equitable manner and as quickly as possible. Although not always practical, it is best to resolve all problems *before* the contractor begins any work under the contract, because if problems are not resolved ahead of time, the government has no control or ability to negotiate regarding the contract requirements. In seeking mutual agreement between the government and the contractor, the COR's actions can include:

- Holding further discussions with the contractor's top management
- Recommending that the contract be modified by the CO.

If a contract change seems necessary, the COR must clearly define the extent of the proposed change and submit it to the CO promptly.

211. How is the postaward orientation conference documented?

The official contract file should include the conference report as well as all other material, correspondence, or actions developed or acquired from the conference. The COR should provide the CO with copies of all technical material and correspondence. In the event of any subsequent disagreements with the contractor, this material can be used to reconstruct facts and events as they occurred. A well-documented contract file will identify and verify the government's initial position on any performance problems that were anticipated during the conference or in the early stages of implementation.

THE COR'S DELEGATED DUTIES

212. What tasks will the COR need to perform to validate delegated duties, establish and maintain files, and plan for the performance of COR responsibilities?

The COR must:

- Accept/reject delegated duties in his or her letter of designation
- Establish and maintain appropriate record-keeping files that support actions under the contract
- Develop and follow a COR workplan.

213. Why should the COR carefully review and accept or reject delegated duties in the letter of designation?

Refer to Chapter 1, Figure 1-1, for a sample letter of designation. As stated therein, this letter is the document used by the CO to accomplish COR designation. The COR must ensure that the information contained in his or her designation letter, including his or her name, role, authorities, and the limits on his or her authority, is complete and accurate (i.e., that the role of COR is not a misdirected assignment). The COR must also be certain that the delegated duties are within his or her technical capability and that no authority that is reserved exclusively for the CO is being delegated to the COR. A review of the problems that can arise from inappropriate delegation of responsibility, as discussed in Step 3 of Question 214 ("Identify any problems with the scope of delegations to the COR"), will explain why the COR must carefully scrutinize his or her letter of designation.

214. What steps are involved in the review of the letter of designation?

In reviewing the letter of designation, the COR should:

1. *Identify the scope of his or her responsibilities from the letter and relevant documents.*

There are basically two sources from which the COR may ascertain his or her responsibility under a contract—the letter of designation and the contract.

Letter of designation. While there is no established format for letters of designation, the letter should address a COR's role and responsibilities by citing:

- *Tasks to be performed.* Tasks to be performed by a COR may include:

  - Providing the CO with a copy of all technical direction issued, within 48 hours of issuance.

  - Providing the CO with written notification of any disputes that cannot be resolved between the COR and the contractor regarding performance of the contract.

  - Keeping a daily log of all contract-related activities while the COR is onsite at the contractor's plant. These activities could relate to any aspect of contract performance by the COR, the contractor, or other personnel with responsibilities related to the contract.

  - Turning over all records pertaining to this contract to the successor COR if the COR designation is terminated for any reason before completion of the contract; notifying the CO that such action has been taken.

- *Specific authorities being delegated.* The COR may furnish the contractor with technical assistance and guidance with all aspects of the contract. This assistance to the contractor may be formalized by written technical direction, provided the direction does not affect the price or duration of the contract. Written technical direction must contain both a signed acknowledgment of the technical direction from the contractor and the following statement: "In accepting this technical direction, the contractor agrees that the price and all other terms and conditions of the contract remain unchanged."

- *Limitations on any delegations.* A COR may not make changes that would affect the cost or duration of the contract. In addition, the CO may restrict the COR from delegating responsibilities to others by including in the letter of designation specific instructions such as this statement:

> You will have the following responsibilities, which may not be re-delegated to any other individual: To verify invoices and, upon receipt, promptly certify them for prompt payment. After verification, you will send me a copy of the certified invoice, and send the original to Finance.

Or instructions to the COR may appear as general statements:

> Please note that you may not re-delegate any of the contractual authority listed above, except for clerical tasks associated with that authority.

A COR may obtain help from other officials for any responsibility not specifically identified in the limitation. When the COR is in doubt about any of his or her responsibilities or the limitations placed on the COR, the CO should be contacted for guidance.

The contract. To fully anticipate the extent of responsibility delegated, the COR should thoroughly read the contract. The letter of designation may identify only overall responsibilities being delegated to the COR, while the contract details the methods, procedures, reports, and time-frames that must be performed or adhered to by the contractor. Information detailing the government's responsibilities may also be found in the contract itself. Both the letter and the contract aid the COR in determining the level of commitment required from both parties to ensure successful contract performance.

2. *Identify items that may have been omitted from the letter.*

Letters of designation should:

- Address the individual by name and position title
- Specify the contract number that applies to the delegation
- Specify the authorities, responsibilities, and tasks being delegated
- Emphasize limitations of the delegation
- Specify any record-keeping requirements and the disposition of those records
- Specify whether the designee may further designate any authority or task

- Include a requirement for the individual to certify that he or she has read and will abide by the agency's procurement integrity or conflict of interest requirements

- Be signed by the CO.

The CO *must* be notified of omissions of any of these elements in the letter.

3. *Identify any problems with the scope of delegations to the COR.* There are three basic problem areas to consider:

   - *Misdirected assignment.* Is the CO delegating responsibilities to the wrong official or office?

   - *Qualifications.* Is the CO delegating responsibilities for which the COR is not qualified?

   - *Unauthorized delegations.* Is the CO delegating responsibilities inappropriately? Delegations should not include responsibilities reserved exclusively for the CO. Unauthorized delegations to a COR include giving him or her the responsibility to:

     - Award, agree to, or execute a contract or contract modification

     - Authorize work outside the scope of the contract

     - Obligate, in any way, the payment of money by the government

     - Give direction to the contractor except as provided in the contract

     - Make a final decision on any matter that would be subject to appeal under the disputes clause of the contract

     - Resolve any dispute concerning a question of law or fact arising under the contract

     - Cause the contractor to incur costs not specifically covered by the contract except for costs that will be reimbursed by the government

     - Terminate for any cause the contractor's right to proceed.

   The CO must also be notified of any problems with delegation.

4. *Notify the CO of acceptance or rejection of the letter.*

   CORs are responsible for understanding the contract terms and conditions as well as knowing the scope and limitations of their authority. CORs are encouraged to contact the CO for guidance if they are unclear about their authority or any aspects of the contract. By signing the letter of designation, CORs accept full responsibility for rejecting the delegation if problems arise.

The COR's supervisor may be asked to concur with the duties outlined in the letter to indicate a recognition of the demands on the COR's work schedule. A copy of the letter should be provided to the project officer and the contractor so they will understand clearly the COR's roles and responsibilities.

Record-Keeping and the Contract File

215. What are the COR's record-keeping responsibilities during performance of the contract?

CORs are required to keep records in a file that document their actions under the contract. The documentation must constitute a complete history of the COR's actions, in order to:

- Provide background information that will help the COR make informed decisions at each step of the acquisition process
- Provide support for actions taken by the COR
- Provide information for reviews and investigations
- Furnish essential facts in the event of litigation or congressional inquiries.

FAR 1.604 states:

The COR shall maintain a file for each assigned contract. The file must include, as a minimum:

(a) A copy of the CO's letter of designation and other documents describing the COR's duties and responsibilities

(b) A copy of the contract administration functions delegated to a contract administration office which may not be delegated to the COR, and

(c) Documentation of COR actions taken in accordance with the delegation of authority.

Specific record-keeping functions will be identified in the letter of designation. The COR may be required, as noted in the letter of designation, to maintain portions of the official contract file.

216. What are some good practices for the COR to follow in maintaining the contract file?

The COR should:

- Include the contract number on each record in the file and on all correspondence relating to the contract
- Be sure that the CO receives a copy of all correspondence
- Give the utmost care to proprietary data, as well as classified and business-sensitive information
- Not rely on memory, but document events on the day or next working day after they occur
- Document telephone conversations
- Be prepared to take notes at even informal meetings
- Create separate files for each contract when keeping records on his or her computer and identify each for ready access (this will be helpful when speed in gathering materials is important).

217. What if the COR is not asked to maintain a contract file?

Responsibility for keeping the contract files may be decentralized and responsibility for their maintenance assigned to various organizational elements or to other outside offices. In accordance with FAR 4.801 and 4.802, each office performing contracting, contract administration, or paying functions is required to establish files containing the records for all contractual actions. Files to be established include:

- A file for cancelled solicitations
- An official file for each contract that consists of:
    1. The contracting office contract file
    2. The contract administration office contract file (if contract administration duties are delegated by the CO)

        and
    3. The paying office contract file
- A file, such as a contractor general file, containing information about:
    1. No particular contract, but a number of projects performed by the contractor

        or

2. The contractor in general (e.g., the contractor's management systems, past performance, or capabilities).

Additionally, the CO may delegate portions of the contract administration office contract file (a part of the official contracting office contract file) to be maintained by the COR. This file should contain copies of all documents supporting actions taken by the COR in performance of the contract. When the COR is not asked to maintain the contract administration file or portions of it, he or she should nonetheless document and maintain records in a COR work file, because CORs are routinely asked for copies of documents by the CO and other government officials involved in the contract.

218. What does the contract file include?

A *contract file* may consist of items in paper, electronic, or microfilm format and should contain sufficient information to constitute a complete history of the transaction (see Figure 5-5).

219. In establishing a contract file, what must the COR consider?

The COR's contract file must be characterized by the following:

- Effective documentation of contract actions

Contract File	Who Maintains It?	What Is Documented?
Award	The CO making the award	The basis for the acquisition and the award; the assignment (listed by individuals and their responsibilities) of contract administration duties (including payment responsibilities); and any subsequent actions taken by the contracting office. See Exhibit 5-3, Records Contained in the Contracting Office Contract File.
Administration	The CO and authorized delegatees (i.e., the COR)	Records documenting actions taken in the performance of contract administration responsibilities. See Exhibit 5-3, Records Contained in the Contract Administration Office Contract File.
Payment	Paying office, to support payments made under the contract	Actions prerequisite to, substantiating, and reflecting contract payments. See Exhibit 5-3, Records Contained in the Paying Office Contract File.

FIGURE 5-5. Contents of the Contract File

- Ready accessibility to principal users
- A minimal number of files; avoid duplicate files and multiple working files as much as possible
- The safeguarding of classified documents or source selection information
- Conformance with agency regulations for file location and maintenance.

220. Why is the maintenance of the contract file so important?

In any dispute with a contractor, the government will enter into litigation, whether the contractor appeals to a court in the judicial system or to an administrative board. In civil cases, the legal system deals mainly with facts, usually coming from files. Consequently, the more accurate and complete contract files are, the more likely the government will prevail in a dispute with a contractor. There are cases in which an administrative board reviews only the files that are submitted and makes a decision based on what they contain. Files prepared for the court will probably be heavily based on COR input. COR files are a part of the contract file and must be maintained in accordance with agency and CO instructions.

The COR and Past Performance Information

221. What is the agency past performance file?

This file, which is a part of the contractor general file, documents general information regarding the contractor's past performance (e.g., information on the contractor's management systems, past performance data, or other historical files). These types of data are routinely collected by the government when contracting for supplies or services and are relevant for future procurements. The information in the file is usually not based on the contractor's performance of a specific contract; it may cover more than one contract. Each agency determines the content and format used to maintain the past performance file.

222. What are the COR's responsibilities with regard to past performance information?

One of the responsibilities of a COR may be to provide information regarding the contractor's:

- Record of conforming to contract requirements
- Standards of good workmanship

- Record of forecasting and controlling costs
- History of reasonable and cooperative behavior
- Commitment to customer satisfaction
- Business-like concern for the interest of the customer.

CORs may be asked to provide regular input on the contractor's performance during the contract period. These interim reports are then incorporated into a final evaluation at the end of the contract period. The evaluation is provided to the contractor, who may review and dispute the content.

CORs may also be asked to respond to contractor rebuttals or consider additional information that might shed new light on the performance issues involved. CORs need to be aware of these requirements and should be prepared to provide responses to rebuttals or new data as needed. An official ranked above the CO will consider and decide the outcome of any disagreements between the government and the contractor.

THE COR WORKPLAN

223. What is the COR workplan, and when should it be developed? What are the COR's responsibilities with regard to the plan?

The *COR workplan*, or contract administration plan, documents a plan of action encompassing strategies and monitoring techniques to be used in the administration of the contract.

OFPP's *Guide to Best Practices for Contract Administration* states the purpose for a COR workplan as follows:

> Contract administration starts with developing clear, concise performance-based statements of work to the extent possible, and preparing a contract administration plan that cost-effectively measures the contractor's performance and provides documentation to pay accordingly.

There is no set format to follow in preparing a COR workplan. It can be simple or complex, but it must specify the performance outputs of the SOW and describe the methodology by which the government will conduct inspection and acceptance of the contractor's performance, as required by the contract.

The workplan should be developed as soon as the COR is appointed and may be modified as needed throughout the acquisition process.

A COR workplan serves as:

- A baseline for project management and scheduling
- A simple tool for tracking contract progress
- An aid for the postaward orientation conference.

With regard to the workplan, CORs are responsible for:

- Developing a cost-effective COR workplan
- Following the plan to monitor contract performance and perform other delegated responsibilities.

224. How does the COR prepare the COR workplan?

Preparing a workplan involves six steps:

1. *Include basic contract administration information in the plan*

   The COR workplan should include the following information:

   - The contract title
   - The identity of the contractor and key contractor personnel
   - The physical location of files related to the contract and the contractor
   - A brief description of the work to be performed
   - The place of performance and delivery points
   - Assigned tasks, milestones for each task, and milestones for functions, including:
     - Monitoring the contractor's quality assurance program
     - Furnishing government property and monitoring its use
     - Reviewing and responding to contractor reports and requests
     - Receiving, inspecting, and accepting the contractor's work
     - Certifying costs incurred and physical progress for payment purposes
     - Monitoring compliance with the small business subcontracting plan.

2. *Consider historical factors*

The COR workplan should indicate the level of commitment or amount of time and effort that will be necessary to monitor the contract to ensure successful performance. The COR determines the level of effort by considering general historical factors and the contractor's performance history.

The COR can review *general historical factors* to determine the necessary level of effort (see Figure 5-6).

The COR should also review the *contractor's past performance* for the last three years, paying close attention to the most recent information. This review should be focused on determining the level of effort the government will have to expend and the amount of attention necessary to monitor the current contract.

Issues to Consider	Questions to Explore
Type of contract	What type of contract is this? If there was a previous procurement for the same product or service, has the type of contract now changed?
Past or present experiences with this type of requirement	Has this requirement ever been purchased before? What are current problems associated with this product or service?
Contractor's past experience on previous contracts	Did this contractor previously deliver on time? Did the contractor perform as expected?
Type of specification	What type of specification was used in the past to describe the requirement: design, function, performance, or a combination of specification types? Have there been any changes in the specifications?
Type of requirement	Does this type of requirement necessitate extensive monitoring to ensure compliance?
Warranty provisions	Does the contract include any warranty provisions? Are the provisions the same as those offered commercially? Were there problems in the past with reliability beyond the warranty period?
Urgency of the requirement	How soon is this requirement needed and what would happen if delivery were delayed? Has this contractor established that it can expedite delivery, if needed?

FIGURE 5-6. Historical Factors to Consider in Determining Level of Effort

Performance history data will usually be filed by the contractor's name and will include the following information:

- Contracts awarded and dollar amounts of each contract
- Items/services purchased
- Key personnel involved with the contract
- Delivery/performance results
- Contractor-provided past performance information.

Any deficiencies in the contractor's past performance should be noted. Some of these deficiencies might include:

- Missed delivery dates
- Labor problems
- Shortfalls in technical performance capabilities
- Financial difficulties
- Failure to meet reporting requirements (e.g., progress reports, submission of subcontracting reports).

At a minimum, the COR should look for the contractor's:

- Record of conforming to contract requirements
- Standards of good workmanship
- Record of forecasting and controlling costs
- History of reasonable and cooperative behavior
- Commitment to customer satisfaction
- Business-like concern for the interest of the customer
- Reaction to remedies that were used by the government to correct problems.

3. *Determine the techniques to be used for monitoring the contract*

   Contract monitoring is a typical function delegated to CORs. The level of effort that will be necessary for monitoring and the monitoring technique that will be used should be addressed in the COR workplan. The appropriate type of effort depends on the complexity and scope of the contract, as well as the contract's specific requirements for monitoring, inspection, and acceptance.

Numerous techniques and procedures can be used for monitoring. A combination of techniques may be appropriate. Selecting a technique for monitoring will depend on what is to be monitored: the contractor's technical and schedule performance, costs, the contractor's financial condition, and the contractor's statutory compliance. The COR can choose to:

– Do nothing (i.e., rely on the contractor's inspection system)

– Conduct progress or status meetings with the contractor and other government officials

– Make onsite visits and other personal observations of the contractor's performance

– Contact other government officials for input

– Make telephone calls to the contractor and to other government officials

– Review the contractor's requests and other correspondence

– Review the contractor's required progress or status reports

– Review the contractor's tracking and management systems.

4. *Determine how to document performance under the contract*

Based on the letter of designation, there may be a requirement that the COR document or provide the documentation necessary for two types of files: the *official contract file*, which can include the contracting office contract file as well as the contract administration office contract file, and a *contractor general file*, which contains information regarding the contractor's past performance as well as other documentation. (Refer back to the section entitled Record-Keeping and the Contract File and Question 217 in this chapter for details regarding these file types, if necessary.)

5. *Identify areas of concern or conflict*

Contract requirements and the contractor's ability (or lack thereof) to meet those requirements may at times cause concern or present a conflict for the COR. Examples of a conflict a COR might face include:

• The delivery time indicated in the contract is after closing hours

• There is a need for government-furnished property that does not exist

- The technical review cannot be accomplished within the allotted timeframe
- The address listed in the contract to which deliverables should ship is incorrect
- The government property being used by the contractor is defective.

All areas of concern and possible solutions should be identified and addressed in the COR workplan.

6. *Prepare the COR workplan*

   While no specific format is required for the COR workplan, it is suggested that the following elements be included or described:

   - Administrative items (e.g., contract number, dollar amount, type of contract)
   - Historical factors
   - Monitoring techniques
   - Documentation of the contractor's performance
   - Areas of concern or conflict

   The workplan should be completed, signed, and dated as soon as possible after the contract is awarded and before work commences under the contract. The COR should forward copies of the workplan to the contracting office and should place one copy in the established contract administration file.

   For additional information, see Exhibit 5-4, Example of a COR Workplan, at the end of this chapter.

Task Order Contracting

225. What is task order contracting?

Chapter 4 discussed contract types, including the three types of indefinite delivery contracts. One of those was the indefinite quantity contract, commonly referred to as an IDIQ (indefinite delivery, indefinite quantity) contract. IDIQ contracts are often used as task order contracts, which are defined by FAR 16.501-1 as contracts for services that do not procure or specify a firm quantity of services (other than a minimum or maximum quantity) and that provide for the issuance of orders for the performance of tasks during the period of the contract. FAR 16.501-1 also defines the delivery order contract similarly, but a delivery order contract is used when procuring supplies instead of services.

226. What responsibilities will the COR need to carry out when working with task order contracts?

The COR must:

- Oversee and coordinate initial efforts regarding preparation of the task order and associated documents

- Review and reconcile differences between the task order and the contractor's task cost plan

- Understand and be prepared to make recommendations to the CO on single- versus multiple-award issues

- Make recommendations to the CO regarding the ordering officer's and task monitor's duties.

Task Order Documentation and Cost Plan

227. What does the COR do to prepare the task order and associated documents?

The COR must:

- Prepare the task order SOW
- Prepare the independent cost estimate
- Determine whether funding is available
- Evaluate the contractor's task plans
- Monitor contractor performance under the task order, or assign task monitors as authorized by the CO
- Avoid personal services relationships.[2]

The work proposed in the task order must fall clearly within the scope of the contract under which the task order is to be issued.

---

[2] A *personal services contract* is a contract that, by its express terms or as administered, makes the contractor personnel appear to be, in effect, government employees (FAR 37.101; also see FAR 37.104). These contracts are illegal unless specifically authorized by statute.

In addition to reviewing the proposed task order to make sure the work falls within the scope of the contract, the CO will also check to ensure that:

- Direct supervision of contractor personnel by government personnel does not transform the contract from non-personal services into a personal services contract (see Chapter 3, Questions 86 and 87)
- The direct labor hours proposed are consistent with the work described
- The estimated cost appears reasonable
- The proposed length of time for performance of the task order appears appropriate.

228. What is the contractor's task cost plan?

The contractor, on receiving the task order, prepares and submits a *task cost plan* to the COR, describing how the contractor intends to accomplish the assigned task. The COR provides a copy of the plan to the CO.

229. What is the COR's role in reviewing the task cost plan?

The COR reviews the task cost plan to determine if the contractor's estimates of hours and dollars needed to accomplish the contract work are consistent with the requirements of the task order. If the task cost plan differs from the task order, the COR prepares, for the CO's approval, a revised task order incorporating the approved task cost plan estimates of hours and dollars and any other required revisions. The COR provides the CO with a copy of the revised task order and task cost plan.

Single- and Multiple-Award Task Order Contracts

230. What are the differences between single- and multiple-award task order contracts?

IDIQ contracts will usually be awarded to multiple contractors to provide for competition on task orders. Multiple-award task order contracts will require significantly more administrative effort than single-award task order contracts, as there will be not only the initial competition for the contracts, but also a series of selections for the award of individual task orders.

231. What must the CO do, and what must he or she consider, when working on a multiple-award task order contract?

COs will draft selection criteria and ordering procedures that will be included in the multiple award solicitation. COs have broad discretion regarding the factors that are relevant to the placement of task orders.
When drafting such procedures:

- Prior to placing each order, the CO will avoid methods such as allocation that would not result in fair consideration being given to all awardees. (However, each awardee is usually guaranteed a minimum amount of the work, so it may be necessary to place an order with each participating contractor to satisfy that minimum requirement.)

- The CO will allow the use of oral proposals and streamlined ordering procedures. (The placing of orders need not comply with the competition requirements of FAR Part 6.)

- The contract's ordering procedures and selection criteria may expressly state that the government need not contact every awardee prior to placing the order. This may be appropriate when:

  - The CO has sufficient information to fairly consider every awardee for the order based on selection criteria stated in the contract

  - There is an applicable exception under FAR 16.505(b) to the fair consideration requirement (e.g. urgency, past performance information, the prices charged by awardees).

232. When must a multiple award be made?

The CO *must* make multiple awards if a contract for *advisory and assistance services* (refer to Chapter 3, Questions 88 and 89 for more information) would exceed three years and would cost more than $10 million (including options).[3]

233. When is a single award made?

The CO plans on a single award when it can be demonstrated that a single award is in the best interest of the government for such reasons as the following:

- Only one contractor is capable of providing performance at the level of quality required because the deliverable is unique or highly specialized

---

[3] An *option* is a unilateral right in a contract by which, for a specified time, the government may increase quantities or extend the term of the contract. (See Chapter 3, Question 74, for further details.)

- Market research indicates that the government will get more favorable terms and conditions, including pricing, if a single award is made
- The cost of administration of multiple contracts would probably outweigh any potential benefits
- Probable tasks are so integrally related that only a single contractor can reasonably perform the work
- Estimated value of the contract is less than the simplified acquisition threshold.

234. **What type of contract is used for a single award?**

For single awards, a *requirements contract*, the other type of indefinite delivery type contract, is used.

235. **What are mandatory sources and what type of contract is typically used to acquire services or supplies from these sources?**

Task order contracts are also frequently used to acquire supplies or services from mandatory sources in accordance with FAR Part 8. These sources include GSA Federal Supply Schedules, Federal Prisons Industries, Inc. (UNICOR), and the Committee for the Blind and Severely Disabled.

Ordering Officers and Task Monitors

236. **What is ordering officer authority?**

If the COR is involved in task order contracting, he or she may be designated an ordering officer by the CO in the letter of designation. Usually, an *ordering officer* deals with multiple program office personnel using the individual task SOW developed by the program office engineers or project officers. Ordering officers are not involved individually in development of the SOW and administering it under the IDIQ; they function exclusively as the ordering officers for other individuals.

237. **When does the CO delegate ordering officer authority?**

The CO should delegate ordering authority only to individuals who have the proper training and ability to properly carry out delegated authority. The key issue for the CO on task order contracts is determining whether he or she should delegate the authority to place orders to CORs or to other ordering officials. This delegation of authority may be possible when the task order contract establishes a fixed price for each task (e.g., $2,000 and travel expenses to conduct each "System Inspection and Operational Report"). Delegating such authority may not be advisable if the task order contract only establishes labor rates and provides for negotiating labor hours and material costs order by order. In such cases, the CO will delegate ordering authority only to personnel trained in cost analysis and negotiation techniques and will usually establish a ceiling amount for each order that may be issued without CO review and approval.

238. What are task monitors and when does the CO appoint them?

Sometimes the CO will appoint, or allow the COR to appoint, *task monitors* in situations involving significant (high-cost or complex) task orders. If the COR is involved in such a case, he or she must make sure the task monitor arrangements are set forth in the letter of designation, because these monitors do not have COR authority. Task monitors only assist the COR in monitoring individual tasks; therefore, ultimate responsibility for monitoring the contractor's performance remains with the COR.

EXHIBIT 5-1. Postaward Orientation Checklist

PART I: GENERAL

Contract No. _____ Total Amount _____

Type of Contract _____ Date of Conference _____

Pre-Award Survey ☐ Yes ☐ No

Contractor Name _____

Contractor Address _____

_____

PART II: CONFEREES

1. Government _____

_____

_____

2. Contractor_____

_____

_____

PART III: CONFERENCE PROGRAM

Subject	Is the topic to be discussed or addressed?	Contract clause number, if applicable	Significant conclusions, further action to be taken (attach additional sheets if necessary)
A. General			
1. Function and authority of assigned personnel			
2. Routing of correspondence			
3. Omissions or conflicting provisions			
4. Other (specify)			
B. Reports: Preparation and Submission			
1. Work progress			
2. Financial			
3. Other (specify)			

C. Subcontracts			
1. Consent to placement			
2. Prime's responsibility for administration			
3. Cost or pricing data			
4. Source inspection			
5. Other (specify)			
D. SB, SDB, and WOSB Subcontracting			
1. Contractual requirements			
2. Program to facilitate			
E. Contract Modifications			
F. Government Property			
1. Use of equipment and tooling			
2. Maintenance and preservation			
3. Property procedure approval			
4. Property disposal procedures			
5. Other (specify)			
G. Special Clauses			
1. Issuing task orders			
2. Liquidated damages			
3. Government financing			
4. Special tooling			
5. Overtime			
6. Bill of materials			
7. Data/copyrights			
8. Warranties			
9. Work performed at government installations			

10. Other (specify)			
H. General Clauses			
1. Limitation of cost			
2. Allowability of cost			
3. Other (specify)			
I. Delivery/ Performance Schedules			
J. Transportation			
K. Invoicing and Billing Instructions			
L. Processing of Cost and Price Proposals			
M. Labor			
1. Actual and potential labor disputes			
2. Davis-Bacon Act			
3. Work Hours Act			
4. Walsh-Healey Act			
5. Copeland Anti-Kickback Act			
6. DoL posters and notices			
N. Quality Assurance and Engineering			
1. Quality control system			
2. Waivers and deviations			
3. Drawing/design approval			
4. Manuals			
5. Pre-production sample			
6. Qualifications and environmental tests			
7. Inspection and acceptance			
8. Specification interpretation			

9. Laboratory facilities			
10. Value engineering clause			
11. Other (specify)			
O. Production			
1. Production planning			
2. Milestones and other monitoring devices			
3. Production surveillance			

EXHIBIT 5-2. Suggested Procedure for Chairing the Postaward Orientation Conference

Introduce the participants	At the opening of the conference, the chairperson (this will be the CO or the COR, if the COR is delegated to do so by the CO, or the CO and the COR could share the chairperson duties, as decided and delegated by the CO) introduces each government attendee by name and title, along with a one-sentence explanation of the role that person will play in contract administration. The contractor makes the same introductions for its team.
Explain the purpose of the conference	Go over the agenda, making clear that the conference is not intended to change or alter the contract in any way. Emphasize that the only way the contract may be changed or altered is by a written modification signed by the CO.
Summarize the roles of key government personnel	Clarify the limits, authorities, roles, and responsibilities of each government representative. Ask the contractor to advise the government of the roles, responsibilities, limits, and authorities of each contractor representative. Emphasize that: • The CO is the only official who can change or alter the contract. Any exception to this must be clearly specified. • No action may be taken at the orientation which in any way changes or alters the contract. • There is no obligation to make any contract adjustments as a result of an action taken by a government representative, unless the action has been specifically authorized in the representative's letter of designation or by the contract itself.
Provide general instructions	General contract administration instructions include information necessary for the contractor regarding the risks it faces as well as the risks the government must face, and they address contractor responsibilities for: • Management and supervision of the workforce • Protection and control of government property, data, and reports • Compliance with contract clauses • Other appropriate areas of concern. Advise contractors of the proper routing of correspondence: • Matters pertaining to technical performance may be addressed directly to the COR or project officer • Matters pertaining to questions of fact dealing with contractual terms and conditions must be sent to the CO.
Provide the contractor with posters, notices, and other data	The government is responsible for providing contractors with required labor posters and notices. Distribute these and other data as needed at the postaward orientation conference.

Hear presentations and address questions

Each official makes his or her presentation as determined at the preliminary briefing. Questions can be raised during the presentation or held until the end of all of the presentations. Responses to questions should be accurate and complete and statements made cannot bind the government in any way that alters the contract.

Secure agreement on milestones or interpretation of terms and conditions

For milestones that require the contractor's input, seek the contractor's agreement. Focus further action issues on key discussion items that would affect:

- Performance
- Interim delivery
- Payment
- Resources needed.

During the conference, request any needed information or responses from the contractor to ensure a uniform understanding of key terms and conditions. All government participants should be made aware of any actions they must take to resolve outstanding issues.

EXHIBIT 5-3. Recommended File Contents

Records Contained in Contracting Office Contract File

Normally, records kept in this file include:

- Purchase requests, acquisition planning information, and other presolicitation documents
- Justifications and approvals, determinations and findings, and associated documents
- Evidence of availability of funds
- Synopsis of the proposed acquisition as published in the government- wide point of entry or associated reference
- A list of sources solicited and a list of any firms or persons whose requests for copies of the solicitation were denied, together with the reasons for denial
- Set-aside decisions (i.e., the reserving of an acquisition exclusively for participation by small business concerns)
- The government estimate of contract price
- A copy of the solicitation and all amendments
- Security requirements and evidence of required clearances
- A copy of each offer or quotation, the related abstract, and records of determinations concerning late offers or quotations. Unsuccessful offers or quotations may be maintained separately if cross-referenced to the contract file. The only portions of the unsuccessful offer or quotation that need to be retained are:
  - Completed solicitation sections A, B, and K of the contract, according to the uniform contract format
  - Technical and management proposals
  - Cost/price proposals
  - Any other pages of the solicitation that the offeror or quoter has altered or annotated.
- The contractor's certifications and representations
- Preaward survey reports or references to previous preaward survey reports relied upon
- Source selection documentation
- The CO's determination of the contractor's responsibility
- Small Business Administration Certificate of Competency
- Records of contractor's compliance with labor policies, including equal employment opportunity policies
- Cost or pricing data and a certificate of current cost or pricing data, or a required justification for waiver of the need to require cost/pricing data
- Information other than cost or pricing data determined by the CO to be necessary to establish a fair and reasonable price. This might include, for example, a contractor's cost breakdown of selected material or labor costs to establish the reasonableness of the total amount
- Packaging and transportation data
- Cost or price analysis
- Audit reports or reasons for waiving the audit report
- A record of negotiation
- Justification for type of contract

- Authority for deviations from any regulation (e.g., the FAR, statutory requirements, other restrictions)
- Required approvals of award and evidence of legal review
- Notice of award
- Original documentation of:
  - Signed contract or award
  - All contract modifications
  - Supporting modifications executed by the contracting office.
- Synopsis of award or associated reference
- Notice to unsuccessful quoters or offerors and record of any debriefing
- Documentation of assignment of the COR
- Acquisition management reports, or a reference thereto, and notices to *sureties* (individuals or corporations legally liable for the failure of the contractor, e.g., through a payment or performance bond for a contractor)
- Report of postaward orientation
- Notice to proceed, stop orders, and any overtime premium approvals (i.e., contractor overtime pay rates versus regular pay rates must be approved by the agency), granted at the time of award
- Documents requesting and authorizing modification in the normal assignment of contract administration functions and responsibility
- Approval or disapproval of requests for waivers or deviations from contract requirements
- Royalty, invention, and copyright reports (including invention disclosures) or reference thereto
- Contract completion documents
- Documentation regarding termination actions for which the contracting office is responsible
- Cross-references to pertinent documents that are filed elsewhere
- Any additional documents on which action was taken or that reflect actions by the contracting office pertinent to the contract
- A current chronological list identifying the awarding and successor COs, with inclusive dates of responsibility
- For contracts and contract modifications in excess of $100,000, a record of all persons or classes of persons authorized to have access to proprietary or source selection information and, to the maximum extent practicable, the names of all individuals within the class.

Records Contained in Contract Administration Office Contract File

Normally, records kept in this file include:

- A copy of the contract and all modifications, together with official record copies of supporting documents executed by the contract administration office
- Any document modifying the normal assignment of contract administration functions and responsibility
- Security requirements
- Cost or pricing data, including:
  - Certificates of current cost or pricing data
  - Information other than cost or pricing data
  - Cost or price analysis

  - Other documentation supporting contractual actions executed by the contract administration office.
- Preaward survey information
- Purchasing system information
- Consent to subcontract or purchase
- Performance and payment bonds and surety information
- Postaward orientation records
- Orders issued under the contract
- Notice to proceed and stop orders
- Insurance policies or certificates of insurance or references to these policies and certificates
- Documents supporting advance or progress payments
- Progressing, expediting, and production surveillance records
- Quality assurance records
- Property administration records
- Documentation regarding termination actions for which the contract administration office is responsible
- Any additional documents on which action was taken or that reflect actions by the contract administration office pertinent to the contract
- Contract completion documents
- Cross-references to other pertinent documents that are filed elsewhere
- Any additional documents on which action was taken or that reflect actions by the contract administration office pertinent to the contract
- Contract completion documents.

Records Contained in Paying Office Contract File

Normally, records kept in this file include:
- A copy of the contract and any modifications
- Bills, invoices, vouchers, and supporting documents
- Record of payments or receipts
- Other pertinent documents.

EXHIBIT 5-4. Example of a COR Workplan

1. **Contract**

   FCA88-10-C-2121 Janitorial and Related Services at Federal Office Building No. 3

   Criticality Designator: C

   Contract Amount: $375,732 (base year); total of $2,076,132 for all 5 years

   Contract Type: Firm fixed price

   Date of Award: December 29, 2010

2. **Responsibilities under Contract**
   - Determining the adequacy of contractor performance
   - Representing the government in directing work
   - Ensuring compliance of work with requirements
   - Advising the CO.

3. **Government Points of Contact**

   Terry O'Day, Contract Administrator: Federal Contracting Administration

   Responsible for:
   - Day-to-day inspection and monitoring
   - Documenting inspections
   - Following through on deficiencies.

4. **Contractor**

   Profitable Building Services, 9191 Crosstown Boulevard, Capital City, DC 11811

   Mr. John Mahoney, General Manager (101) 595-0202

5. **Location of Files**

   Federal Contracting Administration, 1000 First Street, Capital City, DC 11777

6. **Contractor's Scope of Work**
   - To provide all management, supervision, labor, materials, supplies, and equipment (except as specified)
   - To plan, schedule, coordinate, and ensure effective performance of janitorial and related services at Federal Office Building No. 3, Capital City, DC 11811

7. **Place of Performance** Federal Office Building No. 3, 2900 Lost Lane, Capital City, DC 11777

8. **Contractor Reporting Requirements**
   - Annual Daily/Periodic Cleaning Schedule submitted five workdays prior to start date and then annually
   - Daily Work Report (GSA Form 64 or equivalent), submitted daily to the COR
   - Quality Control Program, submitted five workdays prior to start date
   - Resumes of initial and replacement supervisors.

9. **Contractor Milestones**

Date	Task
January 25, 2012	Annual Cleaning Schedule due five workdays prior to base year start date (February 1)
January 25, 2013–2016	Annual Cleaning Schedule due five workdays prior to each option year start date
January 25, 2012	Quality Control Program due five workdays prior to base year start date.

10. **Previous Contracts**

    This is a first-time contractor. There is no information on file for this contractor.

11. **Potential Problem Areas**

    - All supplies, materials, and equipment used by the contractor must conform to specifications and must, on request, be identified; possible problems could be avoided by requesting a listing prior to the start date and prior to any substitutions.

    - Space for locker rooms for contractor personnel, for storage of equipment and supplies, and for use as the contractor's onsite office is to be government-furnished; this space should be identified and inspected prior to the start date.

    - Contract does not specify which official will determine when the contractor's personnel will be diverted for snow removal or emergency conditions; when given, these instructions should be in writing to avoid disputes over deductions.

    - The contractor is to have the opportunity to re-perform deficient services and ensure future services before deductions are taken; however, no time limit for remedial action is specified.

12. **Monitoring**

    Contractor technical and schedule techniques to be used:

    - Making onsite visits and personal observations
    - Contacting the quality assurance specialist
    - Reviewing progress or status reports.

13. **Documentation**

    The contractor's performance will be documented in the contract file using Agency Form 631: Monitoring Report.

14. **Action Requirements**

    Attend postaward preliminary briefing on January 13 with CO to discuss roles and responsibilities for postaward conference with contractor, scheduled for January 15.

CHAPTER 6

Contract Monitoring, Inspection, and Acceptance

Chapter 5 covered the tasks and events involved in planning for contract administration. This chapter deals with the COR's primary duties actually performed during the contract administration phase, which relate to the monitoring of contract performance and inspection and acceptance. These duties are the "heart and soul" of the COR's job. All other functions that the COR performs lead up to his or her monitoring, inspection, and acceptance duties, which are the most important duties he or she performs. The COR's responsibilities culminate in the final acceptance (or rejection) of the contractor's work.

Another very important duty of the COR, documenting past performance information, is covered again in this chapter. The COR may also be assigned responsibility for the direct administration of government property, if applicable to the contract. However, a property administrator may be assigned to the contract, in which case the COR would still have overall monitoring responsibilities relating to government property.

Finally, as the primary monitor of contract performance, the COR may find it necessary to report fraud or other suspicious conduct during contract performance. This chapter also provides guidance for the COR in this area.

MONITORING THE CONTRACTOR'S PERFORMANCE

CORs must know how to monitor contract performance. The COR's monitoring responsibilities, in part, consist of documenting a contractor's performance and preparing a technical analysis of the contractor's performance.

Monitoring is successful if:

- All potential problems with performance and delivery requirements are reported to the CO
- Any noncompliance with other terms and conditions of the contract is identified and reported to the CO
- Sufficient documentation of a contractor's performance exists to support payments under the contract
- Technical analysis is sufficient to support the CO's negotiations and final decisions.

239. What tasks must the COR perform to successfully perform monitoring actions as authorized by the CO?

The COR must:

1. Respond to requests from contractors
2. Monitor contract performance
3. Resolve constructive changes.

Responding to Requests from Contractors

240. What is the COR's role with regard to contractor requests during performance of the contract?

There are times when the COR is responsible for reviewing and approving reports, test results, or production schedules; making decisions; or taking other actions at the request of the contractor during the performance of a contract. A COR can best handle contractor requests by performing the following three actions:

1. Identifying all contractual terms allowing for contractor requests
2. Determining the contractor's obligations in accordance with specific contract terms
3. Providing a timely response to the contractor's request.

1. *Identifying all contractual terms allowing for contractor requests*

   The terms laid out in the contract provide guidance for the COR's response to a contractor request. The contract may address such issues as:

   - A contractor's right to request government action
   - The government's responsibilities when a contractor makes a request
   - The impact from not complying with a request (e.g., the government's liability for late delivery or other non-conforming performance issues).

2. *Determining the contractor's obligation*

   Contract terms generally specify whether the contractor is required to:

   - Submit requests in writing
   - Respond within a pre-established timeframe
   - Notify government personnel, other than the COR, when a request for a particular action is required
   - Stop work in a given situation.

3. *Providing a timely response to the contractor's request*

   Depending on the contractual requirement regarding responses to contractor requests, the COR must either:

   - Respond to the request within the timeframe set by the contract term

     or

   - Forward any request outside the scope of delegated authority to the CO in sufficient time to permit a timely response.

   When no timeframe for responding to requests is identified, the COR will need to provide a response to the contractor that is reasonable and does not delay the contractor from performing under the contract. An untimely response to a request may have major consequences: The contractor may legitimately point to the government's inability to act on its request as the reason for not meeting a delivery or performance schedule.

241. How can the COR anticipate, and therefore most effectively respond to, contractor requests?

Knowing in advance when and what a contractor should be requesting aids in monitoring contractor performance. The COR can:

- Identify and chart the contractual terms that allow contractor requests
- Identify and chart the government's need to respond to those requests
- Identify the contractor's obligations when making a request and the government's responsibilities for responding to that request.

For a listing of possible contractor requests and relevant contract terms, contractor obligations, and the COR's responsibilities as a government representative, see Figure 6-1.

Contractor Request	Relevant Contract Term	Contractor's Obligation	COR's Responsibility
Interpreting technical specifications	Statement of work (SOW)	Submit a letter to the COR	Respond within 30 days
Obtaining approval of contractor entry on a government site	FAR clause (e.g., 52.236-3)*	Request via telephone or letter	Respond within a reasonable amount of time to avoid delay in the contractor's performance
Providing an escort in controlled areas	FAR clause (e.g., 52.236-3)*	Request via telephone or letter	Ensure escort availability on agreed date and time
Arranging for utility outages when required by the contractor for maintenance or installation purposes	FAR clause (e.g., 52.236-14)*	Submit a letter to the COR	Respond within a reasonable amount of time
Authorizing the use of overtime under certain types of contracts	FAR clause (e.g., 52.222-2)*	Submit a letter or other written document to the COR	Respond within a reasonable amount of time for the contractor to assign overtime
Authorizing used or surplus material as substitutes for new material	FAR clause (e.g., 52.211-5)*	Submit a letter or other written document to the COR	Respond within a reasonable amount of time to permit the contractor to proceed with the contract and not delay the delivery schedule

* Specific relevant clause will depend on the type of contract and the supplies or services being acquired.

FIGURE 6-1. Possible Contractor Requests/Obligations and Government Responses

Monitoring Contract Performance

242. Why is careful monitoring of a contractor's performance essential?

When a contract is signed, it is the intent of both parties to perform their respective obligations. However, not all contracts are performed according to specification or other terms and conditions or within the required timeframe. Poor quality of work or deliverables or late deliveries may cause costly delays in the program. The government monitors contract performance closely to ensure that desired end items work as intended and are delivered on time.

243. What steps are involved in monitoring contractor performance?

Monitoring a contract requires that the COR:

1. Determine what functions need to be monitored
2. Select the techniques used for monitoring
3. Determine how to document monitoring actions
4. Monitor performance under the contract.

Determining What Functions Need to Be Monitored

244. What monitoring functions are CORs routinely delegated?

CORs often monitor:

- Contractor technical and schedule compliance, for both commercial and noncommercial requirements
- Costs (in cost-type contracts)
- The financial condition of a contractor
- The contractor's statutory compliance.

245. What are commercial requirements?

FAR 2.101 offers a lengthy definition of a commercial item, but in general terms, a *commercial item* is an item (a requirement) that is customarily used for non-governmental purposes and that has been sold to the general public. The FAR also refers to items that can be modified or tailored in accordance with standard commercial practice to meet the government's requirement. It is the policy of the government in accordance with the Federal Acquisition Streamlining Act (FASA) to acquire commercial items to the maximum extent practicable.

246. What is involved in monitoring technical compliance for commercial requirements?

Contracts for commercial items rely on a contractor's existing quality assurance system as a substitute for government monitoring, inspection, and testing. Customary market practices for the requirement may, however, permit a buyer's (the government) in-process monitoring and inspection. Any government in-process inspection must be conducted in a manner consistent with commercial practice; if in-process inspections are a customary commercial practice for requirements outlined in the contract, then the government may conduct them. For example, when it is determined through market research that commercial firms that buy airplane generators typically perform in-process inspections during production of those generators, the government may include the same practices in its contracts for airplane generators.

247. What are noncommercial requirements?

Noncommercial items (requirements) are those that do not meet the definition of a commercial item, i.e., they are items that must be provided in accordance with unique government specifications or statements of work.

248. What is involved when monitoring technical compliance for noncommercial requirements?

When monitoring technical compliance for noncommercial requirements, the COR:

- Identifies potential contractor delinquencies
- Isolates specific problems with the quality of contractor work
- Supports contractor requests
- Points out any need for government assistance with monitoring
- Reveals actual or anticipated default (i.e., the contractor's failure to perform the contract as required).

Formal monitoring and inspections of supplies are likely to become increasingly less commonplace under the new rules of FASA. Reliance will instead be placed on the integrity of the contractors to deliver acceptable products, with the government retaining contractual protection in all other instances. This means the government will include clauses and terms and conditions in the contract that will allow for government rejection or termination of nonconforming supplies or services or otherwise permit the government to legally protect its contractual interests.

249. What techniques are used to monitor technical compliance?

The COR monitors technical compliance through techniques such as:

- Site visits
- Testing of items to be delivered, if applicable
- Visual inspections of the work the contractor has done
- Analysis of progress charts and technical reports.

250. What tools are best used to monitor schedule compliance?

Many types of contracts may require the contractor to submit graphic displays to compare actual progress with scheduled progress. It is relatively easy to create these graphics with computer graphic software programs. Graphic displays on which contractor progress can be charted include the following:

- *Bar and milestone charts.* Bar and milestone charts are simple graphic displays, but they are difficult to revise when changes in the data must be documented. These charts can display only events, tasks, time, and contractor progress.

- *PERT and CPM charts.* Program evaluation review technique (PERT) and critical path method (CPM) charts provide a more elaborate graphic display. These charts are useful when a contract involves a complex web of interdependent relationships between what has to be done, when it must be done, and the relationship among various tasks; the order in which events and decisions will take place; and the need for specific resources (materials, equipment, and labor). These charts serve as a planning, contract performance, and management tool. When the contractor makes these charts available to the government, they can be an important contract monitoring tool. In some instances, the government may also develop these charts to use for comparison in monitoring the contract.

Cost Monitoring

251. What is cost monitoring?

Cost monitoring involves using various procedures and techniques to:

- Monitor *individual* costs to verify the appropriateness of costs
- Monitor *total* costs to detect variances in planned or budgeted expenses.

Cost reimbursement contracts, as compared to fixed price contracts, require the most cost monitoring because of the potential risk to the government that a cost reimbursement contract creates.

252. How are individual costs monitored?

The COR examines the following factors when monitoring individual costs:

Categories of costs. Under cost reimbursement contracts, payments are made to contractors for incurred expenses plus the agreed-upon fee (or profit). These payments include costs in the following categories:

- Direct costs
  - Labor
  - Materials
- Indirect costs
  - Overhead expenses.

A *direct cost* is any cost that can be identified specifically with a final cost objective (e.g., a particular contract). Examples include:

- Wages of employees working directly on the production of a product
- Cost of materials incorporated in the product
- Cost of subcontracts needed to accomplish the work.

FAR cost principles state a preference for charging costs directly if the direct cost:

- Relates to a specific cost objective or contract, or can be identified with any work unit for which costs are separately accumulated
- Benefits no other cost objective.

Indirect costs are defined as those costs that cannot be tied to any one final cost objective (a contract), but are instead common to multiple cost objectives. These costs generally include the following expenses:

- Management
- Rent and utilities
- Accounting
- Sales and similar business expenses.

Indirect costs are distributed or allocated proportionally among the contractor's various final cost objectives using accepted accounting principles.

253. **What techniques are used to monitor individual costs?**

Techniques used to monitor individual costs include:

- Reliance on the contractor's financial (accounting) system
- Analysis of the backup information (substantiation) to vouchers (e.g., employee time records, material purchase orders)
- Periodic analysis of data obtained from the contractor, government reports, and government site visits
- Reliance on scheduled audits
- Analysis of costs through specific audit requests.

Techniques used to monitor individual costs and typical problems encountered in doing so are outlined in Figure 6-2.

254. **What are the criteria for determining when payments to the contractor are allowable under a contract?**

For such payments to be proper (i.e., allowable under a contract), the costs must be:

- *Reasonable*: Not exceeding that which would be incurred by a prudent person in the conduct of competitive business
- *Allocable*: Properly assigned to one or more cost objectives under the contract
- *Consistent* with applicable accounting standards and prohibitions on the allowability of certain costs.

Monitoring Techniques	Typical Problems in Using This Technique	Restrictions
Reliance on contractor's financial system	None. Problems identified by other means would indicate that this technique might not be appropriate.	Contractor must have obtained financial system review and approval by government auditors.
Analysis of the backup information to vouchers	Inconsistencies between costs billed and the products or services delivered. Inconsistencies between costs billed and costs allowed by the contract price agreement or the auditor-approved billing rate.	Invoicing requirements must include enough information to identify inconsistencies; if contract invoicing requirements are insufficient, negotiate additional requirements.
Periodic analysis of data obtained from contractor, government reports, and government site visits	Problems identified depend on the focus of the report or visit. Onsite observations by government personnel can identify inaccuracies in costs billed (e.g., a COR's daily log indicates that five accountants were working on site on the second Tuesday of the month, but the contractor bills the government for seven accountants for that day).	Written periodic contractor reports can be required only when the contract specifies that they be submitted. However, the contractor may agree to submit a written report without being required to by the contract. Reports are most useful when the government will gain a real advantage commensurate to the contractor's cost to write the report.
Reliance on scheduled audits	Timing and quality of audits reflect the extent of resources and funds available.	Audits are regularly scheduled at the end of cost reimbursement contracts to finalize billing rates and otherwise identify inaccuracies in costs billed for contract performance.
Analysis through specific audit requests	Specific audits confirm the extent of a problem identified or tentatively identified by other monitoring techniques.	Timing and quality of audits reflect the extent of resources and funds available and should never become routine.

FIGURE 6-2.   Individual Costs: Monitoring Techniques

255.   Why is it important to track planned or budgeted expenses?

Cost monitoring involves tracking and analyzing the overall rate of contract expenditures to determine whether the contract will be completed within budget and according to schedule.

If expenses are considered . . .	Then . . .
too **high**	Contract funds may not be sufficient to complete the work.
too **low**	Performance may be falling behind schedule.

256. What documents can be consulted when monitoring total costs in a cost-type contract?

Various documents can be referenced when monitoring the total cost of a cost reimbursement contract or other cost-type contract. These documents include:

- The contractor's cost proposal
- Reports required by the contract
- Contract terms in accordance with FAR text and clauses that address cost and cost monitoring, such as:
  - Award and incentive fee contract provisions
  - Labor-hour contract provisions
- Prior acquisition histories.

Figure 6-3 provides further guidance on monitoring total costs.

Financial Monitoring

257. What is financial monitoring?

Financial monitoring means detecting changes in a contractor's financial condition that have the potential to endanger a contract's performance, then taking the appropriate actions to preserve performance.

258. When does the government initiate financial monitoring?

Three events must take place before the decision is made to monitor a contractor's financial condition:

1. A surety or financial institution involved with the contractor indicates to the government that the contractor is in financial trouble.

Information Sources	Typical Total Cost Monitoring Applications
Contractor's cost proposal	Used as the baseline for measuring whether cost expenditures are under control and within budget.
Reports required by the contract	Used as a tool in deciding whether the contract is progressing satisfactorily and within budget. The inclusion of these reports in the contract usually reduces the need for other proactive monitoring techniques.
Contract terms that address cost and cost monitoring: award and incentive fee contract provisions	Used to evaluate and document variable elements upon which the fee is based when the contract type requires or allows a fee that is not fixed.
Contract terms that address and cost monitoring: Labor-hour contract provisions	Used in assessing whether hours expended are cost reasonable to accomplish the work. hour labor-contract types do not have cost control considerations simply because the hourly rate is fixed in the contract. Labor-hour contracts do not motivate the contractor to use labor efficiently.
Prior acquisition histories	Used in determining how closely to monitor cost and performance. Past performance provides the basis for this determination, along with other considerations such as the dollar value of the contract. Contractors with a history of cost overruns should be monitored more carefully than those with histories of cost efficiency.

FIGURE 6-3.   Monitoring Total Costs

2. A determination is made that the government would be harmed by the contractor's financial difficulties.

3. A determination is made that the government could take positive steps to protect its interests.

The government's interest is *not always* in jeopardy as a result of a contractor's failing financial condition. For example, contractor financial problems on service contracts with monthly payment terms and no up-front materials costs should not cause substantial concern; service workers are typically not paid until after the service is provided, which means that the government is not at risk even if the contractor is in financial difficulty.

259. What steps are involved in monitoring financial conditions?

Four steps are involved in monitoring financial conditions:

1. Determining whether to monitor financial conditions when alerted to circumstances that might endanger government interests

2. Protecting the government's interest if a lien is placed against a contractor's inventory

3. Protecting the government's interest if the contractor is facing bankruptcy

4. Furnishing information to interested parties upon request.

The CO or the agency's financial advisors should be notified when financial conditions may warrant intervention by the government.

Monitoring Statutory and Regulatory Compliance

Monitoring government contracts for legal (statutory) and regulatory compliance means ensuring that contractors take or refrain from taking specific actions as a matter of public policy. The CO may delegate any or all of the statutory monitoring functions to the COR.

260. What steps are involved in monitoring statutory and regulatory requirements?

The steps involved in monitoring statutory and regulatory requirements are:

- Identifying contract clauses related to statutory or regulatory compliance
- Monitoring compliance and responding to notices involving:
  - Labor laws
  - Privacy Act and Drug-Free Workplace issues
  - Hazardous, non-domestic, or recovered materials and environmental issues
  - Insurance and tax issues involving intellectual property.
- Monitoring compliance with the subcontracting plan, if applicable, and:
  - Providing the contractor with written notice of plan violations
  - Invoking remedies in cases of noncompliance, when appropriate
  - Determining any incentive for exceeding goals.

- Continuing actions as needed to encourage and enforce statutory compliance, and keeping the CO informed.

Statutory and regulatory clauses are generally incorporated by reference in the contract. The full text of these clauses is found in the FAR. Proper administration of a contract requires familiarity with the full text of these clauses.

Selecting the Techniques Used for Monitoring

261. What techniques does the COR use to monitor the contract?

Monitoring techniques include:

- Conducting meetings
- Making onsite visits and other personal observations
- Making phone calls
- Reviewing contractor reports
- Reviewing contractor requests
- Contacting other government officials to discuss contractor performance
- Reviewing tracking and management systems.

262. How does the COR select the monitoring techniques to be used?

There are no set rules for selecting the technique to be used; a combination of techniques might be necessary. The contract itself may indicate exactly how the government will monitor various aspects of the contract. If no such indication is given, the contract must be evaluated to determine what monitoring techniques will best suit it.

263. With whom should the COR have meetings and what are the basic benefits of such meetings?

The COR should have meetings with the *requiring activity*, i.e., the program or project office that initiated the requirement originally. Individuals in the program or project office may or may not be the end users, but sometimes the requiring activity does represent the end users. In the case of the Department of Defense (DoD), a technical requiring activity often contracts for a weapon that will be used by soldiers in combat; it may be advisable, during the contract performance phase, to bring in representatives of the soldiers for their specific and unique end-user perspective.

Holding periodic meetings with the requiring activity and end users allows the COR to obtain, as well as provide, pertinent information on the status of the contract. These meetings help foster the government's team approach to contract administration and can provide early warning of any potential performance problems.

The COR should also have meetings with the contractor as deemed necessary to ensure adequate monitoring and communication with the contractor. However, the COR should be careful—more contact is not necessarily better. Unless the contract specifies that pre-planned meetings with the contractor be held at certain intervals, they should be held as infrequently as possible and should focus on problem resolution. The COR needs to be aware of the costs incurred by the contractor when unscheduled meetings are requested. In cost-type contracts, the government will have to pay the costs associated with the meetings. In fixed price contracts, the contractor may balk at attending meetings that were not accounted for (priced) in the contract.

264. What are the advantages of onsite visits?

Holding periodic onsite visits with the contractor allows the COR to obtain monitoring data through observation. Onsite visits allow both the government and contractor personnel an opportunity to identify, as well as resolve, problems at the operating level.

265. What rules of conduct does the COR need to follow when making an onsite visit?

The COR must follow six basic conduct requirements, as specified by the contract administration office (CAO). CAO notification requirements for contractor facility visits (see FAR 42.402) are as follows:

1. Provide names, official positions, and security clearance information for all visitors.

2. Identify the date and duration of your visit.

3. Identify the name and address of contractor facility and personnel you wish to contact.

4. Identify contract number, any overall program involvement, and the purpose of your visit.

5. Request CAO representation, if you desire it (note that the CAO may decide to accompany you, whether you desire it or not).

6. Identify data you may wish to obtain in conjunction with the visit.

In addition to these notification requirements, CORs are expected to inform the agency of any agreements reached with contractor personnel or of any other results that may affect CAO operations and decisions.

266. When may onsite visits not be necessary?

Prior notification is required when making onsite visits to a contractor's site where another agency has an ongoing onsite contract administration activity. If the other agency has already gathered data that fills the COR's current need, personnel within the agency will provide the existing data and inform the COR that the visit is not necessary. When available, CORs should rely on the other agency's documentation rather than gathering the same information.

267. When are phone calls best used in monitoring performance?

Telephone contact with the contractor may be used to:

- Check on contract progress
- Identify any performance problems
- Determine if the government is creating any problems (e.g., creating a contract delay by not responding to a government required action in a timely manner).

268. What kind of documentation should be created when making phone calls?

Telephone communications must be documented, as must other discussions. Some agencies have a "telephone contact record" to use for this purpose. Generally, the documentation is handwritten and kept in the COR contract file. A contact record should include:

- Date and time of the conversation
- Parties involved
- Synopsis of the conversation
- Action items resulting from the conversation.

269. What is the advantage of reviewing contractor reports or daily logs?

Required daily logs or progress reports provide the COR with indicators of:
- Potential changes
- Delays
- Issues with contract performance, such as failed tests or rejections.

The contractor will provide reports when they are required by the contract. CORs may initiate written reports identifying potential or actual delays in performance.

COR reports should:
- Be prepared in sufficient time for necessary action by the contracting office
- State a specific recommendation for action.

Progress and other monitoring reports supplement the scientific and technical reports required by the contract, and they all should become a part of the permanent record of the work accomplished under the contract. These reports include:
- Progress reports
- Production contract reports
- Research and development contract reports.

270. What kind of information do progress reports include?

Different contracts require that different records be kept by the contractor, so there are no standard FAR clauses addressing content requirements for progress reports or other reports. However, progress reports do tend to have some common features. Information on the following is usually documented in progress reports:
- Actual deliveries or performance milestones met
- Scheduled deliveries or projected performance milestones
- Factors causing delays
- Status of the contract work in general and of specific elements of the work
- Reasons for any difficulties or delay factors

- Actions taken or proposed to overcome difficulties or delay factors
- Assistance needed from the government.

Normally, the COR reviews and verifies the contractor's progress reports, but some contracts require direct submission of these reports to the contracting office. In such a situation, a copy of the report should be provided to the COR.

Progress reports do not relieve the contractor of its obligation to notify the proper government official of any anticipated or actual delay as soon as the delay is recognized. Once the contractor notifies the government of the delay or the possibility of a delay, the reports can be used to track the status of the delay.

271. What do production contract reports include?

Some production contracts require a phased schedule for reporting progress on the contract. There is no standard format for a phased schedule, but these schedules often report on the actual amount of time that was required to pass through various stages of the production cycle. The following procedures are documented in a production contract report:

- Planning
- Purchasing
- Plant rearrangements
- Tooling
- Component manufacture
- Subassembly and final assembly
- Testing
- Shipping.

272. What is included in R&D contract reports?

Since the primary purpose of research and development (R&D) contracts is to advance scientific and technical knowledge, they represent some unique monitoring problems; thus, the government must closely monitor technical progress. R&D contract reports usually include the following data and descriptions (see FAR 35.002):

- Number and names of key personnel working on the project during the reporting period

- Facilities currently set aside for the work
- Direction of the work
- Experiments being conducted
- Other work in progress
- Positive or negative results of R&D work
- Problems encountered.

Efforts taken to resolve problems are discussed in terms of:

- Cost
- Schedules
- Technical objectives.

Reviewing Contractor Requests

273. What may a COR review of contractor requests reveal?

Contractor requests for government action may indicate that the contract is not running as smoothly as written. By reviewing contractor requests, the COR may determine whether the contractor is:

- Complying with a contractual term allowing for a contractor request
- Notifying the government of proposed changes to the terms of the contract.

CORs need to be aware of contractor requests that are not a requirement of the contract. Such requests need to be brought to the CO's attention as quickly as possible.

Because the contractor is responsible for the management of the work, the contractor is in the best position to determine when to submit requests to the government. A COR should be prepared to:

- Track contractor requests
- Provide a timely response to the requests as defined in the contract or in applicable regulations.

274. Why is a timely response to contractor requests important?

A timely response to contractor requests:

- Sets a positive tone for the government/contractor relationship.

- Minimizes the amount of contract administration required for contracts that are running smoothly. (An untimely response to a request could cause delays in performance that would increase the administrative effort by both parties.)
- Ensures that the *contractor* is held accountable for delivery and performance terms. The government could be held accountable for delays resulting from untimely responses to contractor requests.

275. Why does the COR need to document and report meaningful communications with the contractor?

CORs involved in contract administration should report any meaningful communications that they have held directly with the contractor to any other government officials who might be impacted by the communications. Certainly the CO is the first and foremost government official to whom the COR should report, but other individuals, such as the paying office or security personnel, might need to be informed of issues related to the contract. *Meaningful*, or substantive, *communications* are communications that include information that might potentially affect:

- Performance (i.e., the quality of the contract work)
- Contract price
- Delivery schedule
- Other contract requirements (e.g., quantity, place of delivery, additional security requirements).

A contractor may change how it is performing the contract based on discussions with government officials involved in the contract. The government is usually held responsible for the legal consequences of changes, even if the employee who gave the oral direction to make a change did not have the general authority to make the directed change. It is always best to document *all* discussions with the contractor and provide a copy of the documentation to the CO.

276. What must the COR be aware of when reviewing tracking and management systems?

Both the contractor and the government use a system to track progress. Posing an informal question or two to the contractor regarding its tracking system may be sufficient to ensure that adequate procedures are being followed. However, the more complex the contract performance requirements or financial accounting requirements, the more sophisticated the tracking system must be.

For example, using a higher-dollar-value cost-type contract requires both parties to keep track of all expenditures as follows:

- *Contractor tracking systems.* Preaward audits scrutinize whether the contractor has the financial accounting systems needed to adequately identify potential contract overruns or underruns[1] and provide notice of overruns to the government. The COR needs to make sure that the contractor is using the audit-approved systems and including necessary information in them as part of monitoring the cost-type contract.

- *Government tracking systems.* A more elaborate technique for monitoring costs is the Cost/Schedule Control System. Many agencies use this method to track contract costs against work actually accomplished, rather than using spending forecasts.

Determining How to Document Monitoring Actions

277. What types of documentation should the COR use to document monitoring of contractor and government performance?

The COR should document *both* the contractor's and the government's performance under the contract. Various types of documentation should be considered when determining how best to monitor contractor and government performance. Types of documentation that may be used include:

- Memorandums to the file

- Trip reports

- Contact records of telephone communications

- Required reports, such as progress reports required by the contract terms

---

[1] A cost-type (or cost-reimbursement) contract does not have a price. Instead, the parties to the contract establish (usually as a result of negotiation) an estimate of total cost for the purpose of obligation of funds. The estimate represents a ceiling that the contractor may not exceed, except at its own risk. However, if the contract cannot be completed within the original total cost estimate, the government may approve and fund a *cost overrun*, raising the estimated cost for the contract. An *underrun* occurs when the contract is completed at a cost less than the original total cost estimate.

- Input in tracking systems
- Minutes of meetings
- Correspondence between the government and the contractor
- Technical analysis of the contractor's performance.

All documents (both contractor and government) generated during the monitoring of a contractor's performance should be submitted to the CO, who will maintain them in the contract administration file.

278. What should be included in memorandums to the file?

All agencies have their own method of preparing memorandums. Memorandums usually include:

- Date of the memorandum
- Author of the memorandum
- Subject
- Description of the situation
- Action items
- Recommendations
- Signature of the individual generating the memorandum.

Memorandums to the file can be prepared at any time for any reason and are especially useful when a contract problem must be documented. Copies of memorandums may be sent to the CO for inclusion in the contract administration file, or they may serve as notification that a problem has been encountered. A copy may also be sent to the contractor to notify it that the government has found a problem if the contractor is not otherwise aware of the problem.

279. Why use trip reports? What should be included in them?

Trip reports are useful for documenting visits made to a contractor's facility. These reports are generally required by agencies when money was expended for the trip (e.g., airfare, per diem). A copy of the trip report can be used to notify the CO of contract status, problems, or any issue that needs attention. There is no set format for a trip report. At a minimum, it should cover:

- The date of the trip

- The location visited during the trip
- The contract number
- A description of the trip
- Discussions with the contractor
- Issues needing attention
- Recommendations for action
- Follow-up actions.

Trip reports should be signed, as required by agency procedures, and a copy included in the appropriate files (i.e., the COR's file and other files) as required by the agency.

280. Why use telephone records? What should be included in them?

Similar to meeting minutes, contact records of telephone communications can be an excellent source of information. Contact records document discussions held with the contractor and other government officials for the purpose of preserving the conversation for the file. Contact records:

- Must be dated
- Must show the applicable contract number
- Need not be written according to any set format, but usually summarize "he or she said/I said" conversations.

There may be an opportunity, when documenting a telephone conversation, to identify action items and recommendations based on the conversation, but this may not be necessary because action items usually must be documented separately on specified forms. Copies of the contact records should be provided to the CO for inclusion in the contract administration file.

281. Why use required reports? Who prepares them?

Reports can be a good tool for documenting the contractual situation, and they should be required by the original requirements document to ensure effective and adequate communication of contract performance status during the contract administration phase. Unlike memorandums to the file, reports are generally prepared by the contractor in accordance with contract requirements in a format suitable for review by others, such as:

- The contracting officer
- Attorneys
- The contractor
- The financial officer
- Small business administrators
- Auditors.

The content of a report is based entirely on the purpose for the report. Reports can:

- Describe contract status
- Identify problems
- Provide background information
- Justify actions taken by the contractor
- Request assistance or resources.

At a minimum, reports must identify the contract number and the date the report was written.

282. What is included when inputting information in tracking systems?

There are two types of tracking systems.

- *Paper-based tracking.* This method is used when the contract is not routinely procured and when an agency does not have an electronic tracking system.
- *Electronic tracking.* This is the preferred method of tracking and requires input from appropriate officials.

The COR may be required to input various data as might be required by the particular contract, including progress of work under the contract, cost expenditures, results of tests on contract products, or other technical information. The format for inputting data in the tracking systems will vary. The COR should follow the direction provided by the CO or other official in charge of the tracking system.

283. What should be included in minutes of meetings?

Minutes generally document:

- Discussions that took place at a meeting
- Situations (e.g., status of product testing or delivery schedule)
- Problems discussed at a meeting
- Attendees of a meeting
- Decisions made at the meeting
- Action items
- Recommendations for action.

284. Who should keep the minutes? To whom should they be distributed?

Minutes can be written by anyone attending a meeting. Minutes of meetings should be provided to all attendees and to the CO for inclusion in the contract administration file.

285. Why is correspondence a good method of documentation?

Corresponding with the contractor and other government officials involved in the contract is a good way to document contract performance because it provides a written record of the contract status. Correspondence, along with other forms of contract-related documentation, serves to further ensure satisfactory contract completion because it explains what is going on with the contract at a given time. Written correspondence between the government and the contractor also ensures that both parties have a common understanding of all aspects of contract performance.

Contractors use correspondence as a way to notify the government of issues they wish to be addressed by the government. Regardless of the author, correspondence is prepared for the purpose of:

- Notifying others of a problem
- Providing routine status updates
- Notifying the government that delivery was made
- Responding to a request
- Transmitting a document
- Providing general guidance and other information.

A copy of all correspondence should be provided to the CO for inclusion in the contract administration file.

286.   What is a technical analysis?

A *technical analysis* is a report prepared by the COR that focuses on the technical aspects of the contractor's response to a government request. The CO uses the technical analysis to make decisions to change the contract. The technical analysis is critical to the CO's work, as it may provide a basis for contract modifications, the contractor's entitlement to payment (as in the case of a dispute pertaining to the scope of work originally required by the contract),[2] and future work with a particular contractor.

287.   What should the technical analysis include? Who should receive copies of the technical analysis?

The format for the technical analysis will be based on the purpose of the analysis and should include:

- Date of the analysis
- Contract number
- Purpose of the technical analysis
- Actions taken (e.g., discussions with the contractor)
- Results (e.g., the contractor's response to discussions with the COR)
- Recommendations for future action.

The CO should be provided copies of the analysis and should determine who else will receive a copy.

288.   What is the overall role of the COR in monitoring the contract?

Having determined which functions need to be monitored, selected the monitoring techniques to be used, and determined how to document monitoring actions, the COR should have formulated an overall plan to monitor

---

[2] Disputes often arise as to whether a work requirement was included or not in the original scope of the contract. These disputes usually result from a difference of interpretation by the parties. The decision as to which interpretation is correct will determine whether the work was already paid for in the original contract price or must be paid for separately by one of the parties. The technical analysis by the COR provides the CO with the information to make this determination and thus decide who pays, the government or the contractor. Of course, if the contractor is not satisfied, the CO's final decision could be appealed in accordance with the disputes process.

the contract. Using this monitoring plan, the COR will be able to ensure that the contract is progressing as required in terms of performance, schedule, and cost requirements. The COR's documentation of monitoring actions should provide a complete picture of the contract progress, and reports provided as a result of this documentation will aid immensely in ensuring successful completion of the contract.

Resolving Constructive Changes

289.   What is a constructive change?

To understand constructive changes, a brief discussion of the "changes clause" included in government contracts is necessary. John Cibinic, Jr., and Ralph C. Nash, Jr., write of the changes clause that:

> . . .most government contracts include a *Changes* clause which gives the government *the unilateral right to order changes* in the contract work during the course of performance. In exchange, the contractor is promised an *equitable adjustment* in the contract price, period of performance, or both.

> The *Changes* clause is one of the most important standard clauses contained in government contracts. The clause is central to the government's contractual approach, since the provisions of the clause directly affect the rights and obligations set forth in numerous other clauses. For example, problems concerning inspection, acceptance, warranties, defective specifications, impossibility of performance, and acceleration of performance will all most likely be involved with the *Changes* clause.

The four basic purposes of the *Changes* clause are:

1.   To provide flexibility by giving the government the unilateral right to order changes in the work to accommodate advances in technology and changes in the government's requirements

2.   To provide the contractor a means of proposing changes to the work, thereby facilitating more efficient performance and improving quality of contract end products

3.   To furnish procurement authority to the CO to order additional work within the "general scope" of the contract without using the procedures required for new procurements

4. To provide the legal means by which the contractor may process claims through the administrative disputes process.[3]

The administrative dispute process is also known as the *constructive change order doctrine*. In this context, the word "constructive" is derived from the word "construed." Therefore, the use of the word "constructive" means that a change to the contract has occurred, and the change can be "construed" or inferred to have the same effect as if the CO had issued a written change order pursuant to the changes clause of the contract.

As Cibinic and Nash state:

> . . .when a contractor performs *work beyond that required by the contract* and it is perceived that such work was ordered by the government or caused by government fault, it is usually found that a constructive change has occurred. Under common law contractual analysis such fact patterns would more likely be placed under theories of implied contract or breach of contract. However, the administrative procedures developed for the resolution of disputes in federal contracts prevent the boards and courts from using these theories. Hence, the alternate theory, or doctrine, of constructive changes.[4]

They further note:

> The doctrine of constructive changes is the basis upon which boards of contract appeals and courts have held numerous types of government action or inaction to be within the scope of the *Changes* clause, thereby entitling the contractor to an *equitable adjustment* to compensate for the additional costs generated by the government's conduct. Both the government and the contractor benefit from the relatively efficient and inexpensive method of resolving constructive change claims through this administrative disputes process.[5]

---

[3] John Cibinic, Jr., and Ralph C. Nash, Jr., *Administration of Government Contracts* (Washington, D.C.: George Washington University Press, 1981), pp. 140–141.

[4] Ibid., p. 167.

[5] Ibid., p. 142.

Moreover:

Categories and examples of constructive changes [include]:

- *Disagreements between the parties over the contract requirements . . .* where due to the government's misinterpretation of a contract provision, a contractor is required to perform more or different work; the contractor is entitled to an equitable adjustment pursuant to the *Changes* clause.

  Examples:

  1. Suggestions by government personnel that the contractor perform work in a specified manner

  2. Rejection of a method of performance selected or used by a contractor that was not otherwise precluded by the contract

  3. The government's refusal to permit use of an item equal to a specified item where the contract contained an "or equal" clause.[6]

- *Defective specifications. . .*[when] the government provides defective specifications [. . .], the contractor incurs additional expense in attempting to perform in accordance with those specifications. Courts have ruled in numerous cases that the costs of a change issued to overcome defective specifications should include *costs incurred from the inception of the contract*, since the contractor had incurred expenditures made useless by the faulty specifications.

  Example: The defective or impossible specifications cause confusion and increase the time and cost of performance until the specifications are corrected or relaxed.[7]

- *Acceleration*, which is a speeding up of the work in an attempt to complete performance earlier than otherwise anticipated. In some instances, a contractor may accelerate on its own initiative to assure completion within the contract schedule or for some other purpose. The costs of such acceleration are, of course, not recoverable from the government.

---

[6] John Cibinic, Jr., and Ralph C. Nash, Jr., *Administration of Government Contracts* (Washington, D.C.: George Washington University Press, 1981), pp. 170–173.

[7] Ibid., p. 178.

The compensable acceleration and constructive change occur where the *government* requires the contractor to meet the current contract delivery schedule in the face of excusable delays.[8]

- *Government failure to cooperate*, such as the government failing to prevent one contractor from interfering with the work of another contractor.

  Example: [A] contractor had the right to remove topsoil from an area for use in [its] portion of the work. The government permitted a second contractor to perform in a manner [that] restricted efficient use of the topsoil. This government action in the face of written notice from the contractor constituted a constructive change."[9]

290. What is the COR's role in resolving constructive changes?

The COR must ensure that a technical analysis, sufficient to support the CO's final decision, is prepared for all constructive changes.

There are three steps in preparing an analysis of constructive changes:

1. Identifying the actual changes to the contract
2. Preparing the technical analysis and notifying the CO that a technical analysis has been prepared
3. Assisting the CO with negotiations.

Identifying the Actual Changes to the Contract

When a COR provides guidance (also known as technical direction) to the contractor under performance of the contract, he or she may go beyond his or her scope of responsibility, resulting in a change to the contract known as a *constructive change*.

---

[8] John Cibinic, Jr., and Ralph C. Nash, Jr., *Administration of Government Contracts* (Washington, D.C.: George Washington University Press, 1981), p. 181.

[9] Ibid., p. 191.

Technical Direction	*Constructive Change*
Technical direction is technical guidance within the boundaries set by the statement of work. More technically complex contracts require direction from government officials, usually the COR. The need for and the ramifications of technical direction are different depending on whether the contract is fixed price or cost reimbursement. Work statements are normally more precise under fixed price contracts than under cost reimbursement contracts. When a work statement is precise, there is little or no need for technical direction.	A *constructive change* occurs when the CO, or his or her duly authorized representative (e.g., the COR), changes the contract without going through the required legal or regulatory formalities. A constructive change can result from either a specific action or a failure to act. Examples of constructive changes include: • Errors of interpretation • Issuance of changes outside the scope of the contract • Failure to issue a change to correct a defective specification • Acceleration of performance.

Preparing the Technical Analysis and Notifying the CO That a Technical Analysis Has Been Prepared

Although there is no set format for a technical analysis, it should be documented in writing and a copy provided to the CO. The technical analysis may be in the form of a:

• Memorandum to the file

• Letter

• Report

• Any other format used to document meaningful communication.

291. Who may identify a potential constructive change?

Constructive changes may be identified by either the COR or the contractor. Because only the CO can change the contract, the CO should be notified if a possible constructive change is identified, and he or she will determine if a constructive change has occurred.

292. How should a COR notify the CO after identifying a potential constructive change?

There are no set rules for how a COR should notify the CO; notification can occur by telephone or mail, or as an action item in a report. It is essential only that the CO is notified that a constructive change may have been made to the contract. Notification should include sufficient information describing the events that led to the possible constructive change.

293. How and when does a contractor notify the CO of a potential constructive change?

A contractor can use any method it chooses to notify the CO of the possibility of a constructive change. Whether the CO is notified or not depends on whether the contract is a fixed price or cost reimbursement contract. A contractor is not likely to perform extra work under a fixed price contract without firm assurance of additional compensation from the CO. Such assurances are not needed under a cost reimbursement contract because the contract stipulates that the government will pay for the extra work. However, if the contract contains a clause requiring a notification of changes, the contractor must notify the CO using a *notice of change*.

294. What format should the notice of change follow?

The *notice of change* should include:

- The date, nature, and circumstances of the conduct the contractor regards as a change
- The name, function, and activity of government or contractor personnel who are aware of this conduct
- The identification of any relevant documents and the substance of any oral communication involved
- The basis for any allegation of accelerated performance or delivery
- Any element of contract performance that the contractor may use as a basis for seeking an adjustment in time or money, including:
  - Contract line items affected
  - Specific labor or material categories affected
  - To the extent practicable, delay and disruption in the manner and sequence of performance and the effect of such delays or disruptions on continued performance

    – Contractor estimates of adjustments to contract price, delivery schedule, or other contract terms.

- The contractor's estimate of a reasonable government response time that would minimize cost, delay, or disruption of performance.

295. What does the COR do if the CO determines the change is permissible?

Upon receipt of notification, the CO must determine if the event in question was permitted as a technical direction or if it results in a constructive change to the contract. No further action will be required of the COR if the determination is made that the event was permitted under technical direction.

Assisting the CO with Negotiations

296. What is the COR's role in the event of negotiations?

The CO may require the participation of the COR at negotiations. The COR should not respond to any contractor statements during the negotiations unless directed to do so by the CO. At the conclusion of negotiations, the CO will make a final decision as to whether the event in question was permitted as technical direction, or whether a change must be made to the contract.

Inspection and Acceptance

The purpose of *inspection* is to determine whether a completed product or service conforms exactly to what the government ordered from a contractor and can, therefore, be accepted. The extent of inspection varies with the dollar value of the contract and the type of product or service being procured.

    Inspections and acceptances are considered successful when:

- Supplies or services tendered by contractors meet contract requirements

or

- Nonconforming supplies or services are rejected, or the nonconformance is otherwise resolved (e.g., by the government accepting nonconforming end items at a reduced price).

The COR is often the individual responsible for performing inspections and recommending product acceptance or rejection to the CO. The government's policy on quality assurance is presented in FAR Part 46, Quality Assurance. Section 46.102 states:

Agencies shall ensure that:

a. contracts include inspection and other quality requirements, including warranty clauses when appropriate, that are determined necessary to protect the government's interest

b. supplies or services tendered by contractors meet contract requirements

c. government contract quality assurance is conducted before acceptance (except as otherwise provided in this part), by or under the direction of government personnel

d. no contract precludes the government from performing inspection

e. nonconforming supplies or services are rejected, except as otherwise provided in 46.407

f. contracts for commercial items shall rely on a contractor's existing quality assurance system as a substitute for compliance with government inspection and testing before tender for acceptance unless customary market practices for the commercial item being acquired permit in-process inspection (Section 8002 of Public Law 103-355). Any in-process inspection by the government shall be conducted in a manner consistent with commercial practice

g. the quality assurance and acceptance services of other agencies are used when this will be effective, economical, or otherwise in the government's interest.

297. What is the contractor's performance responsibility?

When the government awards a contract, the contractor assumes responsibility for timely delivery and satisfactory performance. *Performance* includes furnishing the government with the quantity and quality of items the contractor agreed to deliver and for which the government agreed to pay.

298. What tasks will the COR need to perform to successfully inspect contractor delivery or performance and to inform the CO when accepting or rejecting deliverables?

The COR will need to:

1. Inspect products or services
2. Recommend acceptance if products conform to requirements
3. Recommend rejection if products do not conform to requirements
4. Assist the CO in evaluating the contractor's reply to a notice of rejection.

Inspecting Products or Services

299. What are the three steps the COR should follow in performing his or her inspection and acceptance duties?

The COR should:

1. Identify the inspection method required by the contract
2. Determine if acceptance has occurred
3. Perform inspections.

1. *Identifying the inspection method required by the contract*

Before accepting the product or service, the government must be assured of the quality of the deliverable or performance of the work. Various inspection methods are used for ensuring quality and are incorporated in the various contract inspection clauses discussed below. The full text of the inspection clause may be included in the contract, or the number of the FAR inspection clause may be noted in the contract so that the clause can be referenced. The statement of work (SOW) may provide further clarification of inspection and acceptance requirements. A quality assurance plan (QAP) outlining the monitoring and inspection requirements may also be developed specifically for the contract.

FAR clauses detailing inspection methods include the following:

- *Clauses relating to government reliance on inspection by the contractor*

   (Refer to FAR clauses 52.246-1 and -4.)

   The contractor is required to accomplish all inspection and testing needed to ensure that supplies or services conform to contract quality requirements before payment is made. The government may test the supplies or services in advance of acceptance when:

- It has determined that the contractor's quality assurance processes are inadequate

  or

- Customary market practices for the specific commercial item being acquired specify this type of inspection.

- *Standard inspection requirements clause*

  (Refer to FAR clauses 52.246-2 and -3 through -10.) The standard inspection requirements clause:

  - Requires the contractor to provide and maintain an inspection system that is acceptable to the government

  - Gives the government the right to make inspections and perform tests while the contractor's work is in progress

  - Requires the contractor to keep, and make available to the government, complete records of its inspection work.

- *Higher-level contract quality requirements clause*

  (Refer to FAR clause 52.246-11.)

  This clause is applicable to contracts for complex or critical items or in situations in which the technical requirements of the contract require the government to:

  - Maintain control of work operations, in-process controls, and inspection

  - Concentrate its attention on organization, planning, work instructions, and document controls

  - Comply with a government-specified inspection system, quality control system, or quality program.

2. *Determining if acceptance has occurred*

   Prior to performing inspections or testing, the government has to determine if it still has the right to reject nonconforming supplies or services.

   The determination should resolve whether:

   - The work has been explicitly accepted by acceptance notice sent, acceptance made on a receiving report when the items were received by the government, or a letter indicating that acceptance has been provided to the contractor

- There is evidence of implied acceptance because:
  - The government has not voiced concerns about the procured supplies or services, and the time allowed for rejection has passed
  - Payment has been made

    or
  - Delivered items or performed services have been retained or used.

It is critical to determine whether acceptance has occurred because acceptance is final, except in limited situations, and the government may not reject deliverables or services post-acceptance.

3. *Performing inspections*

   General considerations when conducting inspections include:
   - Minimum inspection requirements
   - Inspection methods and occurrences
   - Interim inspections
   - Improper inspections
   - Unusual or incompetent inspections.

Minimum inspection requirements. At a minimum, the government is required to inspect contractor deliveries in order to determine whether:

- The proper types or kinds of supplies were provided
- The correct quantity of supplies was provided
- Any changes or deviations from contract requirements exist
- The product operates as intended
- There are signs of spoilage or age deterioration
- The item is properly identified or marked
- Appropriate packaging was provided.

Inspection methods and occurrences. Appropriate types of inspection methods and occurrences may be covered in the contract clause or SOW. Inspection methods can include:

- *Sensory and dimensional checks*

  Sensory checks are examinations by an inspector, who measures the procured supplies for the following defects using his or her senses of sight, hearing, and touch:
  - Missing pieces

- Noisy operations
- Surface defects
- Parts that may be out of alignment.

Dimensional checks use gauges and micrometers to measure whether the dimensions of the procured items conform to contract specifications.

- *Performance or physical tests*

   These types of inspections allow the inspector to obtain actual performance data and indicate whether the procured product can perform as required by the contract. Requiring that a motor run or an operating system perform at a certain level for a specified period of time is an example of performance testing. Determining the hardness of an item's chemical composition is an example of a physical test.

- *Destructive tests*

   Some contracts require that end products meet certain reliability standards or can withstand a set level of stress. Destructive tests simulate abuse until the item is destroyed. For instance, to test the fireproofing of a product, the product is heated until it burns.

   The COR will (or will not) be required to run tests of procured items according to one of the following inspection occurrence guidelines:

- No government inspection; the contractor is required to perform all inspections and testing
- Evaluation of all procured items
- Random or spot checking
- Statistical sampling (testing a representative subset of procured items).

Interim inspections. The government has the right to inspect all materials and workmanship in a manner that will not unduly delay the work being done by the contractor. Interim government inspections, conducted while the contract work is in progress, may be used to determine if:

- On-schedule performance can be expected
- Cost will be within the initial estimate for cost-reimbursement types of contracts or fixed-price types of contracts with progress payments
- Resources are being applied at originally predicted levels

- The quality of end products will be consistent with the requirement
- Progress payments are warranted
- New components need to be incorporated in major systems
- A contractor's own inspection system is adequate.

Improper inspections. The government has certain rights in the application of inspection procedures. Tests are considered to be improper when they:

- Impose a stricter standard of performance than is otherwise prescribed
- Do not reasonably measure whether the contract end items conform to the specified requirements
- Are inconsistent with prior inspections
- Result in unnecessary delays due to inspections that take place at unreasonable times and places.

Unusual or incompetent inspections. Any test used to overturn the results of another test is considered an unusual test. The CO must be involved when a case such as this arises.

Inspections made by incompetent inspectors may result in government negligence. If the negligence of a government agent causes financial damages to a contractor, it is likely that the government will be held liable for those damages.

300. How does the COR document inspections?

The format to be used for documentation and the results of inspections that need to be documented are specified by:

- The contract
- Agency policy
- Office procedure.

Documentation can take the form of a letter, memorandum, or report. The documentation should support one of the following conclusions:

- The item conforms to contract specifications
- The item shows minor nonconformance
- The item does not conform but can be made to conform
- The item does not conform and cannot be made to conform.

Recommending Acceptance if Products Conform to Requirements

301. What should the COR take into consideration when determining whether to accept supplies or services?

Supplies or services should be accepted when they conform to contract requirements. Some other acceptance criteria are:

- Nonconformance
- Time of acceptance
- Point of acceptance
- Transfer of ownership
- Evidence of final inspection or acceptance
- Finality of acceptance.

302. When is nonconformance determined?

A *nonconformance* occurs when the contractor presents a deliverable to the government that does not strictly conform to the contract requirements. A nonconformance is evaluated to determine if it is a major (substantive) departure from contract requirements or a minor one.

303. When may nonconformance be accepted?

Minor nonconformities may be accepted "as is" when the savings realized by the contractor do not exceed the cost to the government for processing a formal modification.

Usually, nonconformance may be accepted if it does not adversely affect one or more of the following:

- The safety or health of the product user
- Reliability, durability, or performance
- Interchangeability of parts or assemblies
- Any other basic objective of the contract.

304. What should the COR do in the case of minor nonconformance?

Minor nonconformance may be accepted without modifying the contract. Written documentation to support the decision to accept nonconformance should be placed in the contract administration file. The COR should note and remind the contractor that accepting a nonconformance on one contract does not provide relief for correcting similar defects on pending or future work.

305. What should the COR do in the case of major nonconformance?

The acceptance of supplies or services with critical or major nonconformities requires:

- A modification to the current contract
  and that

- The government obtain an equitable reduction in price, or the contractor offer the government another type of adjustment, such as additional units of end products.

306. How much time is allowed for acceptance?

After delivery is made, a reasonable period of time is allowed for government acceptance or rejection. There is no specified time period because the government's ability to respond depends on numerous factors, such as the complexity of the delivered item(s), acceptance test requirements, and the particular circumstances of the contract.

307. When may acceptance be implied?

Although the government may not have formally accepted items, acceptance may be *implied* by:

- The government's conduct (e.g., government personnel are using the items)

- The government's delay in making a formal statement of acceptance or rejection.

308. What and where is the point of acceptance?

The contract determines the physical location where items will be accepted. The *point of acceptance* may be:

- At the contractor's plant, when a contract requires government quality assurance actions

- A prescribed destination point, when quality assurance actions are performed at the destination
  or

- Any other location that can be mutually agreed upon.

309. When does the transfer of ownership occur?

Ownership (title) transfers to the government upon formal acceptance. The time of this ownership transfer could be significant if damage or loss were to occur when items were being shipped from the contractor's plant to the government destination.

310. When does the government assume responsibility for damages?

The government could become responsible for any damage or loss based on the following delivery requirements:

- *F.O.B. origin.* The contractor has delivered conforming supplies to the carrier, and if the government has made formal acceptance at this point, the government will be liable for damage or loss during transport.

- *F.O.B. destination.* The contractor has delivered conforming supplies to the carrier, but the government has not made formal acceptance at this point, so the contractor will be liable for damage or loss during transport.

The preferred approach for the government is to *inspect at origin* (the contractor's plant) and to *accept at destination* (the government facility), which places the risk for damage or loss during transport on the contractor.

311. What types of documents are considered to be evidence of final inspection or acceptance?

Evidence of final inspection or acceptance may consist of one or more of the following documents:

- *Receiving report.* The COR, as the official authorized to accept supplies or services for the government, signs the receiving report. This report is usually considered written evidence of final acceptance. The Department of Defense (DoD) uses DD Form 250, Material Inspection and Receiving Report, for formal acceptance. Other agencies usually have their own unique forms for this purpose, as found in agency FAR supplements.

- *Copy of an invoice (or voucher).* An invoice or voucher, signed by an authorized official, can serve as an acceptance document, if permitted by the contract.

- *Commercial bill of lading.* Under a commercial bill of lading (CBL), the transportation carrier is responsible to the contractor for any damage or loss, and the contractor, in turn, is responsible to the government. Under contract terms, a CBL usually signifies that the government is responsible for reimbursing the contractor the cost of freight charges.

- *Government bill of lading.* Under a government bill of lading (GBL), the transportation carrier is responsible to the government for any damage and loss, and the government pays the transportation charges directly to the commercial carrier.

- *Certificate of conformance* (COC). At the discretion of the CO, in accordance with FAR 46.315, the FAR clause 52.246-15, which includes specific wording for the COC, may be included in the contract when it is preferable to have the option to use a COC instead of source inspection. The decision to use the COC is generally made when the items to be delivered are low dollar amount and not critical in terms of acceptance requirements. Reliance on the COC reduces government inspection costs. When using a COC as evidence of final inspection, the COR should confirm that:
  - Acceptance on the basis of a contractor's COC is in the government's interest
  - Small losses would be incurred in the event of a defect
  - The contractor's past performance reputation makes it likely that deliverables will be acceptable and any defective work will be replaced or corrected without contest.

Even with a COC, the government still retains the right to inspect the deliverables.

312. Why is the acceptance procedure important?

The acceptance procedure is important because at the time and place of formal acceptance, title for the procured goods passes from the contractor to the government. Acceptance is final, and can be revoked only when:

- Latent defects exist in the items accepted
- The government determines that fraud has been committed
- Gross mistakes amounting to fraud are discovered.

These three problems are discussed further in Chapter 7.

Recommending Rejection If Products Do Not Conform to Requirements

313. When the COR recommends rejection of items received, what is the first step he or she must take?

A notice of rejection must be furnished promptly to the contractor. The notice may be written or delivered verbally by the COR, followed by written confirmation. However, see Question 315 regarding circumstances under which the notice must be in writing.

314. What must the notice of rejection include?

The COR must include the following information in the notice of rejection:

- The reasons for rejection of the item(s)

  and

- A stated amount of time within which the contractor must reply.

315. When must the notice of rejection be in writing?

The notice of rejection must appear in writing if:

- Supplies or services have been rejected at a place other than the contractor's plant
- The contractor persists in offering nonconforming supplies or services for acceptance
- Delivery or performance was late without an excusable delay.

A written notice of rejection requires a written receipt from the contractor.

316. How does a notice of rejection affect the contractor's delivery schedule?

A notice of rejection does not extend the specified delivery schedule, and the contractor remains obligated to provide supplies or services that conform to the contract within that delivery schedule.

317. What information should the COR provide the CO regarding recommended rejection?

When the COR has recommended rejection of deliverables, the CO should be provided with documentation regarding:

- The nature of government contract quality assurance actions, including:
  - The number of observations made of the contractor's work and work site
  - Actions taken to notify the contractor of nonconformances
- The acceptability of the products or the processes, including:
  - Number and type of defects
  - Impact of the defects on the government's requirements
- Any actions taken by the contractor to correct defects.

Assisting the CO in Evaluating the Contractor's Reply to a Notice of Rejection

318. How may a contractor reply to a notice of rejection?

A contractor may reply to a notice of rejection by:

- Submitting a proposal to repair or correct the work
- Submitting a proposal to provide a downward adjustment in price as a basis for acceptance
- Refusing to repair or correct the work or to offer any consideration to the notice of rejection.

319. If the contractor submits a proposal in response to a notice of rejection, what are the COR's resulting responsibilities?

A COR can assist the CO in evaluating the contractor's new proposal by:

- Providing advice concerning the safety and performance of the proposed items
- Evaluating whether acceptance of the supplies or services would be in the government's best interest after repair, correction, or price adjustments are made
- Providing supporting rationale for rejecting or accepting the contractor's proposal
- Attending any negotiations to respond to the contractor's positions.

Using Past Performance Information and Evaluating and Documenting Performance

320. What is past performance information?

Past performance information is relevant information, for future source selection purposes, regarding a contractor's actions under previously awarded contracts. The information includes the contractor's:

- Record of conforming to contract requirements and to standards of good workmanship

- Record of forecasting and controlling costs

- Adherence to contract schedules, including the administrative aspects of performance, such as reporting and responding promptly and adequately to questions and requests for information/action from the government

- History of reasonable and cooperative behavior and commitment to customer satisfaction

- Business-like concern for the customer's interest.

See Chapter 4, Evaluating Past Performance, for basic policy information and other considerations related to past performance.

321. How is the COR's role in documenting past performance significant to future source selections?

As the official delegated by the CO, the COR may be required to document a contractor's performance in the agency's past performance file. The written evaluation of a contractor's performance is used to provide past performance information relevant to future source selections.

As discussed in Chapter 4, the objective of source selection is to select the proposal that represents the *best value* for the government. Source selection procedures can be carried out through either a formal structured approach or a much more informal process.

Formal source selection is generally used in high-priced acquisitions, but it may be used in other acquisitions as prescribed in agency regulations. Normally, an official above the CO selects the source.

An *informal source selection* occurs when the CO selects a contractor with the assistance of a technical evaluation panel.

The government employs the source selection process when the negotiation method of procurement is being used (i.e., the government is not choosing a contractor through sealed bidding). Source selection is based on:

- Cost or price competition between proposals that meet the government's minimum technical requirements, as stated in the solicitation

  or

- Competition involving an evaluation and comparison of cost or price and other factors, such as superior technical performance or delivery capabilities.

The *contractor performance evaluation report* gives the source selection board historical data about a contractor's performance under previous contracts for the same or similar supplies or services.

The content and format of the contractor performance evaluation report should be tailored to the breadth, content, and complexity of the contractual requirements. The technical office, contracting office, and where appropriate, end users of the product or service should make input to these evaluations. Evaluations should address all significant areas of performance and highlight the strengths and weaknesses of the contractor's performance. Evaluations used to determine award fee or incentive fee payments are a good source of performance information when creating an overall contractor evaluation because additional fees are awarded based on a contractor's performance of contract requirements. Contractors who received award or incentive fees are those that performed well.

Evaluations of contractor performance should be provided to the contractor as soon as practicable after completion of the evaluation. Interim evaluations may encourage a contractor's continued good performance, assist a contractor in improving marginal performance, or identify major deficiencies so that a contractor is not surprised by future government actions based on poor performance.

Once the contractor receives a performance evaluation, it is given a minimum of 30 days to submit comments, rebutting statements, or additional information. Disagreements between the contractor and the government regarding the evaluation are considered by officials at a level above the CO. The ultimate resolution of the disagreement regarding the performance evaluation (i.e., deciding which party is "right") is a decision made by the contracting agency—most likely, the head of the contracting activity will actually make the final decision. Copies of the evaluation, contractor response, and review comments, if any, are retained as part of the evaluation. Because these evaluations may be used to support future award decisions, they should be filed and marked as "source selection information."

Past performance information should not be retained to provide source selection information for longer than three years after completion of the contract.

Past performance collection, evaluation, and documentation processes vary significantly from agency to agency. CORs must determine and comply with specific past performance policies, procedures, and forms prescribed by their particular agency.

General guidance is available in the Office of Federal Procurement Policy's (OFPP) *Best Practices for Collecting and Using Current and Past Performance Information* (commonly referred to as the *OFPP Past Performance Guide*). Also see OFPP's Letter of January 21, 2011, *Improving Contractor Past Performance Assessments: Summary of the Office of Federal Procurement Policy's, Review and Strategies for Improvement*.

Effective July 1, 2002, all federal contractor past performance information (PPI) was made centrally available online for use by all federal agency contracting officials through the Past Performance Information Retrieval System (PPIRS) at *www.ppirs.gov*. Several collection tools will submit data to PPIRS. The database provides the acquisition community timely and pertinent contractor performance information that can be used in making source selection decisions.

322. What tasks does the COR need to perform to document a contractor's performance in the agency's past performance file?

The COR will need to:

1. Document performance information
2. Notify interested parties regarding contractor performance
3. Maintain evaluations.

Documenting Performance Information

323. How does the COR document performance information?

The following steps are useful in identifying what type of documentation is necessary:

1. Determine whether a formal evaluation is required.
2. Document past performance information.
3. Rate past performance.

1. *Determining whether a formal evaluation is required*

   After all work on a contract is completed, a COR should prepare a formal evaluation of the contractor's performance for all contracts over the simplified acquisition threshold.

2. *Documenting past performance information*

   Performance evaluations must be prepared at the time work under the contract is completed. A description of the manner in which the evaluation should be done is usually provided in the contract. This description may specify:

   – Which government officials should be involved in the evaluation and documentation process

   – What information should be included in the documentation

   – The format for documenting the evaluation.

   Contracts that do not specify the evaluation procedures should, at least, require the documentation of performance information that could be used by the government in future source selection situations. Interim evaluations should be prepared on contracts with periods of performance (including options) exceeding one year. Interim evaluations should be conducted at sufficient intervals to be useful to source selection officials seeking current performance information about a contractor.

   FAR 42.15 provides overall guidance regarding contractor performance information. Also, for most contracts, refer to the sample contractor performance report form shown in Appendix I of the OFPP *Past Performance Guide* for additional information.

   Always remember, however, to follow agency-specific policies and procedures.

3. *Rating past performance*

   The COR, as the person most familiar with the contractor's performance, should rate the contractor's performance without bias. The contract or agency policy will specify the manner in which the contractor's performance will be rated. The *OFPP Past Performance Guide* provides examples of possible rating areas and factors and other general guidance.

324. What are the sample rating areas the COR may use to rate contractor performance?

The OFPP sample contractor performance report form in Appendix I of the *OFPP Past Performance Guide* lists four areas of performance on which the contractor can be rated:

1. Quality of work
2. Cost control
3. Timeliness (i.e., how well the contractor adhered to the delivery schedule)
4. Business relations (i.e., the business relationship between the contractor and the contract administration team).

As a COR, questions to consider when rating performance might include:

- How cooperative was the contractor in working with the government to solve problems?
- Did the contractor recommend effective solutions?
- Was the contractor responsive to the administrative issues in the contract (e.g. did the contractor submit adequate and timely progress reports)?
- Did the contractor frequently submit unnecessary contract proposals with cost or price increases?

Ratings should reflect how well the contractor complied with specific contract performance standards for each area. Comments should be concise and should provide answers to questions about the contractor's performance that would be asked by a source selection team.

325. What are the five sample rating factors and their associated scores?

The OFPP sample contractor performance report form suggests that each rated area be assigned one of the following five ratings/scores:

Unsatisfactory	1
Marginal	2
Satisfactory	3
Very Good	4
Exceptional	5

"Unsatisfactory" Contrasted with "Exceptional" Ratings	
An "unsatisfactory" rating may indicate:	An "exceptional" rating may indicate:
• Most performance requirements were not met • Significant cost overruns • Many late deliveries • Delinquent responses and lack of cooperative spirit	• The contractor met all performance requirements • Significant cost reductions while meeting all requirements • The contractor exceeded delivery requirements by making many early deliveries • Highly professional, responsive, and proactive contractor conduct

The "comments" section of the performance evaluation report should clearly explain why the contractor earned a particular rating, enabling source selection boards to understand the rating and give proper credit to the contractor in their evaluation (i.e., when reviewing contractors' past performance ratings before choosing a contractor). An exceptional rating may be given for any single area of performance, or the rating may be based on overall contract performance.

An exceptional rating allows the source selection team the discretion to give an appropriate amount of "extra credit" to the exceptional contractor in its evaluation, commensurate with the anticipated additional value of such performance. Such recognition is important, as these top-rated contractors are those with whom the government should continue doing business.

Notifying Interested Parties Regarding Contractor Performance

326. What steps does the COR take to notify interested parties regarding contractor performance?

The COR should follow these steps to ensure that all interested parties are adequately informed regarding the contractor's performance:

1. Provide appropriate information to the contractor.
2. Notify the CO of recurring performance problems.
3. Assist the CO in preparing reports to debarment officials.

1. *Providing appropriate information to the contractor*

   Copies of the agency evaluation should be provided to the contractor as soon as practicable after completing the evaluation. The contractor should be given at least 30 days to comment on the evaluation. If the contractor disagrees with the evaluation, the COR should contact the CO for further guidance. CORs may be asked to assist the CO in evaluating a contractor's rebuttals. If the contractor fails to provide a response by the established deadline, the appropriate official should sign the form in the appropriate block and the government's comments can stand alone.

   A review of the contractor's comments must be conducted by an individual at least one level above the CO. The decision resulting from this review must be in writing and must be issued within 15 working days from receipt of a rebuttal statement from the contractor.

2. *Notifying the CO of recurring performance problems*

   The COR needs to include the following in such a notification:

   - A description of the performance problems
   - Discussion of mitigating or extenuating circumstances, if any
   - Indexed file or related documents documenting performance problems
   - An analysis of the impact that the contractor's performance problems have had on:
     - Overall cost

- Delays in obtaining needed supplies and services
- Mission accomplishment.

3. *Assisting the CO in preparing reports to debarment officials*

The CO may have to determine whether to report a contractor's malperformance or non-responsibility to the debarment official. The debarring official may debar a contractor for a conviction of or civil judgment for:

- Commission of fraud or a criminal offense in connection with obtaining, attempting to obtain, or performing a public contract or subcontract

- Violation of federal or state antitrust statutes relating to the submission of offers

- Commission of embezzlement, theft, forgery, bribery, falsification or destruction of records, making false statements, tax evasion, or receiving stolen property

- Intentionally affixing a "Made in America" label to a foreign-made product

- Commission of any other offense indicating a lack of business integrity that directly affects the present responsibility of a government contractor.

The debarring official may debar a contractor, based upon a preponderance of evidence, for:

- Willful refusal to perform in accordance with the terms of one or more contracts

- History of failure to perform or unsatisfactory performance of one or more contracts

- Violation of the Drug Free Workplace Act of 1988, as evidenced by:
  - Failure to comply with the requirements of FAR clause 52.223-6, entitled "Drug-Free Workplace"
  - Repeated convictions of contractor employees for violations (occurring in the workplace) of criminal drug statutes.

- Commission of an "unfair trade practice," as defined in FAR 9.403.

Maintaining Evaluations

327. What is the COR's role in maintaining evaluations?

The COR, as instructed by the CO, should employ the following steps to ensure adequate and proper maintenance of evaluations:

1. Retain past performance evaluations.
2. Release information to other government officials.
3. Properly dispose of past performance records, as required.

1. *Retaining past performance evaluations*

   The following documents should be filed in the contract file, agency-specific file, or a database:

   – Performance evaluations

   – Any end item evaluations or test results

   – Contractor responses to evaluations

   – An agency review of contractor rebuttals, if any exist.

   The documents should be marked "source selection information" and should be readily accessible to contracting office personnel.

2. *Releasing information to other government officials*

   The past performance evaluation should be released only to other government personnel with a bona fide need to know and to the contractor whose performance is being evaluated. Disclosure of such information to anyone else could harm both the government (it would be a violation of the Procurement Integrity Act to divulge procurement-sensitive information) and the competitive position of the contractor being evaluated. The agency's prescribed procedures for releasing the evaluations should be followed. The contractor's rebuttal statement and agency review of any contractor rebuttals must be attached to the performance evaluation report and must be provided to source selection officials requesting a reference check.

3. *Properly disposing of past performance records, as required*

   Past performance records are to be disposed of in accordance with agency procedures within three years after completion of contract performance.

ADMINISTRATION OF GOVERNMENT PROPERTY

The COR is often the individual responsible for assisting the CO in monitoring government property under a contract. This section will identify the tasks that the COR will be required to perform to ensure that the property is properly transferred, used, and disposed of. See Chapter 3, Government Property Considerations, for basic definitions and information regarding the decision to furnish property under the contract.

328. What is the FAR's policy on administration of government property?

FAR 45.102 states that:

> Contractors are ordinarily required to furnish all property necessary to perform government contracts. Contracting officers shall provide property to contractors *only* when it is clearly demonstrated:
> - To be in the government's best interest
> - That the overall benefit to the acquisition significantly outweighs the increased cost of administration, including ultimate property disposal
> - That providing the property does not substantially increase the government's assumption of risk, and
> - That government requirements cannot otherwise be met.
>
> The contractor's inability or unwillingness to supply its own resources is not sufficient reason for the furnishing or acquisition of property.

329. What are some key terms the COR needs to know to successfully carry out his or her property administration duties?

The following are key terms related to the administration of government property:

- Property
- Government property
- Government-furnished property
- Contractor-acquired property
- Contractor's property management system
- Property records

- Property administrator
- Plant clearance officer.

Property denotes all tangible property, both real and personal, and may include:

- Equipment
- Material
- Special tooling
- Special test equipment
- Plant equipment.

Government property refers to all property owned or leased by the government under the terms of a contract. It includes both government-furnished property and contractor-acquired property. Government property includes material, equipment, special tooling, special test equipment, and real property. Government property does *not* include intellectual property and software.

   Government-furnished property (GFP) is property in the possession of, or directly acquired by, the government and subsequently furnished to the contractor for performance of a contract. It includes, but is not limited to, spares and property furnished for repair, maintenance, overhaul, or modification. It also includes contractor-acquired property if the contractor-acquired property is a deliverable under a cost contract when accepted by the government for continued use under the contract.

   When contractors are issued GFP, the government will:

- Eliminate to the maximum practical extent any competitive advantage that might arise from using such property
- Require contractors to use government property to the maximum practical extent in performing government contracts
- Permit the property to be used only when authorized
- Charge appropriate rentals when the property is authorized for use on other than a rent-free basis
- Require contractors to review and provide justification for retaining government property not currently in use
- Ensure maximum practical reutilization of contractor inventory within the government.

Contractor-acquired property is property acquired, fabricated, or otherwise provided by the contractor for performing a contract and to which the government has title.

A contractor's *property management system* is a method of recording, identifying, and marking government property, used while working under a government contract, that the government requires the contractor to establish.

However, agencies will not generally require contractors to establish property management systems that are separate from a contractor's established procedures, practices, and systems used to account for and manage contractor-owned property.

Agencies must allow and encourage contractors to use *voluntary consensus standards* and industry leading practices and standards to manage government property in their possession.

Voluntary consensus standards means common and repeated use of rules, conditions, guidelines or characteristics for products, or related processes and production methods and related management systems.

Property records are the records created and maintained by the contractor in support of its stewardship responsibilities for the management of government property.

At a minimum, the contractor's property management system should:

- Be reasonably accessible to authorized government personnel
- Provide a complete, current, and auditable record of all transactions
- Contain basic information about the GFP being used, including:
  - The name of the agency from which the property was acquired
  - A description of the property
  - The quantity of items being used
  - The unit price of each item
  - The contract number
  - The location of the property
  - The disposition or transfer of GFP.
- Include other information, such as:
  - Records of all government-furnished materials
  - Special reports, including information on property being returned for rework, if applicable

- A listing of GFP being used for other contracts
- An explanation of how property will be safeguarded from tampering or destruction.

Information on the contractor's property management system will become part of the government's official contract administration office contract file.

A *property administrator* is a government employee designated as responsible for monitoring and maintaining the GFP inventory.

A *plant clearance officer* is an authorized representative of the CO, appointed in accordance with agency procedures, responsible for screening, redistributing, and disposing of contractor inventory from a contractor's plant or work site.

330. What tasks will the COR need to perform to successfully administer government property?

The COR must:

1. Supervise the initial transfer of government property
2. Monitor the contractor's use of government property
3. Monitor the disposition of government property.

Supervising the Initial Transfer of Government Property

331. What is the COR's role in supervising the initial transfer of government property?

The administration of government property starts at the beginning of the contract (i.e., when work on the contract begins) and ends when the government contract expires. (Refer to FAR Subpart 45.5.) The COR may be required by the CO to perform the following three steps at the start of the contract:

1. Monitor delivery of government property.
2. Monitor the contractor's property management system.
3. Resolve deficiencies in the contractor's property management system.

1. *Monitoring delivery of government property*

   The COR should examine the contract at its onset to see what, if any, data, equipment, or other property the government has agreed to furnish the contractor. When monitoring the delivery of government property to the contractor, the COR should:

- Establish an inventory list of the property being delivered
- Set up management requirements (i.e., review the contractor's property management system)
- Inspect government-provided equipment
- Coordinate agency property information with the contractor to ensure complete inventory and accountability for all property or equipment furnished
- Prepare a report documenting all of the above actions and information.

Also, the COR should discuss the following with the contractor:

- The date specified in the contract for delivering the property to the contractor
- If no contract date is specified, the date that the contractor will need the property in order not to impair its ability to meet the contract completion date
- Location of the property★
- The condition of the property and any needed repairs, corrections, or other actions that must be taken to avoid delaying contract completion★
- Any special instructions or limitations regarding use of the property.★

Because the government may become subject to a claim by the contractor if there are any changes to the contract's terms, the COR must ensure that any inconsistencies or delays in the delivery of government property can be remedied by the CO.

Possible claims a contractor could make against the government include the following:

- GFP was not delivered to the contractor by the date agreed to in the contract, or, if no date was specified, the GFP was not delivered by a sufficiently early date to permit the contractor to finish the contract work by the agreed completion date

---

★ This information may or may not be specified in the contract. If not, the COR will need to be sure to document these discussions with the contractor for future reference.

- GFP was not delivered in a condition suitable for the intended use of the property (e.g., poor copies of documents, illegible data)

- GFP was delivered without crucial information concerning techniques or conditions of the property's use, and the contractor is unable to use the property effectively or for its intended use.

Once a contractor has identified a problem with GFP or its delivery, it should be advised to submit a notice, in writing, to the CO. The following might occur:

If the property:	Then . . .
was delivered late	the CO may: • Extend the time for completion of the contract • Increase the estimated cost of, and fixed fee for, the work • Make some other equitable adjustment.
is not in a condition suitable for the intended use	the CO might direct the contractor to: • Repair the property • Modify the property • Return the property • Otherwise dispose of the property.

The contractor's right to claim contractual adjustment in these circumstances is granted by the government property clause in the contract. The contract adjustments that the contractor is entitled to claim include:

- An extension of the time for completion of the contract

- An increase in the estimated cost of, and fixed fee for, the work.

2. *Monitoring the contractor's property management system*

The property management system is a tracking method designed by the contractor to monitor and control the proper use of GFP in its possession. Once the contractor takes possession of the GFP, the COR should:

- Prepare reports on the contractor's overall property management system
- Perform periodic property audits
- Record any notification from the contractor that the government-furnished equipment is in need of repair
- Submit a written report of any shortages, losses, damage, destruction, or misuse of GFP to the CO.

Once the contractor takes possession of the government property, the contractor should:

- Incorporate the property into the contractor's property management system
- File a statement of any overages or shortages of or damages to the property as shipped
- Identify, mark, and record the property
- Furnish a receipt to the government, if necessary.

After reviewing the contractor's property management system, the COR should ensure that the contractor:

- Maintains an approved property management system
- Obtains all required approvals for use of the property
- Uses the property only for those purposes authorized in the contract
- Maintains, protects, and preserves the property
- Discloses the need for major repair, replacement, or other capital rehabilitation work.

3. *Resolving deficiencies in the contractor's government property control system*

   The agency responsible for contract administration will conduct an analysis of the contractor's property management policies, procedures, practices, and systems. This analysis is to be accomplished as frequently as conditions warrant, in accordance with agency procedures. The property administrator will notify the contractor *in writing* when the contractor's property management system does not comply with contractual requirements.

   The CO may request that the COR review the contractor's property management system to ensure compliance with the government property clause of the contract. If the contractor's property management system does not adequately maintain and monitor government property under the contract, the COR should:

– Notify the contractor of deficiencies in the system

– Specify, in writing, the required corrections needed and establish a schedule for completion of corrections

– Monitor compliance with the schedule of corrective actions.

If the deficiency is not corrected, the COR will notify the CO, who will send a written deficiency notice to the contractor advising it that its property management system will not be approved.

Monitoring the Contractor's Use of Government Property

332. How does the COR monitor the contractor's use of government property?

The COR can monitor the contractor's use of government property by:

• Conducting physical inventories of GFP and how it is being used at the contractor's work site

and

• Reviewing the contractor's preventive maintenance program.

333. In what cases might the CO ask the COR to investigate and resolve government property problems?

To ensure that the use of government property complies with the government property clause in the contract, and is in accordance with sound industrial practices, the COR may be required by the CO to investigate and resolve the following problems:

Reported loss, damage, or destruction (LDD) of government property. Generally, contractors are not held liable for loss, theft, damage or destruction of government property under the following types of contracts:

• Cost reimbursement contracts

• Time and material contracts

• Labor hour contracts

- Fixed price contracts awarded on the basis of submission of certified cost or pricing data.

The CO may revoke the government's assumption of risk when the property administrator determines that the contractor's property management practices are inadequate and/or present an undue risk to the government.

A prime contractor that provides government property to a subcontractor may not be relieved of any responsibility to the government that the prime contractor has under the terms of the prime contract.

The COR may be asked to evaluate and document evidence that indicates that government property has been lost, damaged, or destroyed. The COR should:

- Identify the extent to which the contractor is liable for LDD
- Prepare written conclusions on the extent and value of the LDD, including:
  - Proposals from the contractor to repair, replace, or otherwise mitigate damage
  - Government estimates or audit reports of the damages or loss
  - The government's position on the amount of damages and remedy
  - An opportunity for the contractor to present additional facts and the contractor's position on the LDD.
- Issue the contractor a written demand for payment or make any equitable adjustment for the repair of property when the government has assumed the risk.

Reported unauthorized use of government property. The COR may be required to investigate and resolve reports of unauthorized use of government property. The COR should:

- Determine whether there has been unauthorized use
- Evaluate and document any evidence of unauthorized use that is discovered
- Provide the contractor with an opportunity to present additional facts and its position
- Assess the contractor for the contract clause amount, if it is determined that unauthorized use has taken place.

334. When may government property be commingled with the contractor's property?

Normally, government property is to be kept physically separate from contractor-owned property. However, when advantageous to the government and agreeable to the contractor's management, government property may be commingled with the contractor's property. The COR should check with the CO, agency policy, or the property administrator to determine when commingling is permitted.

Monitoring the Disposition of Government Property

335. When government property is no longer needed, what should the COR do?

The COR should refer to FAR Subpart 45.6 and, if assigned the responsibility, assist the *plant clearance officer* in ensuring that the contractor:

- Discloses excess contractor inventory
- Prepares inventory disposal schedules
- Corrects inventory disposal schedules that are not accurate or complete
- Documents the inventory disposal schedule.

When the contract is completed, the government may:

- Request that the contractor deliver government property back to the government
- Request that the contractor deliver government property to another government contract site
- Dispose of the property.

When disposing of property, the government may choose one of the following options (listed in preferred priority order):

- Allow the contractor to purchase or retain the government property at cost
- Return the property to the suppliers
- Use the property within the government
- Donate the property to eligible entities (e.g., schools, charitable organizations)

- Sell the property
- Donate the property to other public agencies (e.g., state and local governments)
- Abandon the property.

Once the method of disposition is determined, the CO or the plant clearance officer may request the COR's assistance in:

- Preparing funding requirements for disposition, if applicable
- Providing information to support the *disposition modification*; if the government decides to allow the contractor to retain GFP at cost or to purchase GFP, the government will then modify the contract price to reflect the contractor's purchase of inventory
- Resolving reported property disposal problems.

REPORTING FRAUD

336. What should the COR do if he or she suspects that fraud or other civil or criminal offenses have been committed during the performance of the contract?

The COR's monitoring duties place him or her in a position to potentially observe misconduct, including civil or criminal offenses and fraud.

If the COR suspects that the contractor has committed such an offense, the COR must:

1. Assist the CO in briefing the contractor on the COR's suspicions
2. Identify and report any suspicions to responsible officials
3. Provide additional information to the CO and others, as requested.

337. To whom should the COR report any suspicions of fraud or other civil or criminal offenses?

The COR should report suspicions of fraud or other illegal activity to "responsible officials." The CO is a responsible official; others might include legal counsel, requiring activity officials, the Inspector General (IG), and the Department of Labor (for labor law violations). The COR must *be alert*; he or she must report any suspicions (conclusive evidence of illegal activity is not needed), and he or she must cooperate with all investigative officials who might be involved in the case. It is essential that the COR keep the CO informed of any suspicious contractor behavior.

338. Should the COR investigate his or her suspicions of fraud or other illegal activity?

The first and foremost duty of the COR is to report any suspicions—the COR should not try to become a private investigator! Investigation is not the COR's responsibility and is certainly not his or her area of expertise.

339. How are postaward orientation conferences used to brief the contractor on, and prevent, fraud or other civil or criminal offenses?

Normally, a briefing on fraud will be included in the postaward orientation conference (see Chapter 5). These briefings are intended to reduce the chances of violation of laws out of ignorance. Remember that government personnel may also be involved in fraudulent or criminal conduct.

340. What constitutes a violation of a federal statute during contract performance?

Violations of federal statutes by both contractor and government personnel during contract performance can include:

- False statements
- False claims
- Conspiracy to defraud
- Bribery
- Illegal gratuities
- Conflicts of interest under criminal statute (18 U.S.C 208), which prohibits a government employee's participation, in an official capacity, in any matter in which the employee has a financial interest.

341. What are some typical indicators of fraud?

Typical indicators of fraud (i.e., grounds for reasonable suspicion) include:

- False invoices
- Cost mischarging on cost reimbursement contracts
- Falsification of records and test results
- Product substitution
- False or misleading technical progress reports.

CHAPTER 7

Administering the Contract

This chapter continues coverage of seven specific contract administration functions that will require significant involvement by the COR. The COR will first need to ensure that the CO is notified immediately of the need for action related to these functions; any delay in notifying the CO could greatly endanger the rights and remedies of the government. Next, the COR will need to provide thorough and competent technical support in determining the best course of action when issues relating to these functions arise. Finally, it is essential that the COR understand that these contract administration functions all have their foundation in technical considerations that rely heavily on the expertise of the COR.

The seven specific contract administration functions with which the COR will be involved are:

- *Contract modifications.* Most contracts will require modifications for numerous reasons. The COR must identify the need to change the contract and must provide technical support as requested by the CO.

- *Options.* An option is the unilateral right of the government to purchase additional supplies or services, as provided in the contract. The COR must provide technical assistance to ensure proper exercise of an option by the CO.

- *Delays.* The COR will need to inform the CO of potential or actual delays and provide technical documentation regarding the delay.

- *Stop work orders.* The COR has primary responsibility for identifying situations in which the CO should issue a stop work order to minimize government risk and avoid unnecessary costs.
- *Claims.* The COR must notify the CO of potential disputes and assist the CO in resolving those disputes and processing formal claims, if needed.
- *Remedies.* In the event of a breach in the contract, the COR must notify the CO, suggest an appropriate remedy for the breach, and assist in evaluating the contractor's response to the suggested remedy.
- *Payment.* The COR will have responsibility for processing payment documents, assisting the CO in determining the amount properly payable, and authorizing payment.

CONTRACT MODIFICATIONS

342. What is the COR's role in the contract modification process?

The COR plays a key role in the contract modification process. He or she reviews and recommends contract modification requests and prepares a technical analysis to support the determination of whether a requested modification falls within the scope of the contract.

343. What key terms does the COR need to be familiar with regarding modifications?

Key terms relate to *contract modification* and *value engineering*.

Contract modification is used to describe any written change in the terms of the contract. There are two types of contract modifications:

Unilateral modification. Unilateral modifications are changes to a contract that are signed only by the CO. This type of modification is used to:

- Make administrative changes that are minor in nature and that do not materially affect contract performance
- Issue *change orders*, which are actual issuances of changes authorized by the changes clause in the original contract
- Make changes authorized by other contract clauses, which may include:
  - Issuance of a stop-work order
  - Issuance of a termination notice
  - Exercise of an option.

Bilateral modification. Bilateral modifications, or *supplemental agreements*, are contract modifications accomplished by mutual action of the involved parties. Both the contractor and the CO sign these changes. CORs may be required to provide advice to the CO on the technical aspects of the proposed change. Bilateral modifications are used to:

- Make *negotiated equitable adjustments*[1] resulting from the issuance of a change order

- Approve changes, such as economic price adjustments, required by the terms of the contract

- Reflect other agreements of the parties that modify the contract's terms.

Most bilateral or supplemental agreements involve the negotiation of price, cost, and other terms. These agreements usually entail tasks that are similar to those involved in the award of a basic contract (e.g., analyzing the contractor's proposed labor and material costs related to the modification).

Value engineering is the formal channel through which contractors may *voluntarily* suggest methods for performing more economically (and share in any resulting savings), or by which contractors may be *required* to establish a program to identify and submit to the government methods for performing more economically. Value engineering is a program that attempts to eliminate, without impairing essential functions or characteristics, any factor that increases acquisition, operation, or support costs.

344. May the COR make a contract modification?

No—the CO is the only individual authorized to commit to a contract modification. CORs may be asked to assist the CO in the *processing* of contractual modifications. FAR 43.102 (a) limits a COR's contract modification powers by stating that:

Other government personnel [personnel other than a CO] **shall not:**

1. Execute contract modifications

---

[1] When the CO issues a change order, *equitable adjustments* to price, estimated cost, delivery schedules, or other areas impacted by the change must be reflected in a supplemental agreement, known as a bilateral modification. The term *equitable* refers to both parties remaining contractually or legally whole as a result of the adjustment (i.e., neither party should gain an advantage or suffer a loss).

2. Act in such a manner as to cause the contractor to believe that they have authority to bind the government

    or

3. Direct or encourage the contractor to perform work that should be the subject of a contract modification.

345. How does the COR assist the CO in making contract modifications?

The COR provides:

- A technical evaluation addressing quality, quantity, price, and other factors or *considerations* ("something of value given in return for performance"[2]) that will impact contract performance and delivery of the end products on the contract

- Any other necessary documentation supporting the actions taken by the CO to resolve the modification request.

346. What are the COR's primary tasks related to reviewing and recommending modifications?

The COR must:

1. Identify the need to change the contract
2. Prepare the technical evaluation report
3. Assist the CO in negotiating the modification.

Identifying the Need to Change the Contract

347. What are some circumstances that can prompt a change to the contract?

A contract change may be desirable due to:

- A change in agency need
- Inadequate specifications that result in inadequate deliverables
- A need to increase or decrease funding
- A need for an extension to provide additional time for performance
- Suspension of work

---

[2] Steven H. Gifis, *Barron's Dictionary of Legal Terms*, 3rd ed. (Hauppauge, NY: Barron's Educational Services, Inc., 1998), p. 93.

- Revisions to the original terms and conditions in the contract
- A change in performance requirements
- Development of contingencies that require resolution.

348. When should the COR not proceed with a contract modification?

The COR should abandon a proposed contract change if the change is:

- Already covered by the terms and conditions of the contract
- Outside the scope of the contract.

Preparing the Technical Evaluation Report

349. What is a technical evaluation?

A *technical evaluation* is the COR's technical analysis of contract situations that arise during performance that cause costs to increase or decrease or that will cause other changes to the contract to be required. The COR's analysis should focus on whether such changes will impact the government technical requirements, and if so, to what extent, in terms of cost, the technical acceptability of the changed requirement, and delivery schedule. Usually, these types of changes are initiated by the technical requiring activity[3] to make changes such as an upgrade in technology of the items being procured, but the contractor will often initiate a proposed change for the same or similar reasons. The COR must then include documentation supporting the contractor's modification request in his or her technical evaluation. Only changes that fall within the scope of the original contract may be made; the COR must work closely with the CO to determine whether proposed changes do so. (Refer to a discussion of the meaning of "within the scope of the contract" later in this chapter, under Questions 352, 353, and 354.)

During the technical evaluation, the COR determines the:

- Technical validity of proposed changes to the technical requirements (e.g., will the government's needs still be met; is the change really

---

[3] The term *requiring activity* generally refers to the technical activity or program (project) office that originally initiated the contract requirements to satisfy a need. Most of the time, the requiring activity is the end user of the contract deliverables. There are other instances in which a technical activity will generate a contractual requirements package on behalf of other end users (e.g., a DoD program office acquiring weapons in support of troops).

necessary; would a completely different approach on a new contract be a better course of action?).

- Value of proposed considerations, such as the tradeoffs between cost, technical merit, and delivery. For example, a proposed change may be technically superior, but what if it increases costs or significantly extends delivery time? The COR must weigh all of these considerations and develop a recommended position for the government during negotiation of the change (see Question 356).
- Technical acceptability of substitute materials or processes proposed by the contractor.
- Acceptability of a value engineering proposal.

350. What information should a technical evaluation report include?

The technical evaluation report should document:

- The reason for the change
- Whether the proposed change is within the scope of the contract
- Whether the proposed change is already covered by the technical requirements of the contract
- The impact of the proposed change on cost (price), delivery, and performance.

351. What steps should the COR take in preparing the technical evaluation report?

The COR will need to perform the following steps:

1. Gather information regarding a proposed change.
2. Perform a technical analysis and prepare supporting documentation.
3. Notify the CO of the pending change.

1. *Gathering information regarding the change*

   The COR should obtain the necessary documentation from the contractor. This documentation may include:

   - A description of the change
   - Chronology of events, such as
     - Who initiated the change—the contractor or the government?

- Has the technical necessity for the change been established? By whom, and when?

- The current contract performance status pending the change (i.e., is performance ongoing, or is it being held up pending resolution and implementation of the change?)

The actual events documented would be dependent on the particular circumstances surrounding the change and its technical significance for contract requirements.

- A justification for the change

- Pricing information (i.e., how much will the change cost?)

The COR should also obtain input from the requiring activity and other support personnel. Their input may include:

- A statement of facts concerning the technical necessity of the change and any associated cost increases or extension of the delivery schedule

- Documentation of correspondence with the contractor

- Reactions to the request

- Information on the impact of the change request on the mission of the requiring activity.

2. *Performing a technical analysis and preparing supporting documentation*

The COR should assist the CO in determining the impact a change will have on the price or cost, delivery, or performance of the contract. The documentation should address:

- Background information and the reason for the change

- Whether the proposed change is already covered by the technical requirements of the contract

- Whether the change is within the scope of the contract

- Impact of the change on the requirement in terms of quality, quantity, or delivery

- Impact of the change on cost or price

- Consequences if the change is not made

- Available alternatives

- Recommended solutions.

Any attachments (e.g., engineering- or quality-related studies or analyses supporting the technical analysis) should also be included in the documentation.

3. *Notifying the CO of the pending change*

The COR should give the CO notification of a pending change within a time frame that does not:

- Jeopardize the government's mission
- Delay the contractor from performing the contract.

The notification should be made in accordance with the specific agency's procedures; at a minimum, notification should include:

- Relevant memorandums to the file, letters, or other documents. These documents will be used to request, explain, and justify the contract modification request
- Work statement changes that specify deliverables and their due dates
- A purchase request attached with the appropriate signatures, if the change requires additional funds.

352. Why is it important to consider the scope of the contract?

The CO must consider whether any change, initiated by either the government or the contractor, is within the scope of the contract. Adding work under an existing contract permits the government to avoid the costs associated with issuing a new procurement. There are definite limits, however, on adding work based on the determination of what is within the scope of the current contract. If the work is determined to be within the scope of the contract, it can be added, but if it is determined not to fall within the scope of the contract, it cannot be added.

In some cases, it will be fairly obvious that the proposed change is not within the scope of the contract. Changes obviously not within the scope of the contract include those that propose to increase the quantity of items being procured under the contract. In other cases, the determination of whether additional work is or is not within the scope of the contract can be very difficult to make, and sometimes the CO must use his or her judgment, relying on the COR's technical input. Contract scope issues are the source of many disputes between the government and contractors. The COR's technical expertise is needed to provide the CO with the best possible insight regarding the technical aspects of the change and how making, or not making, the change will affect the contract work. The following questions are provided to help the COR accomplish this objective.

353. When is a proposed change considered to be within the scope of the contract?

A proposed contract change that falls within the scope of the contract is usually characterized by the following qualities:

1. The function of the items or services being procured has not changed.

2. The basic contract purpose has not changed.

3. The dollar magnitude of the change is proportionate to the price of the original contract. This is a difficult determination to make, as what is considered acceptable can vary significantly from situation to situation. It is essential to determine how much the price of the change increases the overall price of the contract and whether that increase is proportionate or reasonable (i.e., can a price increase of 30 percent, 50 percent, or more be justified?[4]). Such determinations will be made at the discretion of the CO, relying heavily on technical input from the COR, and will have to be based on the particular circumstances involved.

4. The competitive factors of the original solicitation are unchanged. For example, suppose the original contract was awarded based on a sole source justification and the proposed change is based on that same sole source determination. In this case, the change would be determined to be within the scope of the contract and there would be no competition issues involved. On the other hand, the change may be considered to be an entirely different requirement (i.e., not within the scope of the sole source determination) and therefore would have to be competed. These determinations must be made by the CO with input from the COR.

5. Specification changes or statement of work changes are not extensive.

---

[4] Consider the case of *Axel Electronics, Inc.*, Armed Services Board of Contract Appeals (ASBCA) case 18990, 74-1 BCA (1974), where no changes were found to be beyond the contract scope in a situation in which the contractor was claiming equitable adjustments of 170 percent of the contract price because of alleged over-interpretation of the specifications.

354. What should be considered when determining if a change is outside the scope of the contract?

Questions to consider when deciding if a change is outside the scope of the contract include the following:

- Does the changed work represent what both parties reasonably contemplated at the time of award?
- Is the changed work essentially the same as the work agreed to in the original contract?
- Is the nature of the requirement altered by the change?
- Would this type of change normally be expected for this kind of requirement?
- Was the specification deficient, requiring extensive redesign?

355. What is the COR's role in providing information on the effect of a contract change on cost or price? How can contract changes be classified?

Although regulations make the CO the person ultimately responsible for all decisions on contract modifications, as stated earlier, the CO relies heavily on the COR and other support personnel for the technical and pricing decisions related to any modification.

Changes to basic contract requirements can be classified in three ways, according to the effect the change will have on the contract requirements and the resulting price adjustment. Usually, a single change will embody elements of more than one type of change. The three categories of changes are:

- *Additive changes*. Work is added to the contract, so the contractor is paid more for its work.
- *Deductive changes*. Work a contractor has not yet performed is deleted from the contract, resulting in a reduction of the contract price.
- *Substitution changes*. Added (new) work is substituted for deleted (old) work (e.g., obsolete technology is replaced with current technology). Conceivably, such changes could result in no change to the contract price, but this would be coincidental. Usually, the net change in contract price must be negotiated based on the value of the old work versus the value of the new work. Substitution changes are more difficult to make than additive or deductive changes, in terms of technically defining the change and establishing the monetary value of the old and new

work—especially the old work. The old work may not have been separately priced in the original contract; trying to establish its current value can cause disagreement between the government and the contractor.

Keep in mind that when the government is negotiating a modification with the contractor, the contractor is in a sole source position and therefore has some advantage in the negotiation. This is another significant reason for the COR to provide the CO with the best technical information possible in such circumstances.

The effects of the change on the original contract pricing and the original technical proposal should be considered and addressed. When the CO and COR, working together, determine pricing for a modified contract, they should consider:

- Pricing history for similar requirements, if available
- Current market prices.

When the dollar amount of a change (or changes) is $700,000 or more, a contractor may be required to submit to the CO cost or pricing data as a part of its proposal for negotiation of the contract modification. The CO may ask for the COR's assistance in evaluating the data.

Assisting the CO in Negotiating the Modification

356. What assistance may the COR be asked to provide in preparation for, and during negotiation of, a contract change?

The CO will often solicit assistance from the COR in researching information, preparing the pre-negotiation position, developing negotiation strategies, and conducting the negotiation for changing the contract. Assistance may be provided to the CO through:

- Meetings
- Telephone conferences
- Correspondence.

A COR can assist the CO in evaluating the contractor's proposal for a contract change by:

- Providing advice concerning safety and performance

- Providing guidance on whether acceptance of the supplies or services would be in the government's best interest after repair, correction, or price adjustments are made

- Providing supporting rationale for rejecting or accepting the contractor's proposal

- Attending any negotiations to respond to the contractor's position.

CONTRACT CHANGES	
What the COR *should* do:	**What the COR *should not* do:**
• Identify what needs to be changed to meet the government's requirements • Prepare a SOW for the modification • Estimate the funding required for the contractor to implement the modification • Determine the availability of funds • Coordinate with the CO • Review the contractor's cost proposal and prepare a technical evaluation.	• Direct the contractor to make a modification • Act in a way that leads the contractor to believe that the COR is authorized to direct a contract modification • Encourage the contractor to do work beyond the scope of the contract.

OPTIONS

357. What is an option?

An *option* is a unilateral right in a contract by which, for a specified time, the government may elect to purchase additional supplies or services called for by the contract or may elect to extend the term of the contract.

358. Who is authorized to exercise an option on a contract?

The CO is the *only* individual authorized to exercise an option on behalf of the government.

359. What is the COR's role in exercising an option?

The COR may be asked to assist the CO in processing the option and providing written notice to the contractor within the time specified in the contract.

360. What will the COR need to do to process an option?

The COR will need to perform the following tasks to successfully complete this duty:

1. Evaluate available options
2. Determine the need for additional supplies, services, or time
3. Research the market for the latest pricing information
4. Document the option in the COR contract file and provide written data to the CO.

An option is processed successfully when:

- The option is exercised within the time frame established in the contract
- Relevant market research data are submitted to support the recommendation to exercise the option
- The option represents the most advantageous method of satisfying the government's need, considering price and other related factors.

Evaluating Available Options

361. What role does the COR play in evaluating available options?

The COR should become familiar with the contract in order to assist the CO in evaluating and processing the option. To this end, the COR must:

1. Thoroughly read and review the contract
2. Analyze the government's position.

1. *Thoroughly reading and reviewing the contract*
   The COR should:
   - Understand the requirement, the pricing information, the terms and conditions of the original contract containing the option provision, and the time frame needed to exercise the option
   - Determine if it is in the government's best interest to exercise the option.

The COR should begin this step at least *six months* before the option is due to be exercised to ensure that enough time is allowed to make an informed decision about the option.

In supply-type contracts, options may be appropriate when the basic quantities (quantities provided for in the contract apart from the option quantities) are meant for learning or testing purposes, or competition for the options is not possible once the initial contract has been awarded.

2. *Analyzing the government's position*

   The COR should ensure that:

   – Funding for the option is available

   – The requirements covered by the option fulfill an existing government need

   – Exercising the option is the most advantageous method of fulfilling the need, based on price or cost and other considerations.

   The option can be exercised only:

   – Prior to the date specified in the contract for exercising it

   – In accordance with the terms and conditions of the contract.

Determining the Need for Additional Supplies, Services, or Time

362. How does the COR help the CO determine the need for, and possible impact of, an option?

The COR will submit to the CO a written determination in the form of a letter, memorandum, or report that will include information about:

- Government requirements supporting the need to exercise the option
- The advantages of exercising the option
- The technical impact and the value of the option
- Funding availability for the option.

The COR's documentation will assist the CO in making a decision about the proposed option. After reviewing the documentation, the CO will send a written notice to the contractor advising the contractor of the government's intent to exercise (or not exercise) the option. This notice should be submitted to the contractor at least 60 days (or within the timeframe specified in the contract) before the effective date of the option.

Consideration of whether to exercise the option can proceed if, at this point, the decision is made that:

- There is an existing need for the additional supplies, services, or time and

- There are funds available to exercise the option.

Researching the Market for the Latest Pricing Information

363. What is market research?

Market research is performed by the COR to collect, organize, analyze, present, and maintain data for the purpose of maximizing the capabilities, technology, and competitive forces of the marketplace to meet an organization's needs for supplies or services. When the government must decide whether or not to exercise an option, market research provides information regarding pricing and availability of the additional requirements on the open market. This information is needed to determine the most advantageous method of fulfilling the requirement—exercising the option or purchasing the requirement on the open market. Refer to Chapter 3, Conducting Market Research, for additional information on market research.

364. What market research information regarding a proposed option should the COR submit to the CO?

The COR will submit to the CO market research data that confirm that:

- The option price is lower than prices currently offered by other vendors on the open market and

- The option otherwise represents the most advantageous method of fulfilling the need, price and other factors considered.

The following other factors should also be considered in determining whether the option is economically advantageous:

- Any economic price adjustment clause included in the contract that affects the option price

- The need for continuity of operations
- The potential cost of disrupting operations.

The CO must consider the current market price for the requirement and whether the option price is compatible with current market conditions. The option price does not have to be the lowest available price in order to exercise the option. The CO may decide that the need for continuity of operations, and the potential cost of disrupting those operations, might override the advantage of a lower price in certain circumstances. Remember, if the CO decides not to exercise the option in order to pursue a lower price on the open market, a new contract requirement must be developed, awarded, and delivered. There is always a possibility that problems with that process could arise, in terms of delayed delivery or even non-delivery. Therefore, even if the COR were to find a lower price for the requirement on the open market during market research, it may still be more advantageous to exercise the option, all things considered.

365. What types of market research should the COR consider conducting?

To obtain information on the latest commercial market pricing and industry trends, the COR may employ one of three types of market research:

- *Continuous market research*. This type of research is performed on an ongoing basis and is not related to a specific acquisition. It can provide the COR with current knowledge about:
    - Changes, advances, and trends in technology
    - Products of interest
    - Industry capability (i.e., the state of the art in a particular industry)
    - Product availability
    - Competitive market forces
    - Alternative sources.
- *Initial market research*. Initial market research is related to a specific acquisition and can determine whether sources of commercial items are available to satisfy the specified need. The COR can also use information gleaned from initial market research to determine whether the government's requirement could be modified (to a reasonable extent) to allow the use of commercial items.

- *Subsequent market research.* Subsequent market research is conducted prior to the solicitation of offerors. This research helps the COR determine if the requirement fits existing market conditions by identifying the standards and practices of commercial firms.

366. What if market research information is not available?

The COR should notify the CO when needed information cannot be obtained through market research.

Documenting the Option in the COR Contract File and Providing Written Data to the CO

367. What kind of documentation about an option should the COR develop and provide to the CO?

The COR's written documentation should justify the COR's position and can be in the form of a letter, memorandum, or report. The documentation should include:

- A rationale for exercising the option
- The option period, as stated in the contract
- A technical evaluation that indicates that the option meets the government's requirement
- A funding document or form that certifies that funds are available to exercise the option.

The COR should submit this information to the CO within the timeframe specified in the contract.

DELAYS

368. What is a delay?

A *delay* is a failure to perform a service or provide a product during the performance or delivery period established in the contract. A goal of government contracting is to acquire what is needed when it is needed. Every contract, therefore, includes a completion timeframe or delivery date. Delays occur when the delivery period has passed and what should have been done or delivered was not, or when there is an anticipated lag in delivery or performance and the contractor has advised the government that it will not perform the contract when the time for performance arrives.

Delays can cause serious problems. A delay could have devastating cost impact on both the government and the contractor. The government does not get the needed contract deliverables as scheduled and probably has to pay significantly more for the contract work than anticipated, due to price increases, idle labor or facilities, or other costly factors. If a military acquisition is delayed, national security could be compromised. The contractor could also incur idle labor and facilities expenses in addition to having to pay rising prices for labor and material. It is not uncommon for contracts to be terminated due to delays, and there may be severe consequences for both parties. For example, contractors could end up bankrupt after being terminated for delay.

369. What are the types of delays?

Delays can be either *excusable* or *nonexcusable*.

Excusable delays are beyond the control of, and without the fault or negligence of, a contractor or its subcontractors at any tier. A delay is excusable when the contractor can prove the following:

- An event that caused a delay has occurred
- The event was not its fault
- The event was the type for which an excuse can be granted
- The overall process of the work was delayed
- The event, in fact, caused the delay of the work
- The event was unforeseeable
- The requested additional time is appropriate to compensate for lost time.

The contractor will not be liable for any excess costs if the failure to perform the contract arises from causes beyond the control and without the fault or negligence of the contractor. Excusable delays may also be caused by government performance. When the government's actions cause the contractor to stop performing, the contractor may be "excused" from complying with the schedule.

Examples of *excusable delays* include:

1. Delays for which neither the government nor the contractor is responsible:
   - Acts of God

- Unusually severe weather
- Strikes and labor disputes
- Acts of the public enemy
- Causes beyond the control of the subcontractors and suppliers.

2. Delays caused by actions taken by government personnel (e.g., the CO, the COR, the government inspector) involved with contract performance, such as:

- Directing the contractor to stop work
- Making a change to the contract
- Performing other acts within the government's sovereign capacity.[5]

3. Delays caused by the government's failure to carry out one or more of the following responsibilities:

- Making the performance site available when required
- Processing approvals
- Obtaining funding
- Issuing changes in a timely manner
- Responding to the contractor's requests
- Furnishing government property when required
- Inspecting or accepting delivered goods when required.

Nonexcusable delays occur when a contractor cannot justify a delay as being beyond its control.[6] Contractors are responsible for meeting the contract's delivery or performance schedule requirements and for all costs incurred in making up for the "lost time" associated with a non-excusable delay.

See Exhibit 7-1, Checklist: Is This Delay Excusable? at the end of this chapter for more information.

---

[5] As an example, in *D.D. Montague Electrical Contractor*, ASBCA 11837, 67-1 BCA, a contractor was awarded a six-day delay as a result of its inability to secure normally available railroad cars for delivery of needed supplies. The Board found that the unprecedented volume of government demands for railroad cars due to the ongoing Vietnam conflict was a sovereign act of the government.

[6] As an example, in *E.Carron, Inc.*, ASBCA 19105, 76-1 BCA, the Board denied relief to a contractor who claimed that a copper shortage that caused copper prices to rise steeply caused the delay. The Board found that the contractor had postponed its procurement of copper supplies in the hope of buying later at lower prices, and that a "reasonably prudent businessman" would have obtained and stockpiled needed supplies.

370. What are the tasks the COR will need to perform with regard to delays?

The COR must:

1. Identify and verify a delay in performance under the contract

2. Notify the CO of the technical impact of the delay

3. Assist the CO in evaluating the contractor's response.

Identifying and Verifying a Delay in Performance Under the Contract

371. What steps does the COR take in identifying and verifying a delay in performance under the contract?

Every contract includes a delivery or performance schedule. CORs should assist the CO by performing two steps:

1. *Identifying the existence of a delay*

   A delay has occurred if:

   • The contractor fails to perform in accordance with the delivery or performance schedule in the contract

   or

   • The government causes the contractor to stop performing.

   The COR should review the contract for any applicable clauses and any modifications to ensure that the performance or delivery schedule was not previously extended by the CO before claiming that a delay has occurred.

2. *Verifying the delay*

   The COR can confirm a suspected delay by:

   • Obtaining feedback from government individuals responsible for monitoring the performance or delivery schedule

   • Reviewing the contractor's notice and supporting documents regarding the delay

   or

   • Reviewing the contractor's claim regarding the delay (the contractor files a claim instead of a notice for what it considers to be a government-incurred delay).

Notifying the CO of the Technical Impact of the Delay

372. How does the COR assist the CO after notifying him or her of the delay?

Once a delay is confirmed, the COR should prepare documentation to assist the CO in developing the government's position on the delay. The documentation should include relevant information about the delay, such as:

- A list of persons with factual knowledge of the delay
- A description of the delay
- The history of contract performance, indicating:
  - When work under the contract began
  - When work deviated from the performance schedule
  - When the work stopped.

Other issues that may be covered in the COR's technical analysis of the delay include:

- Information that would support whether the delay was excusable
- The contractor's progress to date and the obligations that remain
- A reasonable estimate of the amount of additional time needed
- Potential alternatives and resolution recommendations
- Pros and cons of each listed alternative or resolution (i.e., the effect of each upon price, quantity, and quality of deliverables).

Assisting the CO in Evaluating the Contractor's Response

373. What are contractors generally asked for in their response to the delay?

CORs may be asked to assist the CO in evaluating the contractor's response (i.e., the contractor's notice or claim of a delay). In their responses, contractors may be asked to:

- Substantiate the evidence of the delay
- Substantiate the costs associated with the delay

- Demonstrate that the delay was excusable (i.e., beyond its control and without its fault or negligence)
- Demonstrate that the delay was void of any concurrent or commingled delays.

374. What are concurrent or commingled delays?

These types of delays fall in a "middle ground"—they are neither excusable nor nonexcusable. A *concurrent delay* occurs when two or more different delays happen at the same time. A *commingled delay* occurs when both parties, the government and the contractor, are at fault for one or more events contributing to that delay.

375. What are recoverable expenses?

Recoverable expenses is a term used to refer to the contractor's costs associated with delays that are compensable (i.e., payable by the government). Before allowing the contractor to recover costs as a result of a delay, the contractor's response must provide verifiable documentation of the expenses incurred due to the delay. The CO, with the assistance of the COR, must consider each expense and determine if the contractor should receive compensation. Compensation may be in monetary form or in the form of time extensions. For further guidance, see Exhibit 7-2, Examples of Recoverable Expenses Following a Delay, at the end of this chapter.

STOP WORK ORDERS

376. What is a stop work order? When are these orders issued by the government?

A *stop work order* is a written or oral order to stop work under a contract. If an oral stop work order is given to the contractor, it is binding only when confirmed in writing by the CO and signed by the contractor. Stop work orders may be used, when appropriate, in any negotiated fixed-price or cost-reimbursement supply, research and development, or service contract if work stoppage may be required for reasons such as advancement in the state of the art, production or engineering breakthroughs, or realignment of programs.

Generally, a stop work order will be issued only if it is advisable to suspend work pending a decision by the government, and a supplemental agreement providing for the suspension is not feasible. Stop work orders are not to be used in place of a termination notice after a decision to terminate has been made.

In accordance with FAR clause 52.242-15, Stop Work Order, the government may issue a stop work order lasting a maximum of 90 days without the contractor's agreement. However, if the government issues a stop work order lasting more than 90 days or issues an extension beyond the original 90 days on an existing stop work order, both the government and the contractor must agree on the order.

377. What is the COR's role in issuing a stop work order?

The COR is often the individual responsible for advising the CO of the need to issue a stop work order. This duty is completed successfully when the COR:

- Can identify and determine the need for a stop work order
- Monitors the administration of the stop work order to avoid unnecessary costs and to minimize government risk.

378. What tasks will the COR need to perform in order for a stop work order to be issued?

For a stop work order to be issued, the COR should:

1. Identify the potential conditions under which a stop work order might be issued
2. Recommend a work stoppage to the CO
3. Assist the CO in issuing the stop work order.

Identifying Potential Conditions Under Which a Stop Work Order Might Be Issued

379. What are the potential conditions under which a stop work order might be issued?

The COR should be able to identify conditions under which a stop work order might be issued. The government or the contractor may request stop work orders. Circumstances in which a stop work order might be requested by the government include the following:

- The government is unable to furnish property or services per the contract schedule

- A change to the contract has been received and a modification cannot be issued
- More time is needed for the government to consider contract modifications that would substantially change the end product.

Circumstances in which the contractor might request a stop work order include the following:

- A proposal has been submitted to materially change the technical requirement of the contract (e.g., a value engineering change)
- Conditions at a government work site make the performance of work unsafe, and these conditions are not immediately correctable.

Recommending a Work Stoppage to the CO

380. May the COR issue instructions to stop work?

CORs should avoid issuing instructions, oral or written, to a contractor to start or stop work. The CO is the official responsible for issuing stop work orders after receiving approval of the order from one level above him or her.

381. What should the COR do if he or she thinks work should be stopped?

To be able to recommend the most cost-effective or practical solution to the problem in terms of the program requirement, the COR should complete the following steps:

1. Determine the impact of a work stoppage
2. Document a recommendation.

1. *Determining the impact of a work stoppage*

   Work stoppages should occur only after the government has made a determination of the impact they will have. Factors the COR should consider when making this determination might include:

   - The estimated cost of delaying the work
   - Any potential effects on labor (e.g., loss of skilled labor, loss of efficiency)
   - The potential damage to perishable goods

- The estimated effect on overhead (e.g., inventory, indirect labor)
- Any adverse effects of the potential delay on contract completion.

The COR should determine if there is a stop work order clause in the contract that allows the government to stop work under the contract. Permitting the issuance of stop work orders under a contract does not give the government an unrestrained hand. This provision gives the government the right to impose a delay on the contractor, but the government cannot impose an overly long, unreasonable delay. See the discussion regarding the 90-day limit imposed by FAR clause 52.242-15 under Question 376. In measuring the reasonableness of the delay, the courts and boards will consider the length of the delay balanced against the impact of the delay on the contractor. How long a reasonable period of time is for the government to complete an action under the contract depends entirely upon the circumstances of the particular case.

2. *Documenting a recommendation*

The COR may be asked to prepare documentation for the stop work order. This documentation may include the following information:

- A description of the work to be suspended
- Guidance on actions to be taken on any subcontracts
- Effective date and time of work stoppage
- The timeframe to resume work
- The contractor's right to file a claim
- The reason and purpose for, and benefits of, stopping the work
- Any costs associated with the work stoppage
- Alternatives to stopping the work (if any exist)
- Reasoning behind the determination of the length of time for which work will be stopped.

Work stoppage information may be transmitted to the contractor over the telephone, but the COR should immediately follow up this notification in writing.

Assisting the CO in Issuing the Stop Work Order

382. When the CO decides to authorize a stop work order, what is the COR's role?

When a recommendation for a work stoppage is made, the CO may authorize the issuance of a stop work order and request that the COR:

1. Select the method for issuing the stop work order
2. Assist in discussions with the contractor
3. Recommend a date for the resumption of work.

1. *Selecting the method for issuing the stop work order*

   There are two methods for issuing stop work orders:

   - *Oral stop work orders.* Oral orders are issued in urgent situations—for example, when safety violations have occurred or a life-threatening situation has arisen. A CO will issue oral orders only when the situation precludes waiting for the issuance of a written one, and a timeframe for work stoppage needs to be conveyed as quickly as possible. Oral orders should be followed up and confirmed in writing as soon as possible.

   - *Written stop work orders.* Written orders include all necessary details related to the stop work order (see Documenting a Recommendation under Question 381) and the requirements for the contractor's compliance. Written orders can be presented to the contractor:

     - In person
     - Through a third-party messenger.

   Whatever method is used to deliver the stop work order, the signature of a contractor employee acknowledging receipt of the stop work order must be obtained for the order to become effective. The signature ensures that the government is released from the responsibility for payment of any unnecessary costs incurred for contract work as a result of the stoppage.

   The COR may be asked to prepare the written stop work order for the CO's consideration.

2. *Assisting in discussions with the contractor*

The COR will assist the CO in discussing the stop work order with the contractor. The following topics may be covered in these discussions:

- Reasons for issuing the stop work order
- The length of the work stoppage being imposed by the government and the probability of revisions of that time frame, depending on circumstances
- The impact of different time frames for the work stoppage
- Estimates of labor costs and other costs of the expected work stoppage
- Alternatives for continuing the stop work order (circumstances that would cause the stop work order to continue)
- Acceptance of the stop work order by the contractor.

Daily communication, preferably in writing, is important because costs associated with the work stoppage compound daily. The CO, COR, and the government office most affected by the stop work order should be involved in any communication with the contractor.

3. *Recommending a date for the resumption of work*

Because work stoppage may result in an increase in the cost of any part of contract performance or may prolong the performance period, the COR should recommend the most cost-effective or practical solution to the problem. Stop work orders are undesirable under any contract and should be discontinued as quickly as possible.

The contractor will resume work:

- When written notice is received from the CO to resume work and the stop work order has not yet expired
- When the stop work order is cancelled
- When the stop work order expires and the contractor receives written notice to begin working again
- When the stop work order expires and no official government action is taken.

CLAIMS AND DISPUTES

383. What is a claim?

The government and the contractor sometimes have disagreements regarding the terms of the contract or the manner of performance of the contract work. Usually, the parties can resolve their differences through informal discussion. However, in instances where this informal resolution is not possible, it becomes necessary to litigate unresolved issues—one party may file a claim against the other. Either the government or the contractor can file a claim.

A *claim* is a written demand by one of the contracting parties seeking:

- Payment of a certain amount of money
- Adjustment or interpretation of contract terms
- Other relief arising under or relating to the contract.

A claim can:

- *Arise* under a contract, meaning that it is *directly* associated with that contract (i.e., the contract itself provides a remedy for the claim)

  or

- *Relate* to a contract, meaning that is *indirectly* associated with that contract (i.e., the contract itself does not provide a remedy for the claim).

A claim under a contract can be resolved with a contract clause that provides for the relief sought by the claimant. However, a written demand by the contractor seeking payment exceeding $100,000 is not a valid claim under the Contract Disputes Act until it is certified in writing.

A voucher, invoice, or other routine request for payment that is not in dispute when submitted is *not* a claim. The submission may be converted to a claim through a written notice to the CO if it is not acted upon in a reasonable time by the government, if the monetary amount being requested is in dispute, or if there is disagreement between the government and the contractor regarding which party is liable for the payment request.

384. What are the COR's responsibilities in the case of a claim?

The COR assists the CO in analyzing the claim, recommending a settlement position, and participating in the resolution process.

The COR is often the individual responsible for analyzing the claim and recommending the settlement position to the CO.

The COR will need to perform the following tasks when faced with a dispute:

1. Notify the CO of potential disputes
2. Assist the CO in resolving disputes
3. Assist the CO in processing formal claims.

The COR must be sure that:

- Information is provided to the CO so that he or she may correctly determine the validity of the claim
- He or she prepares a proper and complete report of the technical or performance aspects of the dispute that fully supports the CO's contractual determination
- The government's interests are protected, and the contractor is treated fairly and equitably within the terms of the contract.

The government's policy is to try to resolve all contractual issues to the maximum extent practicable. This policy includes:

- The use of alternative dispute resolution (ADR) procedures, if permitted and appropriate
- The exercise of all reasonable efforts to resolve controversies prior to the submission of a claim
- The inclusion of clauses or other terms and conditions in the government contract that protect the public's interest for any contract disputes/claims.

385. What is the Contract Disputes Act of 1978?

The Contract Disputes Act (CDA), as amended, establishes procedures and requirements for asserting and resolving claims by or against contractors arising under or relating to a contract subject to the act. The act requires that the dispute procedures listed be used by all federal agencies.

386. How does a contractor notify the government when it has a problem that could result in an equitable adjustment or a claim, and how does the government respond to this notification?

When a contractor has a problem performing the contract work, he or she usually contacts the CO or the COR by phone to inform them that a problem has arisen. This initial contact is not a claim. The government usually responds to the contractor's phone call with a letter, asking that the problem be stated in writing. The contractor will then respond with a letter describing the problem. The contractor's letter might be more than a simple notice that there is a problem. It could request an equitable adjustment to resolve the problem informally, or it could represent a claim that could result in litigation. Usually, at this early stage, the contractor does not know how severe the problem will be, what will be required to correct it, or how much a solution will cost. Without this information, it is too early to proceed with a request for equitable adjustment or a claim.

At this point, the COR must investigate the problem and assist the CO in determining whether the contractor is due more money, time, or both, and if so, how much more.

In the meantime, the contractor will investigate the problem, determine exactly what the problem is, and specify what is needed to resolve it. The contractor will probably send a written request for the CO to make an equitable adjustment to the contract to correct the problem; the government will then agree to pay added costs, adjust the delivery schedule, or provide any other considerations that it deems appropriate. Most of the time, the government will comply with the contractor's request, make the equitable adjustment, and modify the contract to effect the change.

However, there are instances in which the contractor and the government cannot agree, and the contractor decides to file a formal claim demanding that the CO make a final decision. The CO has the authority to make the final decision for the government, either granting the contractor its claim or denying it. Whatever the decision, the CO must issue a formal final decision to resolve the claim. A CO's final decision denying the contractor's claim entitles the contractor to file an appeal to a board of contract appeals or the Court of Federal Claims.

Sometimes, determining whether a notice sent by a contractor is an actual claim can be difficult—the notice may only be a simple notification of a problem, or it could be a request for equitable adjustment that can be resolved informally. Unfortunately, there are no criteria that can be applied in every instance to reach a failsafe decision on whether or not a notice is really a claim. If a COR receives a letter from a contractor in which the contractor's intentions are not made clear, the COR should:

- Initiate discussion of the problem with the contractor to gather information about the contractor's perception of the problem

- Informally attempt to determine what sort of resolution the contractor is seeking
- Talk to someone who may have dealt previously with the problem
- Join the CO in consulting with legal counsel, if necessary
- If considered necessary based on the particular circumstances and with the CO's concurrence, write a letter to the contractor asking if a claim is being submitted.

387. What is a dispute?

A *dispute* is formed under a contract when a controversy develops about:

- Payment for contract work
- The time period allotted for performance
- Money due to either party
- Contract terms.

When the contractor's written request does not include all the criteria for a claim, the CO will return the request along with a written response explaining its deficiencies, as outlined in the disputes clause in the contract.

Notifying the CO of Potential Disputes

388. What conditions can lead to disputes under a contract?

The COR should be aware that controversies can stem from disagreements and can give rise to disputes under the contract. For instance:

- Complex projects may form troublesome interrelationships between the government and contractor personnel administering the contract.
- Lengthy contract documents and multiple revisions of those documents can foster differing interpretations of contract terms.
- Unforeseen events may create problems that cause disagreements between the contractor and the government; for example, changing weather conditions may disrupt delivery schedules.
- Well-intentioned actions can create out-of-scope changes. For example, a contractor may try a different approach than the one initially agreed upon when performing the contract work, thinking that the new approach would be more efficient and cost-effective. The COR might

even have agreed that the contractor could use the new approach. But what if it is later determined that this approach is more expensive than the original approach because of a factor that was not initially considered? At this point, it is likely that a dispute will arise regarding which party is responsible for the added costs associated with the out-of-scope change. Does the contractor have sole responsibility or did the COR's actions or inactions create government liability for the added costs?

389. How does a dispute become a claim?

For a contractor's disagreement or dispute with the government to constitute a claim, the contractor must first initiate a request for a claim and demand that the CO make a final decision on the written request. A CO's final decision can be discretionary, but it must be within the terms and conditions of the contract. The Contract Disputes Act does not require the board of contract appeals to review the CO's decision.

The process of analyzing a potential claim, leading up to the CO's final decision, can be categorized into five phases:

1. Identifying the issue(s) being disputed
2. Performing an analysis of the impact the claim will have on performance and cost
3. Evaluating project documentation (see Question 395)
4. Performing a price/cost analysis of the claim and damage apportionment
5. Preparing a report.

390. What kinds of disputes often develop into claims?

A decision from the CO may be necessary when various types of disagreements arise between the government and the contractor. Disagreements can develop with regard to the following issues:

- Payment of invoices
- Settlement of contract claims
- Reinstatement of a previously terminated contract
- Termination of a breached contract for default
- Acceptance or rejection of nonconforming items.

391. What are the warning signs of a potential dispute?

The COR should be aware of the warning signs of a dispute and should notify the CO as soon as the possibility of a dispute has arisen. These warning signs include:

- Lack of specific information from a contractor during a preproposal conference about how the job will be completed
- Failure of a contractor to begin work within approximately 10 percent of the contract's total period of performance
- Repeated failure of a contractor to meet milestones on the critical path of a project's schedule
- Repeated safety violations or accidents, possibly indicating poor management
- Repeated incidents of poor-quality work or rework
- Complaints from site workers to government personnel about working conditions
- Refusal by a contractor to sign bilaterally negotiated contract modifications or agreements containing the language necessary to release a modification
- Letters from a contractor alluding to field problems, without specific details regarding those problems
- Numerous contractor correspondences about insignificant matters that require replies, creating a nightmare of paperwork
- Persistent complaints, without foundation, from a contractor, concerning the behavior, motives, or requirements of the inspector or contract administrator
- Complaints from subcontractors concerning late payments or nonpayment.

Assisting the CO in Resolving Disputes

392. What does the COR do to assist the CO in resolving disputes?

Two steps in dispute resolution will involve the COR:
1. Preparing supporting documentation for a dispute or claim
2. Participating in ADR procedures.

Preparing supporting documentation for a dispute or claim involves submitting supporting data to the CO that:

- Provides a description of the claim or dispute
- References the pertinent contract terms
- Includes a statement of the areas of agreement or disagreement
- Determines whether the contractor is indebted to the government
- Makes a recommendation to reject, partially accept, or fully accept the claim
- Includes background information covering:
  - Facts, in chronological order, about the claim or dispute
  - All separate issues or allegations involved in the claim or dispute
  - Points of contact for discussion of the dispute.

Methods used in developing this documentation include:

- Discussions with the contractor
- Personal observations at the work site
- Discussions with other government personnel (e.g., audit, quality assurance, or program office employees).

The COR will also participate in ADR procedures.

393. What is alternative dispute resolution?

Alternative dispute resolution (ADR) is any procedure or combination of procedures that the government and the contractor use voluntarily to resolve issues in controversy without the need to resort to litigation. ADR procedures may include, but are not limited to:

- Assisted settlement negotiations
- Conciliation, facilitation, mediation, and fact-finding
- Mini-trials
- Arbitration
- Use of ombudsmen.

ADR procedures may be used at any time and should be employed as often as possible to resolve controversial issues. ADR procedures are best used when:

- An issue in controversy exists

- Officials from both parties who are authorized to resolve the issue voluntarily participate in dispute resolution
- Both parties agree on procedures and terms
- Formal litigation will not be pursued.

Agencies have established very specific ADR procedures. The CO may request, and provide guidance for, the COR's participation in the ADR procedures.

Assisting the CO in Processing Formal Claims

394. How does the COR help the CO process formal claims?

To assist the CO in the claim resolution process, the COR should:

1. Submit a detailed analysis of the claim
2. Participate in appeals proceedings.

1. *Submitting a detailed analysis of the claim*

   The COR will provide information to assist the CO in completing a detailed analysis of the claim. This technical analysis should be submitted in writing to the CO, including the following information:

   - The background of the claim or dispute (including information used to support the dispute)
   - Contract number and date
   - Estimated contractor's claim amount, the amount the contractor may be entitled to, and any reasons for the differences between the two amounts
   - Contractor's labor and equipment usage and cost
   - Documentation (from monitoring reports) of idle time, wasted time, or dragged-out time
   - Possible overstaffing of personnel or overequipping
   - Contractor's cost overage (or overrun) on materials, labor, equipment, and overhead
   - Contractor's diligence and production efficiency (the COR should note the number of days or months the contractor is behind schedule)
   - Number of changes or change orders received and processed under the contract

- The engineering approach that was employed by the contractor, establishing the reasonableness of any additional time and person-hours expended.

Once a claim has been identified, the CO may request that the COR assist with the preparation of the claims file for the appeal proceedings.

2. *Participating in appeals proceedings*

The CO may ask the COR to provide some of the required information for the claims file when the contractor appeals to the government agency, the courts, or the agency's counsel. This required information must support the CO's final decision on the claim and must be:

- Responsive to all issues addressed in the claim

- Impartial and unbiased

- Legally sound.

If the decision following an appeal favors the contractor, the CO may negotiate an equitable adjustment, unless the amount of relief (in terms of money or extra time to perform the contract) has already been established in the decision. The CO may request assistance from the COR in negotiating the equitable adjustment. After negotiation, a supplemental agreement (bilateral contract modification) is used to formally reflect the equitable adjustment.

395. What should a claims file include?

A *claims file* should include the following documentation, whenever possible:

- The contract specification and drawings, including all modifications.

- The COR's correspondence files.

- Copies or documentation of any written or oral technical direction that the COR may have provided to the contractor and that may be pertinent to the claim.

- Contract modifications that include technical changes on a project. Of particular importance are changes that were originally approved, plus those that have been added throughout the course of the contract.

- Inspection records, including daily records, if applicable, and logs or reports by inspectors and contractor personnel.

- Memoranda of meetings (only those pertinent to the claim).
- All progress charts and information, including any bar or other charts and all changes to the charts concerning progress.
- Copies of the postaward orientation meeting notes. These may establish expectations and understandings of both parties concerning a particular provision of the specifications or anticipated problems.
- Copies of contract clauses. These are important for general reference purposes and should be reviewed during the course of a claim's preparation.
- Copies of all photographs pertinent to the claim.
- Copies of pertinent logs, such as change order logs or submittal approval logs.
- Copies of the contractor's interim and final performance evaluations of the contractor's performance. These can be used to support performance disputes.

Information submitted by both parties constitutes the file that will be used during the appeals proceedings, and much of this information will be used as evidence during the litigation process.

REMEDIES

396. What is a remedy?

Government contract *remedies* are forms of relief that can be pursued in light of a contractor's nonconformance or noncompliance with the contract terms or conditions. *Relief* is defined as "the redress or assistance awarded to a complainant, by the court, especially a court of equity, including such remedies as specific performance, injunction, rescission of a contract, etc. The term generally does not comprehend an award of money damages. Thus the term *affirmative relief* is often used to indicate that the gist of relief is protection from future harm rather than compensation for past injury."[7] Relief can be provided by contract clauses or from basic rights provided by government contract law and, occasionally, by commercial contract law.

---

[7] Steven H. Gifis, *Barron's Dictionary of Legal Terms*, 3rd ed. (Hauppauge, NY: Barron's Educational Services, Inc., 1998), p. 414.

397. What is the COR's role regarding remedies?

The COR is often the individual responsible for recommending a formal contract remedy to the CO. The COR:

- Provides remedy notification to the CO that is adequate, timely, and will support the CO's final decision
- Suggests a remedy that will minimize the impact of the contractor's performance problems on the requirement, delivery schedule, and cost.

398. What is a breach of contract?

A *breach of contract* occurs when:

- The government or the contractor fails to fulfill the terms and conditions of the contract, and there is no relief available under the terms of the contract
- The contractor has committed fraud or made a gross mistake amounting to fraud.

399. When a breach of contract has been identified, what should the COR provide to the CO?

The COR should provide the CO with:

- Sufficient evidence of a breach of contract and suggestions for an appropriate contract remedy
- Assistance in evaluating the contractor's response after it is informed that a breach of contract has occurred.

400. What may the government do when a breach of contract occurs?

When a contractual breach has occurred, the government may:

- Issue a forbearance letter deferring termination of the contract
- Modify the contract to correct the problem
- Use a contractual remedy
- Begin proceedings to terminate the contract for the contractor's default.

401. What is a letter of forbearance? When is it issued?

Forbearance is a term used to describe deferring termination action. Forbearance is appropriate when a contractor has provided a workable solution to a performance deficiency brought to its attention. To ensure preservation of the government's right to future remedial action for deficient contract performance, the government issues a *letter of forbearance*, which must:

- Acknowledge the contractor's stated method for and commitment to "curing" performance problems

- Notify the contractor that the government is deferring its right to take future corrective actions only if the contractor fulfills its commitment to remedy deficient performance

- Declare the government's intention to pursue corrective contractual remedies, including default, if the contractor fails to fulfill its commitment.

402. What are delinquency notices?

Delinquency notices are notices that may be sent to the contractor by the CO when it appears a contractual breach has occurred and contract termination is being considered. Delinquency notices are time-sensitive; if the government does not act in a timely manner, it could lose its right to do so, so it is important that the COR notify the CO of any possible breaches of contract as soon as possible. Delinquency notification can take one of two forms: the *cure notice* or the *show cause notice*.

A *cure notice* is used when:

- The contractor fails to make progress and performance is endangered

- The performance problem is not related to contract terms regarding delivery

- At least ten days remain for contract performance, and correction of the problem can reasonably be expected to take place within the time remaining.

A cure notice:

- Specifically states the failure in performance that is believed to be endangering performance

- Allows the contractor at least ten days to "cure" the failure

- Is in writing and is legally sufficient (i.e., legally establishes the government's right to proceed) to support a default termination.

A *show cause notice* is used when:

- There is insufficient time remaining in the delivery schedule for the contractor to cure or correct the delinquency

  and

- The government is seeking evidence that the delinquency was beyond the control of the contractor.

Usually a show cause notice is issued when there are fewer than ten days remaining in the performance period or when the contractor is delinquent; however, it can be used at any time a COR determines that there is an "insufficient amount of time left" to correct the problem.

A show cause notice:

- Informs the contractor of its liabilities in the event of the contract being terminated for the contractor's default

- Requests that the contractor "show cause" why the contract should not be terminated for default

- Informs the contractor that failure to explain the cause of the deficiency may be taken as admission that no valid explanation exists

- Invites the contractor to discuss the matter at a conference, if appropriate.

See Chapter 8 for additional information regarding contract termination.

403. What are liquidated damages?

Liquidated damages are a predetermined rate of payment, specified in the contract, payable to the government by the contractor, for the contractor's delay in performance. They are assessed when:

- Time of delivery or performance is such an important factor in the award of the contract that the government may reasonably expect to suffer damage if the delivery or performance is delinquent

  and

- The extent or amount of such damage would be difficult or impossible to ascertain or prove.

404. What factors must the COR consider when rejecting nonconforming supplies or services?

Supplies or services that do not conform to the terms of the contract should be rejected. Inspection and acceptance clauses in the contract provide the basis for rejecting supplies and services. After a product or service has been accepted, the government cannot later reject it; acceptance is final, except when:

- Latent defects exist in the items accepted
- The government determines that fraud has been committed by the contractor
- Gross mistakes amounting to fraud are discovered.

When a nonconformance is critical or significant, the CO must ordinarily reject the nonconforming supplies or services. Even in those circumstances, however, acceptance may be in the government's best interest (e.g., for reasons of economy or urgency). In such circumstances, a CO must base a decision to accept supplies or services on the following factors:

- The requiring activity's (the program or project office) assertion that the nonconforming deliverable is safe to use and will meet the intended purpose.
- Information concerning the nature and extent of nonconformance.
- A request from the contractor for acceptance of the deliverable.
- A recommendation from the requiring activity for acceptance or rejection with supporting rationale.
- Legal consideration for the nonconformance. A contract adjustment might be considered appropriate, as well as any other adjustment offered by the contractor, such as a reduction in unit price for the end items, or perhaps the provision of additional units at no cost.

405. What are latent defects?

A defect is considered *latent* (hidden) when the defect was not known or could not have been known through reasonable inspection and testing at the time of acceptance. Generally, the contractor is responsible for latent defects discovered at any time after final acceptance. For a defect to be latent, it must be:

- Not susceptible to discovery using inspection methods that are reasonable under the circumstances

  and

- In existence at the time of acceptance.

A "reasonable" inspection of an item is one that would normally be performed as a matter of routine in the industry for that item.

406. What is fraud?

Fraud is "an intentional deception of the government by the contractor and is . . . covered by the False Claims Act, 18 U.S.C. 287, 31 U.S.C. 231, and the False Statements Act, 18 U.S.C. 1001.

If the government charges the contractor with fraud, it will usually elect to proceed under one of these statutes since the remedies include civil penalties of double damages in addition to criminal penalties. If the government proceeds under the terms of the inspection clause, its success will result only in defeating the finality of acceptance."[8]

To demonstrate that the contractor has committed fraud under a contract, the evidence must show:

- A misrepresentation of fact (actual or implied) or a concealment of a material fact

- Contractor knowledge of facts that were concealed or misrepresented

- An intent to mislead the government into accepting a misrepresentation or concealment as fact

- Government injury suffered as a result of the misrepresentation or concealment.

Evidence is defined as "all means by which any alleged matter of fact, the truth of which is submitted to investigation at judicial trial, is established or disproved. Evidence includes the testimony of witnesses, introduction of records, documents, exhibits, or any other relevant matter offered for

---

[8] John Cibinic, Jr., and Ralph C. Nash, Jr., *Administration of Government Contracts* (Washington, D.C.: George Washington University Press, 1981), p. 378.

the purpose of inducing the trier of fact's (fact finder's) belief in the party's contention."[9]

407. What are gross mistakes amounting to fraud?

"The elements of gross mistakes amounting to fraud are the same as those of fraud, except that there is no requirement to prove intent to mislead. This standard would require a knowing misrepresentation of a material fact, inducing acceptance by the government . . . . The requirement of a knowing misrepresentation on the part of the contractor is usually interpreted to mean a misleading statement, act, or omission . . . . In Catalytic Engineering & Manufacturing Corp., ASBCA 15257, 72-1 BCA 9342 (1972), the contractor was to supply dehydrator cartridges with end pieces made of polyvinyl chloride. The contractor's use of polystyrene—an unsuitable material—was a gross mistake, but not one amounting to fraud. The contractor's failure to tell the government of the change, however, was a gross mistake amounting to fraud. The board stated that the lack of an 'intent' element distinguished the gross mistake amounting to fraud from actual fraud."[10]

To prove a *gross mistake*, the government need only prove that the mistake was truly irresponsible or neglectful. A gross mistake can be legally pursued if the mistake is so obvious that the contractor never should have presented the work as complete.

408. What are warranties?

Warranties define the rights and obligations of the contractor and the government concerning defective items and services after acceptance. Warranties extend the rights of the government to correction of defects or replacement of a deliverable for the time period specified in the warranty.

There are two types of warranties:

- An *express warranty* is a written promise or affirmation given by a contractor to the government regarding the nature, usefulness, or condition of the supplies or performance of services furnished under a contract. Express warranties include:

  - A government warranty clause specified in the contract

---

[9] Steven H. Gifis, *Barron's Dictionary of Legal Terms*, 3rd ed. (Hauppauge, NY: Barron's Educational Services, Inc., 1998), p. 165.

[10] John Cibinic, Jr., and Ralph C. Nash, Jr., *Administration of Government Contracts* (Washington, D.C.: George Washington University Press, 1981), p. 379.

- A contractor's commercial warranty incorporated into a contract.
- An *implied warranty* is an unwritten guarantee that the item of supply or a service will live up to the claim of the manufacturer or provider. Oral guarantees made to the government under a specific contract are *not* considered implied warranties. Implied warranties include the contractor's claims for:
  - Warranty of merchantability
  - Warranty for a particular purpose.

409. What are government warranty clauses?

Government warranty clauses provide for various types of warranties in supply and service contracts and generally fall into one of five basic categories:

- *Failure-free or hardware warranty.* The contractor accepts the responsibility to correct any failure or defect that occurs during a specified or measured amount of use or operation.
- *Correction of deficiencies warranty.* The contractor agrees to correct any deficiency in design, material, or workmanship that becomes apparent during a test or early operation and that results in the specific item's performing below the required standard. This type of warranty in a major systems contract usually also applies to spare parts and other supplies included in the contract.
- *Supply warranty.* The contractor is obligated to replace or reperform work on contract items if defects in material or workmanship existed at the time of acceptance.
- *Service warranty.* The contractor agrees to reperform defective services if defects in workmanship existed at the time of acceptance. This is similar to a repair warranty in a retail establishment.
- *Data warranty.* The contractor agrees to either correct or replace data that does not at the time of delivery conform with the specification and all other requirements of the contract. If correction or replacement of the data is no longer required by the government, the government may elect a price or fee adjustment. This warranty lasts for a period of three years after delivery of the data.

410. What is a warranty of merchantability?

This implied warranty provides that an item is reasonably fit for the ordinary purposes for which it is used. The item must be of at least average, fair, or medium-grade quality, and it must be comparable in quality to items of the same description that will pass without objection in the trade or market.

411. What is a warranty for a particular purpose?

This implied warranty provides that an item is fit for the particular purpose for which the government will use the item. The government can rely on this implied warranty when:

- The contractor knows the particular purpose for which the government intends to use an item

    and

- The government relied on the contractor's skill and judgment that the item would be appropriate for the known particular purpose.

412. What tasks will the COR need to perform regarding remedies?

The COR must:

1. Notify the CO of performance failures
2. Provide technical assistance to the CO.

Notifying the CO of Performance Failures

413. What kind of performance failures may occur during contract performance?

While monitoring the contract, the COR may identify performance failures or other breach of contract situations. These may include:

- Anticipated or actual late delivery
- Failure to control costs
- Unsatisfactory performance
- Nonconforming supplies or services.

Once a performance failure or breach of contract has been identified, the COR must notify the CO of the problem in a timely manner. Because many remedies are time-sensitive, any delay in informing the CO may result in harm to the government—it may lose its rights to relief.

Recommendations for remedies for performance failures should:

- Best match the problem
- Include documentation that is adequate and timely to support the decision.

Providing Technical Assistance to the CO

414. What does the COR typically do to provide technical assistance to the CO in the event of a performance failure?

To provide the CO with technical assistance in this situation, a COR may need to:

- Prepare documentation and make appropriate recommendations to support the government's legal position for:
  - Any monetary or non-monetary consideration (i.e., relief)
  - A new delivery schedule
  - Modification of other terms and conditions of the contract.
- Attend meetings with the contractor and provide technical advice as requested by the CO.

The COR can also assist the CO in the remedy process by:

- *Providing technical analysis for delinquency notice situations.* CORs are asked to provide an analysis of performance problems that are so critical as to justify the issuance of a delinquency notice. If a delinquency notice is issued, the COR's technical analysis must be presented to the contractor. The contractor is then given an opportunity to respond to the delinquency notice.

  The COR may be asked to determine the ability of the contractor, in response to a *cure notice*, to:
  - Correct the work
  - "Cure" performance problems
  - Provide a downward price adjustment before acceptance
  - Provide *substantial performance* (i.e., significantly more work or better work than has been done thus far) in exchange for relief from some terms or conditions in the contract
  - Analyze and negotiate a revised delivery schedule for a conforming product with *consideration* (i.e., something of value from the contractor)
  - Present a case for excusable delay.

The COR may be required to assist the CO with the contractor's response to a *show cause notice* by evaluating:

- The impact of no reply or one that offers no justification for performance problems
- A claim for a case of excusable delay
- A claim that performance is impossible under the contract terms and conditions
- A claim that contract work is substantially complete.

- *Calculating liquidated damages.* When assessment of liquidated damages is appropriate, payments are withheld based on an accurate computation of the amount due. The actual computation will depend not only on the specific amount or specific formula in the contract, but also on actual events that occurred during the contract administration phase of the contract. Liquidated damages are calculated by:

  - Identifying all factors that control how these amounts are computed, to reflect an accurate maximum amount authorized under a specific liquidated damages contract clause
  - Subtracting amounts of time that may have constituted an excusable delay from the period for liquidated damages assessment
  - Examining the contract for any restrictions. Generally, the contract will restrict the total amount withheld to the greatest amount that can be withheld under the authority of a single clause.

To ensure that the total liquidated damages amount is reasonable and not a penalty, there may be special contract terms limiting the overall dollar amount that may be charged or the period of time over which damages may be assessed, or both, for liquidated damages assessment. The courts and administrative boards will *not* uphold liquidated damages that are so excessive that they can be construed as a penalty.

- *Preparing a written rejection of noncomforming supplies and services.* The written rejection of nonconforming supplies and services must clearly explain how the supply or service did not conform to the specification. CORs need to provide supporting documentation identifying which part of the contract the contractor did not perform correctly and why. Inspection and acceptance clauses in the contract provide the basis upon which supplies and services may be rejected.

When a nonconformity seriously affects the requirement, the item should be rejected. It is recommended that the COR discuss the rejection with the contractor before issuing any written notification because the contractor may have additional information concerning the deliverable. Before rejecting the product or service, a determination must be made by the CO or the COR that no changes have been made in the contract requirements. CORs, when authorized by the CO to perform inspections and to determine acceptance, may also be required to notify the contractor of the rejection of nonconforming supplies or services.

The notification of rejection must be in writing if:

- The rejection took place at a location other than the contractor's plant
- The contractor persists in providing items or services with minor nonconformities

  or

- Supplies that were delivered late are being rejected, and no excusable delay factors were involved in the delinquency.

Written notification should:

- Provide the reason for rejection
- Allow time for the contractor's reply
- Be furnished to the contractor promptly. There is no specific time period in which the notification must be submitted to the contractor, but the contractor is entitled to prompt notice of rejection in the interest of mitigating costs and perhaps further delay.

CORs need to note the specific supplies or services that were rejected and must consider the following points when issuing rejection notices:

- The contractor's acknowledgment of delivery of the notice is required.
- A rejection notice does not extend the delivery period.
- *Determining warranty provisions.* The CO may request that the COR assist in collecting some of the following information:
  - A summary of all warranties that apply to a specific product or service

- A listing of the specific components to which a warranty applies if all components are not included (i.e., all components are not delivered at the same time, or some are actually missing)
- Who has government responsibility to report warranty incidents and the authority to implement a warranty's clauses
- The duration of the warranty
- Packaging and transportation requirements.

CORs may also be asked to verify that a warranty clause applies to a specific failure by:

- Confirming that the government has officially accepted the items or services
- Examining the written terms and conditions of the warranty. This examination should reveal:
  □ The duration of the warranty
  □ The extent of coverage for specific defects.
- Determining if any government obligations under the warranty were met or providing assurance that they will be met
- Confirming that the facts support invoking the warranty (i.e., that the technical deficiencies are in fact covered or applicable to the particular warranty).

• *Providing technical review of the contractor's responses.* CORs are asked to assist in evaluating the impact of the contractor's response to the proposed remedy. Contractor responses can include:

- A proposal to repair or correct the work
- A proposal to provide a downward adjustment in price or cost as a basis for acceptance
- No reply
- A refusal to repair or correct the work or to offer any consideration to the government's suggested remedy.

For additional information, see Exhibit 7-3, Decision Table for Selecting a Contract Remedy, at the end of this chapter.

PAYMENT

FAR Subpart 32.9 states that the contractor is entitled to payment under the contract. This payment should conform to agency policies and to the policy outlined in the Prompt Payment Act. The COR should not authorize payment of money in excess of, or less than, the amount to which the contractor is entitled under the terms and conditions of the contract. However, the government has payment alternatives with regard to paying a contractor for services or supplies received or accepted. These are:

- Payment in full
- Payment after certain deductions and withholdings (after written notice to the contractor)
- Rejection of the contractor's invoice (the reason for rejection must be specified) and return of the invoice to the contractor for correction and resubmission.

415. What is a payment?

A *payment* is the monetary amount the contractor is entitled to receive under the contract for services or supplies ordered by the government. The form used to pay the contractor is known as a *payment document*.

416. What is the COR's role in payment authorization?

The COR is often the individual responsible for assisting the CO with the authorization of payment. This duty is completed successfully when the COR recommends to the CO whether to authorize payment for any invoice in full, in part, or not at all.

417. What tasks will the COR need to perform to successfully authorize payments?

The COR must:

1. Accept the payment document for processing
2. Calculate the payment amount
3. Notify the contractor of the final amount calculated to be paid, and submit the correct invoice to the paying office.

The following sections deal with payments to be made in accordance with various types of government contracts with and without government financing. For a discussion regarding the methods of government financing, refer to the Government Financing section in Chapter 4.

418. What is partial payment?

Partial payment is a method of payment based on acceptance of a particular part of contract performance.

419. What is prompt payment?

Prompt payment occurs when the government pays the contractor prior to the invoice payment date. The *prompt payment discount* is an invoice payment reduction voluntarily offered to the government by the contractor for prompt payment that is made prior to the due date stated on the invoice.

Payments under Noncommercial Item Contracts

420. What is a contract financing payment?

A *contract financing payment* is a disbursement of monies to a contractor under a contract clause or other authorization prior to acceptance of supplies or services by the government. Contract financing payments include the following payment types:

- Performance-based payments
- Advance payments
- Progress payments based on costs incurred
- Progress payments based on a percentage or stage of completion
- Interim payments under a cost-reimbursement contract.

Contract financing payments should be made on a timely basis. Contract financing payments *do not* include:

- Invoice payments
- Payments for partial deliveries
- Lease and rental payments.

421. What is government policy regarding performance-based payments?

Performance-based payments are the *preferred* government financing method when the CO finds them practical and the contractor agrees to their use. Performance-based payments are contract financing payments that are not payments for accepted items; they are fully recoverable, in the same manner as progress payments, in the event of default.

Performance-based payments may *not* be used :

- For payments under cost-reimbursement line items
- When the contract provides for progress payments based on a percentage or stage of completion
- For contracts awarded through sealed-bid procedures.

Performance-based payments may be made on either a whole contract or a deliverable item basis, unless otherwise prescribed by agency regulations. Financing payments made on a whole contract basis are applicable to the entire contract, not to specific deliverable items. Financing payments made on a deliverable item basis are applicable to a specific individual deliverable item, i.e., an item with a distinct unit price. Thus, a contract line item for 10 airplanes, with a unit price of $1,000,000 each, has 10 deliverable items— the separate planes. A contract line item for one lot of 10 airplanes, with a lot price of $10,000,000, has only one deliverable item—the lot.

422. What are the prescribed bases for performance-based payments and how are they established?

Performance-based payments may be made on any of the following bases:

- Performance measured by objective, quantifiable methods
- Accomplishment of defined events
- Other quantifiable measures of results.

The basis for performance-based payments may be either specifically described events (e.g., milestones) or some measurable criterion of performance *that was identified in the contract,* including a description of what constitutes successful accomplishment. The signing of contracts or modifications, the exercise of options, the passage of time, or other such occurrences do not represent meaningful efforts or actions and *may not* be identified as events or criteria for performance-based payments. An event need not be a critical event to trigger a payment, but the government must be able to readily verify successful performance of each such event or performance criterion.

The CO establishes a complete, fully defined schedule of events or performance criteria *and payment amounts* when negotiating contract terms. If a contract action significantly affects the price, an event, or a performance criterion, the CO responsible for pricing the contract modification adjusts the performance-based schedule appropriately.

Total performance-based payments are to:

- Reflect prudent contract financing provided only to the extent needed for contract performance
- Not exceed 90 percent of the contract price if on a whole contract basis, or 90 percent of the delivery item price if on a delivery item basis.

The contract must specifically state the amount of each performance-based payment either as a dollar amount or as a percentage of a specifically identified price (e.g., contract price, unit price of the deliverable item).

423. How are performance-based finance payments to be liquidated?

Performance-based amounts are to be liquidated by deducting a percentage or a designated dollar amount from the delivery payments. The CO specifies the liquidation rate or designated dollar amount *in the contract*. The method of liquidation should ensure complete liquidation *no later than final payment.*

424. What is government policy regarding advance payments for non-commercial item contracts?

Advance payments are the *least preferred* method of contract financing and should be used sparingly, if at all. Other types of financing should be available to the contractor in adequate amounts. However, loans and credit at excessive interest rates or other exorbitant charges are not considered reasonably available financing.

Advance payments might be considered useful and appropriate for the following:

- Contracts for experimental, research, or development work with non-profit educational or research institutions
- Contracts solely for the management and operation of government-owned plants
- Contracts for acquisition, at cost, of property for government ownership

- Contracts of such a highly classified nature that the agency considers advance payments necessary for national security
- Contracts entered into with financially weak contractors whose technical ability is considered essential to the agency.

425. What is an invoice payment?

An *invoice payment* is a disbursement of government monies to a contractor under a contract or other authorization for supplies or services accepted by the government; invoice payments are also sometimes referred to as *delivery payments*. Invoice payments include:

- Payments for deliveries (including partial deliveries) that have been accepted by the government
- Final cost or fee payments where amounts owed have been settled between the government and the contractor
- Payments under fixed price construction contracts
- Payments under fixed price architect-engineer contracts
- Interim payments under a cost-reimbursement contract for services.

Invoice payments are subject to payment due dates and interest penalties for late invoice payment. Remember, invoice payments do *not* include contract financing payments; therefore, contract financing payments are not subject to penalties for late invoice payment.

Payments under Commercial Item Contracts

426. What types of payments are applicable to commercial item purchases?

A *commercial advance payment* is a payment made before any performance of work under the contract. The aggregate of these payments may not exceed 15 percent of the contract price. These payments are *not* subject to penalties for late payment; however, they should be paid on a timely basis. A *delivery payment* is a payment for accepted supplies or services, including partial deliveries. Delivery payments *are* subject to penalties for late payment. A *commercial interim payment* is any payment that is not a commercial advance payment or a delivery payment. Commercial interim payments are *not* subject to penalties for late payment. A commercial interim payment is made to the contractor after *some* work has been done, whereas a commercial advance payment is made to the contractor when *no* work has been done.

Accepting the Payment Document for Processing

427. What steps does the COR take in processing a payment?

Processing a payment to the contractor involves the following steps:

1. Determining if payment may be processed
2. Inspecting the payment document for completeness
3. Accepting the invoice or notifying the contractor of any defects found in an invoice.

1. *Determining if payment can be processed*

   Prior to processing any payments, at least one of the following must be true:
   - Acceptance of the product or service must have occurred
   - Contract performance must have been otherwise completed.

   Several documents may need to be obtained in order to determine whether payment can be processed. Necessary documentation may include:
   - Documentation that supports successful delivery or completion of products and services, including:
     - Inspection forms
     - Receiving report forms (see Question 311, Chapter 6)
     - Commercial shipping documents
     - Packing lists.
   - Documentation of the suspension of performance
   - Documentation of the application of remedies, such as liquidated damages or rejection of work
   - Documentation of adjustments to liquidation rates or reductions in progress payments
   - Documentation of interim or final adjustments to the contract price
   - Modifications to the contract
   - Documentation of termination settlements.

2. *Inspecting the payment document for completeness*

   Once a contractor submits an invoice for payment, the COR may be required to:
   - Inspect the submitted invoices

- Determine if the invoice is complete
- Determine if the invoice is for a fixed price or cost-type contract.

3. *Accepting the invoice or notifying the contractor of any defects found in the invoice*

   Once an invoice is received, the COR will evaluate the invoice and either accept it or notify the contractor of a deficiency in the invoice. Incomplete or incorrect invoices should be returned to the contractor prior to acceptance for payment. Contractors must be notified of any specific deficiencies:

   - In writing

     and

   - Within seven calendar days after the receipt of invoice.

If the contractor submits an incomplete invoice, the COR should keep a record of the length of the delay getting a corrected invoice from the contractor causes. Once the invoice is corrected, if the original invoice date appears on the corrected invoice, the invoice should be sent to the payment office with the following statement:

> After receipt of invoice, the Contracting Office waited days for the contractor to supply necessary information for invoicing. Therefore, the invoice was not proper until _____, and any interest payment that may be due the contractor shall be based on this later date.

428. What types of invoices can a contractor submit?

Invoice types under a fixed price contract include *fixed price contract invoices* and *cost-type contract invoices*.

   Under fixed price contracts, the contractor will submit invoices in accordance with the payment clause in the contract. Payment clauses may include specific instructions for the submission of invoices for payment. Depending on the type of fixed price contract, a contractor may use one of two formats for the invoice:

1. *Basic invoices*

   An invoice for a fixed price contract must contain some basic elements in order to be considered complete or proper for payment purposes. These elements are:

- The name and address of the contractor.
- The invoice date and invoice number. (Contractors should date invoices as close as possible to the date of mailing or transmission.)
- The contract number or other authorization for the items or services performed (including order number and contract line item number).
- The description, quantity, unit of measure, unit price, and extended price of supplies delivered or services performed.
- Shipping and payment terms. If any government bills of lading (GBLs) are used, the GBL number and the weight of the shipment must be shown. (See Question 311, Chapter 6, for a discussion of commercial bills of lading and government bills of lading.)
- The name and address of the contractor's official to whom payment is to be sent. (This must be the same name and address as shown in the contract or on a proper *notice of assignment*, i.e., a document demonstrating that the contractor has transferred its right to be paid by the government for contract performance to a bank, trust company, or other financial institution.)
- The name, title, phone number, and mailing address of the person to be notified in event of a deficient invoice, when available.
- Taxpayer Identifiaction Number (TIN), if required by agency procedures.
- Electronic Funds Transfer (EFT) banking information.
- Any other information or documentation required by the contract.

2. *Performance-based payment invoices*

   On a performance-based contract, payment invoices must include:
   - The contractor's name and address
   - The date of request for payment
   - The contract number or other identifier of the contract under which the request is made
   - Information and documentation required by the contract's description of the basis for payment
   - The contractor's certification that the request for payment is true and correct; the certification must be signed by an official authorized to bind the contractor.

Under cost-type contracts, submitted invoices may be verified by reviewing vouchers for compliance. The COR may have to request that the contractor submit vouchers for his or her review to validate the amount invoiced for payment. The voucher must include corroborating information or data concerning all incurred costs.

Calculating the Payment Amount

429.   How does the COR calculate the payment amount?

After the invoice has been accepted for payment, the COR will calculate an amount for payment against acceptable invoices or vouchers. The COR will follow these steps in doing so:

1. Identify terms and conditions of the contract
2. Obtain needed documents and determinations
3. Identify billed amounts that will not be paid to the contractor
4. Determine the total amount due the contractor.

1. *Identifying terms and conditions of the contract*

   The COR should be able to identify applicable contract terms and conditions for payment, such as:

   - Price
   - Type of contract
   - Payment provisions (in-full, partial, performance, or progress payments)
   - Period of acceptance
   - Discounts
   - Liquidated damages.

2. *Obtaining needed documents and determinations*

   Supporting information and data for invoices and vouchers are essential to reinforce a contractor's billings for:

   - Work that has been completed
   - Work in process
   - Costs incurred for a specified period of time.

While the extent of such information and data may vary considerably under different types of contractual arrangements, the principle of reasonable documentation for expended public dollars stands behind every government contract. The COR may request that the contractor support the amount claimed on the invoice through either:

- *Voucher documentation.* Vouchers submitted by the contractor should list corroborating information or data concerning all incurred costs. This data may include:
  - Vendor or supplier billings
  - Contractor internal cost sheets or displays
  - References to files where relevant information can be found.
- *Invoice documentation.* Supporting information and data for invoice payments may include:
  - Inspection or receiving reports
  - Commercial or government shipping documents
  - Determinations[11] on billing rates
  - Reports on contractor indebtedness
  - Determinations for reductions in progress payments
  - Determinations for an adjustment for progress payments.

3. *Identifying billed amounts that will not be paid to the contractor*

   The COR should be able to determine when billed amounts cannot be paid. Reasons for nonpayment include:

   - *Withholdings and deductions in fixed-price contracts.* A contract may include special terms that allow the government the right to deductions or withholdings in certain instances:
     - A *withholding* is an amount of money subtracted from the total billed amount that may be paid at a later date. Figure 7-1 identifies several common withholdings.
     - A *deduction* is an amount of money that is permanently subtracted from the billed amount, unless a contractor provides appropriate supporting evidence for the reinstatement of any

---

[11] The term *determination*, as used in this context, refers to the judgment or opinion of the COR or other individuals (e.g., the auditor) as to the allowability or reasonableness of rates, amounts, or charges.

Common Withholding	FAR Reference
Suspended or reduced progress payments	52.232-16
Retention of 1% of total estimated costs, when appropriate in cost (or no-fee-)-type contracts	52.216-11
Retention of 15% of the target fee for cost-plus-fixed fee or cost-plus-incentive fee contracts	52.216-8, 10
Retention of up to 5% of amounts billed for time charges under time and material and labor-hour contracts.	52.232-7

FIGURE 7-1. Withholdings

deducted amount. For example, some contracts specify deductions for defective products or services that do not meet an "acceptable quality level." It is possible that later, if the contractor improves the service or product, and the government finds it acceptable, the deducted amount could be reinstated. Figure 7-2 identifies some events that can lead to deductions from amounts invoiced.

• *Unallowable costs in a cost-type contract.* In a cost-type contract, the COR should examine each cost element (direct or indirect) to determine if the cost will be allowed under the contract. A COR may request that the contractor submit vouchers in support of the invoiced amounts.

4. *Determining the total amount due the contractor*

Once all appropriate withholdings and deductions are identified, the COR will determine the amount due the contractor. Depending upon the contractual situation, the contractor will then be issued:

• Payment in full

• Partial payment

• Performance-based payment.

When the COR recommends payment in full or issues a partial payment, the amount of payment the contractor receives is self-explanatory. However, when payment is performance-based, the amount due must be *liquidated* by deducting a percentage or a designated dollar amount

Event	Common Reasons for Deductions
Administering fixed price contracts	• Invoiced items that have not been received or accepted (FAR 52.232-1 and 52.232-2) • Invoiced prices that exceed the contract price
Administering a *letter contract* (refer to Chapter 4, Question 149, for a description of a letter contract)	• Invoiced amounts in excess of the limitation of reimbursement and reimbursement rates (FAR 52.216-26)
Terminating a contract	• Invoiced amounts that are greater than the amount authorized for partial payment or final payment of termination settlements (FAR 49.402-6 and 49.402-7(b))
Billing the government for transportation costs	• Improperly supported reimbursement for transportation charges (FAR 52-242-10 and 52.247-1)
Collecting contractor debts	• Setoffs for the collection of contractor debts (FAR 32.611 and 32.612)
Modifying the contract	• Unilateral or bilateral downward adjustments to the contract price, including adjustments that result from the resolution of performance problems (FAR Part 43, 52.243-1 to 52-243-7, and 52-248-1)
Implementing special contract remedies	• Liquidated damages, per specific clauses (FAR 52.212-4, 52.219-16, and 52.222-4)

FIGURE 7-2. Deductions

from delivery payments, and the CO must specify the liquidation rate or designated dollar amount in the contract. Whatever the method of liquidation, complete liquidation must occur no later than final payment under a contract.

In accordance with FAR 32.1004 (d)(1)(2), the CO may use the following methods of liquidation:

- For payments established on a *total contract amount*, payment is liquidated according to predesignated liquidation amounts or liquidation percentages

- For payments established on a *delivery item basis*, the liquidation amount for each line item is the percent of that delivery item price that was previously paid under performance-based finance payments, or the designated dollar amount.

430.   What information must a voucher include?

All vouchers must support whether or not costs are allowable in accordance with certain allowability factors listed below. These costs are subject to a determination of allowability by audit under:

- Government cost principles
- Applicable cost accounting standards (CAS)
- Agreement by the contractor and the government
- Advanced agreements or some form of contract management procedures.

431.   What are cost allowability factors?

Factors for determining whether a cost is allowable include the following:

- *Reasonableness.* A cost is reasonable if, in its nature and amount, it does not exceed that which would be incurred by a prudent person in the conduct of competitive business.
- *Allocability.* A cost is allocable if it is assignable or chargeable to one or more cost objectives on the basis of relative benefits received or other equitable relationship, as defined by the contractor's accounting system, in accordance with FAR Part 31 or generally accepted accounting principles (GAAP).
- *Standards* promulgated by the Cost Accounting Standards Board, if applicable; otherwise, generally accepted accounting principles and practices appropriate to the particular circumstances apply.
- *Terms* of the contract.
- *Any other cost limitations* as set forth in government guidelines for cost principles.

432.   What is the COR's role if there are differences between the submitted invoice and the amount the government will pay?

If there are differences between the amount of the submitted invoice and the amount that the government proposes to pay, the COR must notify the contractor. The government must accurately present all factual data that justify the difference, and the contractor should be provided an opportunity to present its position.

Reasons for a difference between the invoiced amount and the actual amount paid may include:

- Performance problems
- Unallowable costs
- Defective products or inferior service
- Delivery problems.

433. What should the COR do if the contractor disagrees with the amount the government proposes to pay?

If a contractor disagrees with the calculated amount, the COR should notify the CO, who will make a final determination. Once the amount to be paid is agreed to by both the government and the contractor, the COR will submit the correct invoice to the paying office for payment within the time specified in the contract.

EXHIBIT 7-1.   Checklist: Is This Delay Excusable?

A Contractor Delay Assessment Tool

The following checklist will assist you, the COR, in evaluating whether or not contractor delays are excusable. You must rely upon your knowledge of how the contract was executed and consider any additional information that may affect your determination of whether a contractor delay was excusable. Before making a final decision, you must be certain that the contractor had no control over the circumstances that caused the delay. If you can answer "Yes" to any of the following questions, the delay was probably excusable. *Please check the response that most accurately describes your assessment of each statement listed below.*

1. **Was the delay caused by a labor strike?**   ☐ Yes   ☐ No

   If NO, go to Question #2.

   If YES, did the contractor:

File a charge with the appropriate labor relations board to seek injunctive relief in the court?	☐ Yes	☐ No	☐ N/A
Use other available government procedures or seek the assistance of private boards or organizations in an attempt to settle or arbitrate disputes that caused the strike?	☐ Yes	☐ No	☐ N/A

2. **Did government interference or disruption cause the delay?**   ☐ Yes   ☐ No

   If NO, go to Question #3.

   If YES, did the government:

Delay in making payments due the contractor?	☐ Yes	☐ No	☐ N/A
Deliver government-furnished property late?	☐ Yes	☐ No	☐ N/A
Fail to reply to the contractor's request for clarification?	☐ Yes	☐ No	☐ N/A
Fail to disclose all of the facts applicable to performance?	☐ Yes	☐ No	☐ N/A
Misrepresent working conditions?	☐ Yes	☐ No	☐ N/A
Experience scarcity of supplies due to Defense Production Act priorities being placed before commercial or non-rated orders?	☐ Yes	☐ No	☐ N/A
Delay issuing a required notice to proceed?	☐ Yes	☐ No	☐ N/A
Delay issuing changes?	☐ Yes	☐ No	☐ N/A
Delay performance by other government contractors?	☐ Yes	☐ No	☐ N/A
Experience delays because of an interested party protesting the contract award?	☐ Yes	☐ No	☐ N/A
Delay making the site available?	☐ Yes	☐ No	☐ N/A
Delay providing funding?	☐ Yes	☐ No	☐ N/A

Delay inspection or acceptance?	☐ Yes	☐ No	☐ N/A
Delay because of defective or ambiguous specifications?	☐ Yes	☐ No	☐ N/A
Delay granting approvals?	☐ Yes	☐ No	☐ N/A

3. **Did a subcontractor cause the delay?**   ☐ **Yes** ☐ **No**

   If NO, go to Question #4.

   The delay cannot be excused if either of the following occurred:

Did a dispute between the subcontractor and prime cause the delay?	☐ Yes	☐ No	☐ N/A
Were subcontracted products or services available from other sources in time for the prime to complete performance?	☐ Yes	☐ No	☐ N/A

4. **Was the delay caused by any other occurrence specifically characterized as generally excusable in a default contract clause, excusable delays clause, or other clauses?**
                                                                                     ☐ **Yes** ☐ **No**

   If NO, go to Question #5.

   If YES, was the delay caused by:

Acts of the government in either its sovereign or contractual capacity?	☐ Yes	☐ No	☐ N/A
Acts of God or of the public enemy?	☐ Yes	☐ No	☐ N/A
Fire?	☐ Yes	☐ No	☐ N/A
Flood?	☐ Yes	☐ No	☐ N/A
Unusually severe weather?	☐ Yes	☐ No	☐ N/A
Epidemics?	☐ Yes	☐ No	☐ N/A
Quarantine restrictions?	☐ Yes	☐ No	☐ N/A
Labor dispute resulting in strikes?	☐ Yes	☐ No	☐ N/A
Freight embargoes?	☐ Yes	☐ No	☐ N/A
Common carrier delays?	☐ Yes	☐ No	☐ N/A

5. **Was the delay caused by other circumstances not previously mentioned?** ☐ **Yes** ☐ **No**

   If YES, did the contractor:

Not cause the delay?	☐ Yes	☐ No	☐ N/A
Not have any control over the circumstances that caused the delay?	☐ Yes	☐ No	☐ N/A

EXHIBIT 7-2. Examples of Recoverable Expenses Following a Delay

Possible Contractor Expenses	Government Verification Review
Idle time of facilities or equipment	Idleness of rental equipment is not normally a recoverable expense because the equipment can be returned to the rental agency. However, if the contractor can show that it is less expensive to continue renting, these costs are recoverable.
Increase in material prices	The contractor should support these price increases with invoices or letters substantiating the price increases.
Increase in wages	These costs can normally be verified by: • Consulting local labor union officials • Interviewing contractor personnel • Examining payroll records in an audit.
Loss of efficiency	When the contractor has been forced to work out of sequence, that is, in a poorly organized, inefficient manner, rather than according to the originally scheduled sequence of work, learning curve efficiencies will be lost. Note that the loss of efficiency is the most difficult expense to document, although it is also one of the most common delay and disruption costs.
Unusually severe weather	Conditions of unusually adverse weather can be *weather conditions* verified by U. S. Weather Service reports for the affected period. These reports can be compared with those from the original period of performance to verify the degree or extent of unusual weather conditions that could have contributed to the delay. To be recoverable, the conditions being claimed by the contractor would have to be "unusual" relative to the conditions of the original period.
Insurance and bond coverage	If the contractor extended this coverage for the period of the delay, and would not have otherwise done so, a notice from the bonding or insurance company for the amount of the increased premium should be provided.
Protection or storage of materials	These must be actual additional costs. Examples are rehandling and transportation costs necessary to protect or provide alternate storage for materials due to the delay.
Additional make-ready costs	If a production run was interrupted, there will be additional costs for restarting the production line.
Demobilizing and mobilizing the workforce	If the contractor laid off personnel during the delay, there may be administrative rehiring costs. If the delay was long, and the contractor is unable to rehire part of the original workforce, recruitment advertising and employment fees to recruitment agencies may be included within these costs.
Interest	Interest on funds necessary to finance the extended performance time caused by the delay is recoverable.

EXHIBIT 7-3. Decision Table for Selecting a Contract Remedy

Problem	Options	Comments
Late delivery. (The CO has determined that the deliverable has been or will be delivered late and that the delay is non-excusable.)	Reschedule the delivery date in exchange for *consideration* (i.e., something of value in return from the contractor).	Appropriate when (1) no liquidated damages clause was included in the original contract, (2) there is a reasonable probability of delivery by the new delivery date, and (3) the requiring activity can accept the new date.
	Reduce or suspend progress payments under FAR 52.232-16(c)(2). For advance payments, see FAR 52.232.12(k).	Appropriate when (1) progress payments are being made and (2) performance of the contract is endangered by the contractor's failure to make progress.
	Accept late delivery and impose liquidated damages.	Appropriate when (1) the contract provides for liquidated damages and (2) there is a reasonable probability of delivery by a date the requiring activity can accept.
	Send a cure notice (ten days or more prior to the contract's delivery date) or a show cause notice (immediately upon expiration of the delivery period).	Appropriate when there is little probability of delivery by a date that the requiring activity can accept, or the contractor has not offered adequate consideration.
The deliverable has not been accepted and does not conform to the contract's requirements. (The CO has determined that the deliverable has not been implicitly or explicitly accepted and does not conform to the contract's requirements.)	Accept the deliverable without consideration.	Appropriate when the nonconformance is minor and obtaining consideration is not in the government's interests (see FAR 46.407(f)).
	Accept the deliverable in exchange for consideration.	Appropriate when the requiring activity can tolerate non-conformance (see FAR 46.407(c)).
	Accept the deliverable and invoke a warranty to have the deliverable improved to meet specifications after acceptance.	Appropriate when there is an express or implied warranty and immediate acceptance will benefit the requiring activity.
	Reject the deliverable and obtain correction or replacement at no cost to the government. Tell the payment office to withhold payment until an acceptable deliverable has been furnished.	Appropriate when there is a reasonable expectation that a satisfactory replacement will be provided by the delivery date in the contract, or for consideration, within a reasonable time thereafter.
	Reject the deliverable and send a cure or show cause notice.	Appropriate when there is little expectation of receiving an acceptable product within a reasonable time.

The deliverable has been accepted but does not conform to the contract's requirements. (The CO has determined that the government has a reasonably strong case for revoking acceptance based on the terms and conditions of the contract.)	Invoke an express warranty.	Appropriate if an express warranty applies.
	Invoke an implied warranty.	Appropriate if an implied warranty applies.
	Demand that the deliverable be replaced or corrected or that the price be adjusted downward.	Appropriate if there is a latent defect in the deliverable or if acceptance was based on fraud or gross mistake.
Other breaches. (The CO has exhausted all efforts at informal resolution of the problem.)	Invoke whatever remedy (if any) is established in the applicable clause.	Possible solutions for contractor breaches:
	Suspend or reduce progress payments under FAR 52.232-16(c)(2). For advance payments, see FAR 52.232.12(k).	• Liquidated damages (per FAR 52.219-16) for failing to comply with the subcontracting plan • Liquidated damages and withholding for unpaid wages (under FAR 52.222-4, "Contracting Work Hours and Safety Standards ActOvertime Compensation") • Cancellation, suspension, or termination of the contract (under FAR 52.222-26, "Equal Opportunity") • Withholding of payments and contract termination (under FAR 52.222-41, "Service Contract Act of 1965, As Amended") • Suspension of contract payments, termination for default, and suspension or debasement (under FAR 52.223-6, "Drug-Free Workplace").
	Send a cure notice 10 days or more prior to the contract's delivery date.	Appropriate when the breach is of sufficient magnitude to warrant termination for default.

CHAPTER 8

Contract Termination and Closeout

This chapter covers the COR's activities at the end of a contract. Most contracts are completed through normal completion and closeout procedures; however, sometimes the government finds it necessary to terminate a contract for various reasons. The two types of termination are *termination for convenience* and *termination for default* (or *cause*).

No matter which type of termination the government employs, the COR's role is essential. The COR, as the primary government monitor of contract performance, is likely to be the first person aware of the need to consider termination of the contract. Because the COR functions as the government team's technical expert, he or she is also the most likely person to advise the CO about termination or alternatives to termination, depending on the circumstances.

This chapter discusses the termination of noncommercial versus commercial item contracts; it also offers guidance regarding cure notices and show cause notices. The second half of the chapter deals with closeout of the contract. The COR plays a vital role in the closeout procedure. Physical completion of the contract must be affirmed by the COR, and the COR must ensure that final payment should be, and has been, made to the contractor. The COR files must be forwarded to the CO for inclusion in the official closeout file for the contract.

TERMINATION

Termination of a contract is an extremely serious step. It is serious for the contractor, whose business reputation or profits may be diminished, and for the government, because either the desired project has not proceeded as expected or the timeliness of the project has been, or will be, adversely impacted. For these reasons, termination is *not* a desirable action to take to resolve a contracting problem.

434. What are the principles of contract termination?

These principles must be followed if the government is considering terminating a contract:

- Only the CO has the authority to terminate a contract.
- The COR may not terminate a contract or imply that termination action will be taken.
- The contractor has the right to appeal termination.
- The COR must document all performance monitoring, with particular attention to those activities that support the government's position (i. e., those areas in which performance was weak, thus causing the government to consider termination).

435. What is the preferred method of contract termination?

The preferred method of contract termination is to effect a *no-cost settlement* without using formal termination procedures.

A contract can be terminated through a no-cost settlement only if:

- The contractor has not incurred costs for the terminated portion of the contract or
- The contractor is willing to waive the costs incurred
  and
- No amounts are due the government under the contract.

As with any type of termination, the no-cost settlement may be *complete* (i.e., the contract is entirely terminated) or *partial* (i.e., only a portion of the contract is terminated). FAR 49.603-6 prescribes a no-cost settlement agreement to be used for a complete termination:

49.603-6: No-cost settlement agreement, complete termination:

[Insert the following in Block 14 of the SF 30 if a no-cost settlement agreement, under a complete termination, is to be executed.]

(a) This supplemental agreement [insert "modifies the contract to reflect a no-cost settlement agreement with respect to the Notice of Termination dated ...." or, if not previously terminated, "terminates the contract in its entirety"].

(b) The parties agree as follows:

The contractor unconditionally waives any charges against the government because of the termination of the contract and, except as set forth below, releases it from all obligations under the contract or due to its termination. The government agrees that all obligations under the contract are concluded, except as follows:

[List reserved or excepted rights and liabilities. See 49.109-2 and 49.603-1(b)(7).] (End of agreement)

FAR 49.603-7 provides a similar agreement for partial no-cost settlements.

436. What are the government's rights with regard to contract termination?

The government has the inherent right to terminate entire contracts or, occasionally, portions of contracts (partial termination) for the government's convenience or because of contractor default. The CO is authorized to terminate contracts in accordance with standard contract termination clauses, which are required to appear in all government contracts. However, even though termination might be possible in a particular case, COs should terminate *only* when termination is in the *best interest* of the government.

Termination for Convenience and Termination for Default

437. What is termination for convenience, and when does it occur?

Termination for convenience occurs when the government requires the contractor to discontinue performance when a determination is made that completion of the work is no longer in its best interest. The government has the right to terminate without cause and to limit the contractor's recovery to:

• Costs incurred

- The profit on work done

  and

- The cost of preparing a termination settlement proposal.

The recovery of anticipated profit is precluded when a contract is terminated for convenience.

Termination for convenience should be considered when:

- Funds are insufficient to pay the full contract price
- The requirement is no longer needed
- The quantity of supplies or services needed has been reduced

  or

- There has been a radical change in the requirement, and the requirement is now beyond the contractor's expertise.

438.   What is a termination for default (or cause), and when does it occur?

Termination for default (or *cause*) occurs when the contractor fails to perform in accordance with the contract. The government should terminate a contract only when termination is in its best interest. A contract is terminated for default (or cause) when there is no other alternative for obtaining performance, given the current contractor's problems and deficiencies, and the government has a sustainable case for default termination.

The word *default* is traditionally used in government contracting for *noncommercial item contracts* in accordance with FAR Part 49.

Default is defined as "failure to discharge a duty,"[1] referring in this case to the contractor's failure to perform the *noncommercial* contract and the resultant termination of the contract by the government.

The word *cause* is normally used when terminating a *commercial item contract* in accordance with FAR Part 12. *Cause* is defined as "that which effects a result,"[2] referring in this case to the contractor's failure to perform the *commercial* contract and the resultant termination of the contract by the government.

---

[1] Steven H. Gifis, *Barron's Dictionary of Legal Terms*, 3rd ed. (Hauppauge, NY: Barron's Educational Services, Inc., 1998), p. 124.

[2] Ibid., p. 64.

439. What is a wrongful termination for default?

A *wrongful termination for default* occurs whenever a contract is improperly terminated for default. An improper termination may occur when there is an excusable delay or if proper notice of a possible termination is not given to the contractor. Such termination is converted to a termination for convenience, and the contractor can recover cost and profit on the work completed as of the effective date of termination.

440. What is forbearance?

Forbearance means the withholding of a default termination while the government decides whether or not to terminate a contract. Failure to terminate immediately does not necessarily waive the government's right to terminate. The government is allowed a period of time to investigate the facts and determine what course of action is in the best interest of the government. This period of time, however, must be reasonable, because the government's inaction can be considered by a court to constitute a waiver of the right to terminate if the time period is unreasonably long. There is no established time period that is considered reasonable for all cases; the length of time considered reasonable will depend on the facts and circumstances of each situation as judged by the court or a board of contract appeals.

441. What is a waiver in the case of a termination?

To *waive* means to intentionally relinquish a right. If the government does not exercise its right to terminate for default within a reasonable amount of time after default, it will have waived that right. To take advantage of the government's waiver, the contractor must show that it was adversely affected by relying on the government's inaction. Once the government has waived its right to terminate for default, it must establish a new delivery schedule. If the contractor and the government cannot agree on a new schedule, the government may establish a new one unilaterally. Under that new schedule, the contractor must be given a reasonable time to make delivery.

A classic example of a waiver is one in which the government encourages continued performance after the initial delivery date. An important criterion of a waiver is the government's willingness, either express or implied, to accept the contractor's continued performance.

Why Terminate a Contract?

442. What are the main reasons the government may choose to discontinue a contract?

CORs should be aware that the government might need to discontinue the contract and terminate for convenience when:

- There is no longer a need for the item or service called for under the contract
- Funds are not available for continued contract performance
- It is impossible for the contractor to perform as specified in the contract (i.e., according to contract terms defining specifications, acceptance, or delivery methods)
- There has been a radical change in the requirement that goes beyond the contractor's expertise.

A termination for default (or cause) may be triggered by events such as:

- The contractor fails to perform as required by the contract
- The contractor's response to the government's cure notice or show cause notice fails to show that the contract will be completed in accordance with its terms.

The COR may use a default questionnaire to determine whether a contract should be terminated for default (see Figure 8-1).

Occasionally there may be evidence or rumors that a contractor is in "financial trouble." Warnings of the contractor's impending bankruptcy or financial difficulties sometimes go hand-in-hand with a delinquent contract. The COR should be aware of the following signs of a contractor's financial problems:

- The contractor fails to pay subcontractors on time.
- Late deliveries of materials to the job site are being made, and deliveries are usually brought in on a C.O.D. basis.
- The contractor is falling behind schedule.
- Laborers on the job make complaints about late wage payments or lack of pay increases.
- Telephone calls to the contractor go unanswered.
- Sloppy performance and workmanship are evident.

Circumstance	Validating Questions
Issues regarding terms and conditions of the contract and applicable laws and regulations	• Was there a breach of contract? • Do the facts support a finding that the contractor has breached the contract? • Does the breach merit the severe remedy of default? • Has the government met procedural requirements for proceeding with a default termination notice (i.e., has it issued any required notices)? • Has the decision to default been made based solely on the facts of the situation directly related to the contract (i.e., free of outside influence)? • Has the requiring activity proposed any change in the material requirement for the repurchase, which would thereby undermine the government's case for a default termination? (A new requirement by the government would dictate that the current contract be terminated for the government's convenience, as opposed to the contractor's default.)

Mitigating circumstances	• Does the contractor have a good case that it is not at fault, based on such grounds as:
	  – Impossibility of performance
	  – An excusable delay
	  – A breach of contract by the government?
	• Does the contractor have a good case for contending that default would be arbitrary, capricious, or retaliatory?

Impact on the requirement if the contractor is terminated for default	• Have alternatives to termination for default been considered? • Is there any reasonable probability of meeting the requirement by continuing to work with the present contractor? If so, how much additional time and funding would be needed to continue working with the present contractor? • Is the deliverable available from other sources and, if so, what would be the procurement lead-time? • What is the urgency of the need for the deliverable? • What is the potential for recovering the government's current investment in the contractor (e.g., any government-guaranteed loan(s), unliquidated progress payments, or advance payments) and repurchase costs? • Can the contractor afford to repay the government or would it go bankrupt?
Impact on other requirements	• Is the contractor essential to other critical work of the government? • Will the contractor be able to meet other critical government requirements if it is terminated for default on the contract?

FIGURE 8-1. Questionnaire for Determining Whether to Terminate for Default

Noncommercial and Commercial Contract Terminations

443. What are the differences between noncommercial and commercial contract terminations?

Termination of noncommercial item contracts is addressed in FAR Part 49 and applicable clauses in the contract. Commercial item contract termination procedures are contained in FAR Part 12 and applicable clauses, but Part 49 is still used as guidance for instances in which it does not conflict with Part 12.

Noncommercial Contract Terminations

444. How are terminations of noncommercial contracts conducted?

The right of the government to terminate a contract when its completion is no longer in the government's best interest has long been recognized. Noncommercial contracts may be terminated either for convenience or for default.

This right has been the subject of many court decisions and boards of contract appeals decisions. The government has the right to terminate *without cause* and to limit the contractor's recovery (e.g., recovery of anticipated profit is *not* allowed) in a negotiated settlement (i.e., the contractor is allotted allowable costs, profit, and other considerations in the judgment of the CO). The settlement should compensate the contractor *fairly* for the work done and the preparations made for the terminated portion of the contract. Fair compensation is a matter of judgment and cannot be measured exactly.

The use of business judgment by the CO—as opposed to adherence to strict accounting principles—lies at the heart of a settlement. Cost and accounting data may provide guidance, but should not be used as rigid measures of whether settlement is appropriate in a given situation. In fact, in appropriate cases, costs may be estimated and differences and questions settled by agreement.

Termination for convenience:

- May be imposed at any time when termination is in the best interest of the government

- Is a government right that provides flexibility to the government in the procurement process
- Involves no fault or negligence on the part of the contractor
- May be total or partial
- Permits the contractor to propose an amount of compensation that it considers reasonable for accepted work up to the time of termination, costs for work completed plus a reasonable profit, and termination settlement costs. The final settlement amount is subject to negotiation by the CO.

In addition to termination for convenience, the government is also entitled to terminate a contract due to inadequate contractor performance. Such *terminations for default* stem from the government's contractual right to terminate a contract when the contractor is failing to perform its obligations under the contract, usually amounting to a breach of the contract. The breach may be either *actual* (a currently existing failure to perform the contract) or *anticipatory* (a potential failure to perform the contract, e.g., failure to make progress as related to the contract schedule). A contract may be terminated for default when the contractor does *any one* of the following:

- Fails to deliver the supplies or perform the services within the time specified in the contract or within the time limit specified in an extension
- Fails to make progress, so as to endanger performance of the contract
- Fails to perform any other contractual provision.

Figure 8-2 presents additional factors to consider before terminating for default.

Commercial Contract Terminations

445. How are terminations conducted under commercial contracts?

Commercial contracts may be terminated for *convenience* or for *cause*.

The Federal Acquisition Streamlining Act (FASA) of 1994 established a government-wide preference that government contracts acquire commercial items whenever possible. The procedures for terminating commercial item contracts are contained in FAR Part 12.

The CO and COR may consider the following questions to help them make a default termination decision:
- What are the applicable contract clauses, terms, conditions, and regulations?
- What is the nature and severity of the performance problem or violation?
- Does the contractor's failure warrant the severe remedy of default termination?
- Can the contractor present evidence that it is not at fault?
- Is performance impossible?
- Is there an excusable delay?
- Is there any breach on the part of the government?
- What is the impact on the government's requirement if the contract is terminated?
- Were alternatives to default termination considered?
- What is the probability that the requirement will be met if work continues with the present contractor?
- How much additional time is needed to complete the contract with the present contractor?
- What additional funding is needed to complete the contract?
- Is the product or service available from other sources?
- Is the need for supplies or services urgent?
- Can the contractor pay costs identified without going bankrupt?
- What is the contractor's level of participation in the government's acquisition program?
- What effect would the default termination have on the contractor's capability for additional work?

FIGURE 8-2. Factors to Consider before Terminating a Contract for Default

The need to terminate a commercial item contract for convenience is no different from that associated with noncommercial item contracts; for example, a commercial item contract can be terminated when the government no longer requires the item. The difference between termination of a noncommercial item contract and a commercial item contract lies in the applicable settlement procedures. When a CO terminates a commercial item contract for convenience, the government must pay:

- A percentage of the contract price, reflecting the percentage of work performed prior to the notice of termination

  and

- Any costs that the contractor can demonstrate resulted from the termination (e.g., restocking fees charged by a supplier when the contractor returned purchased parts). The contractor may use its standard record-keeping system to demonstrate such costs.

Under commercial item contracts (unlike noncommercial item contracts), the government cannot require the contractor to comply with the cost accounting standards or the contract cost principles outlined in FAR Part 31, nor does the termination for convenience automatically give the government a right to audit the contractor's records. However, the government will not pay for any work or costs incurred that the contractor reasonably could have avoided.

The government may terminate a contract for cause in the event of any default by the contractor, or if the contractor fails to comply with any contract terms and conditions or fails to provide the government, upon request, with adequate assurance of future performance. These causes are essentially identical to the three causes found in the FAR Part 49 default clause.

When an "excusable delay" occurs, the contractor must notify the CO as soon as possible after its occurrence. One possible remedy for an excusable delay is for the CO to issue a modification to the delivery schedule. Show cause letters are not necessary in these cases, as the contractor is responsible for notifying the government of any delay or disruption of the delivery schedule. However, cure notices are required prior to terminating a contractor for any reason other than late delivery.

In the event of a termination for cause, it is crucial that the contractor assure the government that the contractor will afford the government all remedies available to any buyer in the commercial marketplace. When a termination for cause is effected, the government's preferred remedy is to acquire similar items from another contractor and to charge the defaulting contractor with any excess costs associated with the repurchase (e.g., if the price of the items has increased), together with any incidental or consequential damages related to the termination.

Delinquency Notices

446. What is a delinquency notice?

A *delinquency notice* is a written notice from the CO to the contractor to inform the contractor of problems with contract performance as perceived by the government. The CO may also issue a delinquency notice to determine whether delays in contract performance are excusable. FAR Part 49 provides the format for two notices, the cure notice and the show cause notice. These notices are also required by the FAR to be sent with proof of delivery requested, to document the government's action in the event of legal proceedings resulting from the contract termination.

COs will issue cure notices or show cause notices prior to terminating a contract. Generally, a cure notice is used for "action," for example, to request that the contractor advise how it plans to remedy a problem that is causing its failure to progress. A show case notice is generally used for "information, for example, to determine if the contractor has an excusable delay that justifies its problem.

447. What is a cure notice?

A *cure notice* is used if the contractor fails to make progress or fails to perform any other provision of the contract. A cure notice should *not* be sent if delivery is late, because late delivery by itself is cause for a default termination.

The cure notice informs the contractor of the specific failure and gives the contractor an opportunity to cure the defect within 10 days (or any longer period of time the CO may consider reasonably necessary). There must be sufficient time remaining in the contract performance period for the contractor to cure or fix the deficiency within ten days or within the period specified by the CO.

The contract may not be terminated for default until this "cure period" expires.

At a minimum, a cure notice must:

- Be in writing
- Specifically state the failure the CO believes is endangering performance and
- Allow the contractor at least ten days to "cure" the failure.

A cure notice does not require a written reply; rather, it requires action by the contractor to cure the condition. However, the contractor may respond to a cure notice by specifying the progress already made and the steps taken to ensure that contract performance will be on schedule. The contractor may also identify any failures on the government's part and any excusable delays that have contributed to the lack of progress. If the contractor fails to cure the condition endangering contract performance, the CO will ordinarily issue a show cause notice.

448. What is a show cause notice?

A *show cause notice* is used when the contractor has failed to deliver the required supplies or to perform services on time, and the government must ascertain whether the delay was excusable. The show cause notice is *not* required when terminating commercial item contracts. If the contractor fails to deliver the supplies or perform the services within the amount of time specified in the contract or any extension of that time, the CO should send a show cause notice asking the contractor to show why the contract should not be terminated for default. A show cause notice should be sent immediately upon expiration of the delivery period.

The show cause notice ensures that the contractor understands the severity of the situation. The contractor's response to the notice is used to evaluate whether circumstances justify default termination. A show cause notice is generally not mandatory, but it is advisable: Consider what would happen if the government were to terminate a contract for default without giving the contractor a chance to show cause, and an excusable delay actually existed. The default termination could be invalidated and turned into a termination for convenience, and the government would be liable not only for the contractor's costs of performance to date but also its anticipated profit.

At a minimum, a show cause notice must:

- Inform the contractor of its liabilities in the event of default termination
- Request that the contractor "show cause," in writing, why the contact should not be terminated for default
- Inform the contractor that failure to explain the cause of the deficiency may be taken as admission that no valid explanation or excuse exists.

449. What are excusable delays?

A contract cannot be terminated for default if the contractor has an excusable delay. Examples of *excusable delays* include:

- Acts of God or of the public enemy (e.g., terrorism)
- Acts of the government (sovereign or contractual)
- Fires
- Floods
- Epidemics

- Quarantine restrictions
- Strikes
- Freight embargoes
- Unusually severe weather.

In each instance the failure to perform must be beyond the control of and without the fault or negligence of the contractor. In most cases, the CO will need to rely on the COR to investigate and gather facts related to the contractor's excuse to determine its validity.

Termination and the COR's and Contractor's Duties

450. What is the COR's role in a contract termination action?

The COR has a key role in any potential or actual termination action. The COR is the individual responsible for documenting circumstances that may lead to the need to terminate the contract.

If a situation arises that could lead to a termination action, it is the responsibility of the COR to notify the CO in a timely manner. This duty is completed successfully when the COR identifies termination situations and procedures and can recommend a termination for convenience or a termination for default (or cause) when necessary. In the event of a possible termination, the COR should:

1. Identify the event(s) that have led to consideration of termination of the contract
2. Notify the CO of the possible need to terminate
3. Assist the CO with termination proceedings.

451. What are the contractor's duties upon receiving a termination notice?

Upon receipt of a termination notice, whether for convenience or for default, the contractor must comply with the following requirements:

- Stop work immediately on the terminated portion of the contract and stop placing subcontracts.
- Terminate all subcontract work related to the terminated portion of the prime contract.

- Immediately advise the government of any special circumstances preventing work stoppage.

- Perform the portion of the contract that is to be continued and promptly submit any request for an *equitable adjustment* (a price adjustment "marked by due consideration for what is fair and impartial, unhampered by technical rules the law may have devised that limit recovery or defense"[3]) for this continuing portion.

- Take action to protect and preserve property in the contractor's possession that the government has or may acquire an interest in, and deliver the property to the government.

- Promptly notify the government in writing of any legal proceedings arising from any subcontract or other commitment related to the terminated portion of the contract.

- Settle outstanding liabilities and proposals from terminated subcontracts and obtain approvals required by the government.

- Submit a settlement proposal within one year of termination. (If the termination is partial, the contractor may submit a request for equitable adjustment to the government for repricing the unchanged portion of the contract to reflect, for example, new quantities or delivery schedules.)

- Dispose of termination inventory as directed or authorized by the CO.

The COR can assist in making sure the contractor fulfills these responsibilities by communicating the status of these activities to the CO.

Notification of Contract Termination

452. What should be included in the COR's notification to the CO of possible contract termination?

The COR should notify the CO when conditions indicate a contract may need to be terminated. The notification should document:

- Clause(s) of the contract affected by the possible termination

---

[3] Steven H. Gifis, *Barron's Dictionary of Legal Terms*, 3rd ed. (Hauppauge, NY: Barron's Educational Services, Inc., 1998), p. 159.

- The specific failure of the contractor and reasons provided by the contractor for such failure
- The availability of supplies or services from other sources
- The urgency of the government's need and the period of time that would be required for work by other sources, as compared with the time in which completion could be obtained from the delinquent contractor
- The degree of indispensability of the contractor (i.e., consideration of the contractor's unique capabilities)
- The impact the termination would have on the availability of funds
- Any other pertinent facts and circumstances.

453. **What kind of analysis or recommendations should the COR provide to the CO?**

In addition to providing the CO with notification of possible termination, the COR should suggest available alternatives to terminating a contract, indicating the advantages and disadvantages of each alternative. The suggested alternatives should have the least possible impact on the government's requirements (per the instant contract and future contracts), delivery schedule, and overall cost.

454. **What are some available alternatives to termination the CO and COR may consider?**

The CO is not compelled to terminate a contract simply because he or she was asked to do so by the program or project office. Alternatives to termination may include:

- *Continuing the present contract* through such means as:
  - Permitting performance by the contractor, a *surety* ("one who undertakes to perform other acts in the event that his or her principal fails therein"[4]), or a *guarantor* ("one who makes a guaranty, i.e., a promise to be responsible for the default of another"[5]) under a revised delivery schedule

---

[4] Steven H. Gifis, *Barron's Dictionary of Legal Terms*, 3rd ed. (Hauppauge, NY: Barron's Educational Services, Inc., 1998), p. 485.

[5] Ibid., p. 210.

- Allowing the contractor to continue with *consideration* (i.e., something of value given to the government by the contractor in return for the government not exercising its right to terminate the contract)
- Forbearing or postponing termination action
- Permitting the contractor to subcontract with an acceptable third party.

• A *no-cost cancellation* when:
  - The government can obtain the supply or service elsewhere
  - A no-cost settlement is acceptable to the contractor
  - Government property had not been furnished to the contractor
  - There are no outstanding payments, debts due the government, or other contractor obligations.

• *Termination for convenience* if:
  - The requirement is no longer necessary
  - The requirement could be more cost-effectively met by reprocuring it from another source
  - There is no sustainable case for default.

Termination Proceedings

455. What is the COR's role in assisting the CO with termination proceedings?

Termination proceedings may involve meetings, discussions, and conference calls between the contractor and the government. The COR may be asked to assist the CO in preparing for these proceedings by providing documentation supporting the termination decision and by coordinating information related to the termination.

456. What information might be included with the termination decision?

Termination documentation may include the following information:

• The reasons for terminating the contract
• General principles related to the conclusions and agreements reached on any aspects of the settlement proposal submitted by the contractor

(i.e., the CO's judgments or discretionary decisions during negotiation of the settlement), including the contractor's obligations under the termination settlement

- The extent of the termination, the point at which work will be stopped, and the status of any plans, drawings, and data that would have been delivered had the contract been completed
- The status of any continuing work
- The obligation of the contractor to terminate subcontracts and general principles to be followed in settling subcontractor settlement proposals
- The names of subcontractors involved and dates that the termination notices were issued to them
- The names of contractor personnel handling the review and settlement of subcontractor settlement proposals and the methods being used to do so
- Arrangements for the transfer of title and delivery to the government of any material required by the government.

CLOSEOUT

457. When may final payment be made to a contractor?

Even though a contract may have expired, final payment may not be made until the government verifies that the contractor has:

- Fulfilled the terms of the contract
- Resolved all issues concerning government property
- Registered with the government all inventions conceived under the contract
- Submitted all necessary reports (e.g., technical or progress reports) to the government
- Received final technical acceptance

  and
- Submitted all necessary financial information.

458. What is the purpose of contract closeout?

The closeout process verifies that the above conditions have been fulfilled after the contract expires. Once all conditions are met, final payment can be made and the contract closed out. The contract is then physically retired—it is boxed and either stored locally or shipped to a federal records storage facility.

459. When is a contract considered closed?

The contract is considered physically complete and is closed only when one of two events has occurred:

- All required supplies or services have been delivered or performed, inspected, and accepted; all administrative tasks have been finalized; and all existing options periods have expired

  or

- Notice has been issued to the contractor that the contract termination has been completed.

460. What must be done to close out a contract?

The office administering the contract is responsible for initiating automated or manual administrative closeout of the contract after receiving evidence of its physical completion. A review of the funds under the contract is carried out by the COR and the contract specialist administering the contract in coordination with the budget office; where appropriate, excess funds are identified to the CO.

461. What is the COR's role in contract closeout?

The COR should:

- Verify that the contractor has fulfilled the terms of the contract
- Initiate *deobligation action* (i.e., coordinate with the budget office to recoup excess funds if appropriate, or secure additional funding if required)
- Assist in *property certification action* (i.e., perform an inventory and verify that all government property has been returned to the government or otherwise disposed of as required by the contract).

The COR's duty is completed successfully when the contractor and government have fulfilled their obligations in a timely manner, all outstanding contract administration issues have been resolved, and all records are properly stored in accordance with record retention requirements specified by the FAR or the particular contract.

462. What should the COR do with his or her files upon closeout?

Upon completion of the contract, including the making of final payment, the COR should return the COR files to the CO to be retired with the official contract file and kept in records storage. Failure to store the two files together has often resulted in the government's inability to deny post-contract claims for lack of supporting evidence. This is particularly troublesome if finance offices are merged during downsizing and supporting records cannot be accessed.

463. What does the COR do to close out the contract file?

CORs are required to close out the *contract file*, which is used to document actions taken under the contract. The COR is responsible for documenting that the contract file is physically complete. Some agencies provide a checklist or other forms for this purpose. At a minimum, a closing memorandum to the file should be prepared and signed by the COR. All files, correspondence, and other documents pertaining to the contract should then be forwarded to the CO for inclusion in the contract administration file. There are three steps the COR should take when closing out a contract file:

1. Identify any outstanding claims or disputes.
2. Identify and recommend deobligation of excess funds.
3. Verify the return or disposition of government property.

1. *Identifying any outstanding claims or disputes*

   The COR should be aware that a contractor may raise issues after a contract closeout action is taken. To avoid having to reopen a contract file that has been closed, some agencies make it a standard practice to request a release of claims from a contractor as a condition of final payment. If this release is required, the CO may request that the COR document the release in the contract administration file.

   See Figure 8-3 for an example of a release of claim form.

2. *Identifying and recommending deobligation of excess funds*

   An *obligation* of funds is defined as a monetary liability of the government that results from the award of a contract by a CO. The COR should identify any funds remaining on a contract. If there is no known potential for the funds to be used in the future on the contract, a

To: Reference	*(contractor name and address)*
Contract Number	*(agency)*
For	*(#)*
	(describe supplies or services required under the contract)

To expedite final payment and contract closeout, please forward the following items to my attention by _____ *(date)* :

(List only items that apply, renumbering paragraphs after deleting an item.)

1. Any outstanding reports or data items, such as technical manuals or instruction manuals, per *(reference contract line-item number or paragraph citation)*

2. Government-furnished property

3. Inventory schedules for government property

4. Contractor's release of claims *(form enclosed)*

5. Final voucher *(for cost-reimbursement types of contracts only)*

6. Other *(cite specific requirement)*.

(Use the following paragraph only if it applies.)

Under the terms of the contract, a warranty *(describe the warranty)* is still in effect. Final payment and contract closeout do not relieve you of your obligations to the government under the warranty clause.

(signed)

Contracting Officer

FIGURE 8-3. Release of Claim Form

recommendation should be made to the CO for the deobligation of the funds. To *deobligate* funds, the CO issues a bilateral modification to the contract deobligating and removing the excess funds (i.e., removing the monetary liability of the government).

During the closeout of cost-reimbursement contracts, the COR should be aware of the following:

– Audits of final indirect (overhead) rates and incurred costs by the government auditors may take years to complete. The contractor must wait until final rates are established to prepare the final invoice.

- The government must retain sufficient funds to pay the final voucher (same as a final invoice on a fixed-price contract).

- Excess funds should be deobligated if they will not be used.

The contract specialist will consult the COR for a revised estimate of cost:

- To pay for any pending claims

- To identify the amount of excess funds remaining, if any.

3. *Verifying the return or disposition of government property*

   The COR should verify and document whether the contractor has:

   - Returned or otherwise disposed of government-furnished property and

   - Properly disposed of classified material.

464. What other responsibilities might the COR have during closeout?

The COR may also be asked to:

- *Prepare a contract completion statement*

  The *contract completion statement*, which may be in the form of a memorandum, should contain the following information:

  - The CO's name and address

  - The contract administration office address (if different from the CO's address)

  - The contract number

  - The last modification number, if any

  - The last call or order number, if any

  - The contractor's name and address

  - The dollar amount of excess funds, if any

  - Invoice or voucher number and date, if final payment has been made

  - Invoice or voucher number and date, if the final approved invoice or voucher has been forwarded to a disbursing office of another agency or activity and the status of the payment is unknown

  - A statement that all required contract administration actions have been fully and satisfactorily accomplished

- The name, title, and signature of the record-keeping official
- The contract completion date.

- *Annotate the contract administration activities log*

  If the COR should need information from a closed-out contract file, he or she could contact the contract administration office that keeps a log of closed-out files. The closed-out files log should contain such information as:

  - The date the file was closed out
  - The date the file was transferred to a storage center
  - Where the file was sent for storage
  - A filing location provided by the storage facility. (It is of *vital importance* to record and safeguard the container number for stored contracts. The storage facility may not retain such information and may not be able to locate a particular contract without this number.)

Some information in contract files must be kept for a specific number of years. For example, contracts (and related records and documents, including successful proposals) exceeding the simplified acquisition threshold must be retained for six years and three months after final payment. Contracts at or below the simplified acquisition threshold must be retained for three years after final payment. Also, FAR 4.703 requires the contractor to retain contract records and documents for three years after final payment or as otherwise indicated for specific records, whichever period expires first. Other record retention requirements may stem from statutory requirements or administrative regulations as applicable.

COR Duties and Tasks

This appendix provides a listing of all of the major duties and respective tasks to be performed by the COR that are covered in this book. The 18 "units of instruction" contained in the *FAI COR Workbook* are directly related to the 20 listed duties printed in bold. The remaining 12 listed duties (printed in italics) were derived from the *FAI Contract Specialist Training Blueprints* and other references.

This appendix can be used as an index to locate specific information related to the COR's assigned responsibilities. For example, suppose a COR were assigned the responsibility of preparing a technical work package, including a purchase request, to yield the best market response in terms of competition, quality, timeliness, price, and mission needs. If the COR needed more information about developing a work package, he or she could scan the list of duties and tasks in this appendix and would find among the listed duties for Chapter 3, "Duty: Develop the work package for transmittal to the contracting office." Turning to Chapter 3 of this book, the COR would find a section titled "Developing the Work Package," which includes information related to the seven items that are to be included in the work package. The chapter text identifies the seven tasks the COR will need to perform to develop the work package and provides specific guidance and information related to the COR's assigned duties.

DUTIES AND TASKS

Chapter 1: The Contracting Officer's Representative and Contract Fundamentals

Duty: Determine the requirements for designation as a COR in a particular situation.

Tasks:

- Determine the COR training, nomination, and designation requirements of the contracting office making the designation.
- Identify the term (title) that will be used for the designated COR position.

Duty: Establish the source and extent of assigned COR authority.

Tasks:

- Identify the source of the COR's authority.
- Describe the COR's authority.
- Explain the extent of the COR's involvement and authority.

Duty: Explain the selection and designation process for a COR, and identify the elements of a COR letter of designation.

Tasks:

- Describe the COR selection criteria.
- Describe the COR designation procedure.
- Identify the elements of a letter of designation.

Duty: Be able to describe the general duties and responsibilities that may be assigned to a COR.

Tasks:

- Identify and be able to describe the general duties of a COR.
- Describe typical COR responsibilities and be able to list the major areas of contract administration that are usually assigned to CORs.

Duty: Develop an understanding of the communication and documentation duties of the COR and the importance of performing them effectively and thoroughly.

Tasks:

- Identify occurrences that require communication with the CO.
- Compare formal vs. informal communication with the contractor.
- Explain the requirements of proper technical interpretation.
- Describe the technical direction clause.
- Explain the requirements of proper documentation.

Duty: Identify the six types of contracts and the five elements of a valid contract, and describe the concepts of authority under agency law, as related to the COR.

Tasks:

- Define *contract*, be able to list the six types of contracts, and identify the elements of a valid contract.
- Explain *agency* and how it relates to the COR.

Chapter 2: The Federal Acquisition Process

Duty: Recognize and briefly describe the federal acquisition process and its goals.

Tasks:

- Clearly understand the vision and standards of performance of the federal acquisition process.
- Identify the goals of the federal acquisition process.
- Identify the phases, steps, and functions of the federal acquisition process.
- Describe the performance objectives for the COR as a member of the contracting team.

Duty: Identify ethical principles and procurement integrity requirements applicable to COR duties.

Tasks:

- Describe ethical principles that apply to the COR.
- Identify procurement integrity requirements that apply to the COR.

Chapter 3: Planning for the Acquisition

Duty: Participate in updating or preparing the acquisition plan, and provide funding coordination as necessary.

Tasks:

- Assist in identifying acquisition-related information.
- Perform market research.
- Assist in preparation of the acquisition plan.
- Coordinate funding information with the contracting office.

Duty: Develop the work package for transmittal to the contracting office.

Tasks:

- Prepare the Purchase Request (PR).
- Respond to PR deficiencies.
- Prepare the requirements document.
- Prepare a surveillance plan.
- Prepare a government cost estimate.
- Prepare evaluation factors.
- Obtain concurrence and approval for documents as required.

Duty: Recommend to the CO whether to issue government property to the contractor.

Tasks:

- Identify government property for proposed procurements.
- Notify the CO of the use of government property.

Duty: Properly prepare a requirements document to acquire contractor services, or prepare the government statement of work (SOW) under the commercial activities (CA) program.

Tasks:

- Distinguish requirements for services from requirements for supplies and assist the CO with Service Contract Act information as necessary.
- Determine whether the required services are personal or nonpersonal.
- Determine whether the services are of the advisory and assistance type.
- Determine the applicability of performance-based acquisition procedures and assist the CO as necessary.
- Review the procedures and requirements of the CA program and assist the CO as required.

Chapter 4: Preaward Technical Assistance

Duty: Provide presolicitation technical assistance to the CO as required.

Tasks:

- Develop determinations, descriptions, justifications, and other documents as applicable to the requirement.
- Develop and coordinate funding and other documents that require approval.
- Provide a suggested sources list.
- Provide the technical evaluation plan.
- Assist the CO with financing and bond needs assessment.

Duty: Provide solicitation technical assistance to the CO as required.

Tasks:

- Assist in determining the method of procurement.
- Assist in contract type selection.
- Refer preaward inquiries to the CO and provide technical responses and advice on other issues to the CO as requested.
- Participate in prebid and preproposal conferences as requested.

Duty: Provide evaluation and source selection technical assistance to the CO as requested.

Tasks:

- Provide assistance in receipt, processing, and evaluation of proposals.
- Provide past performance survey assistance.
- Provide assistance with other terms and conditions and responsibility evaluation.
- Participate in fact-finding sessions, negotiation preparations, and discussions with offerors.
- Gather facts, prepare technical documentation, and participate in debriefings and protests.
- Review and provide advice on the acceptability of unsolicited proposals.

Chapter 5: Planning for Contract Administration

Duty: Assist the CO in planning for, and participate in, postaward orientation.

Tasks:

- Prepare for the CO's preliminary meeting (or briefing).
- Participate in the CO's preliminary meeting.
- Participate in the postaward orientation conference.
- Review a report of the postaward orientation conference.
- Complete assigned action items.

Duty: Validate delegated duties, establish and maintain files, and plan for the performance of COR responsibilities.

Tasks:

- Accept or reject delegated duties in letter of designation.
- Establish and maintain record-keeping files that support actions under the contract.
- Develop and follow a COR workplan.

Duty: Perform task order statement of work (SOW) preparation and monitoring duties.

Tasks:

- Oversee and coordinate initial efforts regarding preparation of the task order and associated documents.
- Review and reconcile differences between the task order and the contractor's task cost plan.
- Understand and be prepared to make recommendations to the CO on single vs. multiple award issues.
- Make recommendations to the CO regarding the ordering officer's and task monitor's duties.

Chapter 6: Contract Monitoring, Inspection, and Acceptance

Duty: Perform monitoring actions as authorized by the CO, and document contractor performance.

Tasks:

- Respond to requests from the contractor.
- Monitor contract performance.
- Resolve constructive changes.

Duty: Inspect contractor delivery/performance and recommend acceptance or rejection of deliverables to the CO.

Tasks:

- Inspect products or services.
- Recommend acceptance if products conform to requirements or if nonconformities are minor.
- Recommend rejection if products do not conform to requirements.
- Assist the CO in evaluating the contractor's reply to a notification of rejection.

Duty: Document the contractor's performance in the agency's past performance file.

Tasks:

- Document performance information.
- Notify interested parties regarding contractor performance.
- Maintain evaluations.

Duty: Monitor the acquisition, control, and disposition of government property by government and contractor personnel, and assess contractors for any loss, damage, or destruction of property.

Tasks:

- Supervise initial transfer of government property.
- Monitor the contractor's use of government property.
- Monitor the disposition of government property.

Duty: Refer indications of fraud or other civil or criminal offenses to responsible officials.

Tasks:

- Assist the CO in briefing the contractor on the COR's suspicions.
- Identify and report any suspicions to responsible officials.
- Provide additional information to the CO and others, as requested.

Chapter 7: Administering the Contract

Duty: Review and recommend contract modification requests and prepare a technical analysis to support a "within scope of the contract" determination.

Tasks:

- Identify the need to change the contract.
- Prepare the technical evaluation report.
- Assist the CO in negotiating the modification.

Duty: Using market research data, make recommendations to the CO on whether to exercise an option.

Tasks:

- Evaluate available options.
- Determine the need for additional supplies, services, or time.
- Research the market for the latest pricing information.
- Document the option in the COR contract file and provide written data to the CO.

Duty: Notify the CO of a delay in the delivery or performance schedule under the contract.

Tasks:

- Identify and verify a delay in performance under the contract.
- Notify the CO of the technical impact of the delay.
- Assist the CO in evaluating the contractor's response.

Duty: Assist the CO in administering stop work orders.

Tasks:

- Identify the potential conditions under which a stop work order might be issued.
- Recommend a work stoppage to the CO.
- Assist the CO in issuing the stop work order.

Duty: Assist the CO in analyzing a claim, recommend a settlement position, and participate in the resolution process.

Tasks:

- Notify the CO of potential disputes.
- Assist the CO in resolving disputes.
- Assist the CO in processing formal claims.

Duty: Provide sufficient evidence of a breach of contract, suggest an appropriate remedy, and assist in evaluating the contractor's response.

Tasks:

- Notify the CO of performance failures.
- Provide technical assistance to the CO.

Duty: Recommend to the CO whether to authorize payment against an invoice in full, in part, or not at all.

Tasks:

- Accept the payment document for processing.
- Calculate the payment amount.
- Notify the contractor of the final amount calculated to be paid, and submit the correct invoice to the paying office.

Chapter 8: Contract Termination and Closeout

Duty: Be prepared to assist the CO in determining whether to terminate a contract.

Tasks:

- Identify the events that have led to the consideration of contract termination.
- Notify the CO of the possible need to terminate.
- Assist the CO with termination proceedings.

Duty: Perform contract closeout.

Tasks:

- Close out the contract files.
- Submit the files to the CO.

Acronyms

ACO	administrative contracting officer
ADR	alternative dispute resolution
ASBCA	Armed Services Board of Contract Appeals
CA	commercial activities
CAO	contract administration office
CAP	commercial activities program
CAS	cost accounting standards
CBA	collective bargaining agreement
CBL	commercial bill of lading
CDA	Contract Disputes Act
CDRL	contract data requirements list
CFR	Code of Federal Regulations
CICA	Competition in Contracting Act
CID	commercial item description
CO	contracting officer
COC	certificate of conformance
COR	contracting officer's representative
COTR	contracting officer's technical representative
CPAF	cost plus award fee
CPFF	cost plus fixed fee
CPIF	cost plus incentive fee
CPM	critical path method
DoD	Department of Defense

DOL	Department of Labor
EPA	Environmental Protection Agency
FAI	Federal Acquisition Institute
FAR	Federal Acquisition Regulation
FASA	Federal Acquisition Streamlining Act
FFP	firm fixed price
FFP/LOE	firm fixed price/level of effort
FLSA	Fair Labor Standards Act
FOB	free on board
FOIA	Freedom of Information Act
FP/EPA	fixed price with economic price adjustment
FPAF	fixed price award fee
FPI	fixed price incentive
GAAP	generally accepted accounting principles
GAO	General Accounting Office
GBL	government bill of lading
GFP	government-furnished property
GPE	governmentwide point of entry
GSA	General Services Administration
GTE	government technical evaluator
GTR	government technical representative
HCA	head of the contracting activity
ID/IQ	indefinite delivery, indefinite quantity
IFB	invitation for bid
IG	inspector general
IGCE	independent government cost estimate
IHCE	in-house cost estimate
JOFOC	justification for other than full and open competition
LDD	loss, damage, or destruction
LH	labor hour
LOE	level of effort
MEO	most efficient organization
MFR	memorandum for the record
NAFTA	North American Free Trade Agreement
NDI	nondevelopmental item
OFPP	Office of Federal Procurement Policy
OMB	Office of Management and Budget
OPM	Office of Personnel Management

PERT	program evaluation review technique
PCO	principal/procuring contracting officer
POC	point of contact
PPI	past performance information
PPIRS	past performance information retrieval system
PR	purchase request
PWS	performance work statement
QAE	quality assurance evaluator
QAP	quality assurance plan
R&D	research and development
RFI	request for information
RFP	request for proposal
RFQ	request for quote
SAT	simplified acquisition threshold
SB	small business
SBA	Small Business Administration
SCA	Service Contract Act
SDB	small disadvantaged business
SOW	statement of work
SSEB	source selection evaluation board
T&M	time and materials
TCO	termination contracting officer
TEP	technical evaluation panel
UCF	uniform contract format
UNICOR	Federal Prison Industries, Inc.
VE	value engineering
VECP	value engineering change proposal
WOSB	women-owned small business

Index

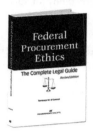

Federal Procurement Ethics:
The Complete Legal Guide
Terrence M. O'Connor

This book provides comprehensive, easy-to-understand descriptions of all the ethics rules that procurement professionals in both government and the private sector need to follow. Summaries of recent and relevant court cases that illustrate the need for full compliance with procurement regulations are also included. Revised to include recent changes in procurement ethics rules, such as the significant additions to the False Claims Act made by Congress in 2009, this book is a complete, all-in-one resource. This plain-English guide focuses on exactly what procurement professionals—both federal officials and contractor employees—need to know to be in compliance with the law and to conduct better business practices.

ISBN 978-1-56726-277-3 ■ Product Code B773 ■ 379 pages

Understanding Government Contract
Source Selection
Margaret G. Rumbaugh

From planning to protest and all the steps in between, this book is the one reference all government acquisition professionals and contractors should keep close at hand. This valuable resource provides straightforward guidance to ensure you develop a firm foundation in government contract source selection.

ISBN 978-1-56726-273-5 ■ Product Code B735 ■ 509 pages

Source Selection Step by Step:
A Working Guide
Charles D. Solloway, Jr., CPCM

Whether you are new to the acquisition team or an experienced practitioner looking to sharpen your skills, this comprehensive, highly readable handbook will guide you through the entire acquisition process, from designing an effective source selection plan, to preparing the solicitation, evaluating proposals, establishing a competitive range, and documenting the source selection decision. With clarity and frankness, Charles Solloway presents government source selection in a step-by-step guide that offers readers quick access to needed information.

ISBN 978-1-56726-300-8 ■ Product Code B008 ■ 407 pages

Federal Acquisition ActionPacks

Federal Acquisition ActionPacks are designed for busy professionals who need to get a working knowledge of government contracting quickly—without a lot of extraneous detail. These books cover all phases of the acquisition process, grounds you firmly in each topic area, and outline practical methods for success, from contracting basics to the latest techniques for improving performance.

Each spiral-bound book contains approximately 160 pages of quick-reading information—simple statements, bulleted lists, questions and answers, charts and graphs, and more. Each topic's most important information is distilled to its essence, arranged graphically for easy comprehension and retention, and presented in a user-friendly format designed for quick look-up.

Earned Value Management Gregory A. Garrett ISBN 978-1-56726-188-2 ■ Product Code B882 173 Pages	**Best-Value Source Selection** Philip E. Salmeri ISBN 978-1-56726-193-6 ■ Product Code B936 178 Pages
Performance-Based Contracting Gregory A. Garrett ISBN 978-1-56726-189-9 ■ Product Code B899 153 Pages	**Government Contract Law Basics** Thomas G. Reid ISBN 978-1-56726-194-3 ■ Product Code B943 175 Pages
Cost Estimating and Pricing Gregory A. Garrett ISBN 978-1-56726-190-5 ■ Product Code B905 161 Pages	**Government Contracting Basics** Rene G. Rendon ISBN 978-1-56726-195-0 ■ Product Code B950 176 Pages
Contract Administration and Closeout Gregory A. Garrett ISBN 978-1-56726-191-2 ■ Product Code B912 153 Pages	**Performance Work Statements** Philip E. Salmeri ISBN 978-1-56726-196-7 ■ Product Code B967 151 Pages
Contract Formation Gregory A. Garrett and William C. Pursch ISBN 978-1-56726-192-9 ■ Product Code B929 163 Pages	**Contract Terminations** Thomas G. Reid ISBN 978-1-56726-197-4 ■ Product Code B974 166 Pages